Advance Praise for *Over the Wall*

"Kevin Hallinan has written a masterful book about his experiences after a long and celebrated career as one of his generation's outstanding New York City police officers. I was privileged to serve as the New York City police commissioner during some of those years, and Kevin brings the streets of the city alive in *Over the Wall*. It is a great read and a must-read."

—**Robert McGuire**, Former Commissioner
of New York City Police Department

"*Over the Wall* is a true tale of teamwork, integrity, as well as incredible adversity, the net result of which was better policing, increased national security, and inventive new programs to protect our national pastime. More than just a truly entertaining and enlightening read, Kevin's tale offers important historical insights and perspectives that many should benefit from for years to come."

—**Peter V. Ueberroth**, Corporate Leader, Former
Olympic Organizer/Summer Games Chairman and
Commissioner of Major League Baseball

"Kevin Hallinan's riveting memoir *Over the Wall* has it all—street cops and drug lords, mobsters and terrorists, FBI agents and the Lords of Baseball. It's a fast-paced and exciting ride through mean streets and boardrooms, the remarkable real-life journey of a hero cop. Start reading, and you won't be able to stop."

—**Howard Blum**, *New York Times* Bestselling Author

"I never believed in the American mythos of 'John Wayne' until I met Kevin Hallinan. *Over the Wall* is a reminder that everyday heroes are walking among us doing their best to make us safer and our lives better. For over forty years, it seems like Kevin was a part of every seminal moment in NYC history while he went from a rising rookie cop on the beat building strong relationships in the neighborhood he was charged with protecting to running the first NYPD/FBI Joint Terrorism Task Force that watched over millions of New Yorkers like myself from those looking to do us harm. Kevin's ideals on police work have never been more relevant than they are today. Kevin's story celebrates the man who single-handedly brought an ethos to his career that centered on honor plus hard work equals a job well done. Congratulations Kevin and thank you for bringing us with you 'over the wall'!"

—**David Gavant**, Business Development, North America at WSC Sports; Former Executive Vice President and Executive Producer at MLB Productions

"This story is a brilliantly lit pathway for young men and women who aspire to success! Kevin Hallinan, a typical NYC kid, had a fabulous career in the NYPD, and became commander of the very first Joint Terrorist Task Force in America. His balance of police skills and people skills led him on a career of achievement, and ultimately, to the dream job of director of security for all of Major League Baseball. His stories are amazing, riveting, and all true. They tell of an average kid rising to the top in everything he cared about, sports, work, and most of all, family."

—**Rick Hahn**, FBI, Retired

"The creation of the FBI/NYPD Terrorist Task Force was a logical response to the upsurge of terrorist activities in the late '70s and early 1980s. Both law enforcement components required intelligent and sensitive leadership to move their agencies from rivals to partners. NYPD Lt. Kevin Hallinan fit the bill perfectly. He was a strong, smart, and sensitive leader who represented his department faithfully and without reservation as the FBI's partner."

—**Tom Sheer**, Former Assistant Director, FBI, New York Office

"Kevin Hallinan doesn't tell stories—he shares experiences. In that way, he delivers examples and lessons about the famous, infamous, and everyday people he has encountered in law enforcement and in life. Few of us may end up doing the kind of work that Kevin has done helping keep New York City, an Olympic Games, Major League Baseball, and many other places and organizations safe and secure. But all of us can learn from someone whose career in law enforcement is really a cover for teaching people and their communities how to investigate, analyze, and improve themselves and society."

—**Lee Igel**, NYU Tisch Institute for Global Sport;
NYU Langone Health Medical Ethics

OVER THE WALL

From the Dangerous Streets of NYC...
Through the Birth of Counterterrorism and Beyond

KEVIN M. HALLINAN
With Rob Travalino

A POST HILL PRESS BOOK
ISBN: 978-1-63758-398-2
ISBN (eBook): 978-1-63758-399-9

Over the Wall:
From the Dangerous Streets of NYC…
Through the Birth of Counterterrorism and Beyond
© 2022 by Kevin M. Hallinan with Rob Travalino
All Rights Reserved

Cover design by Tiffani Shea

Post Hill Press
New York • Nashville
posthillpress.com

Published in the United States of America
1 2 3 4 5 6 7 8 9 10

To Joan,
I'll love you forever.
You made all my dreams come true.

To my children,
Joanne, Kevin, Eileen, Thomas;
all of whom work hard serving others,

And to my grandchildren,
Matthew, Jennifer, Jack, Ryan, Kelly, Kevin,
Michael, Kiera, Erin, Brendan;
work hard and love what you do.

And to my parents Nora and Michael, my
brother Tom and sister Margaret;
I hope I made you proud.

TABLE OF CONTENTS

PART 8: RETURN TO COWBOY LAND

AUTHOR'S NOTE

When I arrived as the commander of the FBI/NYPD Joint Terrorism Task Force in New York in 1981, I told one of my dashing FBI counterparts, Kenneth P. Walton, that I didn't come to lead the parade, but simply to be part of it. With that top of mind, this book will not contain the usual thank-yous as the work itself comprises one grand "thank-you" to the countless parade of people and places, names and faces, those who joined, inspired, led, and accompanied me through my journey.

If you choose to join us on this literary version of a "Ride Along"— which is police lingo for accompanying police personnel for an entire shift of action—please take this journey in honor of these many people and organizations that have been invaluable to my success and career. They are the very same selfless men and women who protect us and keep watch. Celebrate their efforts, their lessons and mentorship; the results of all by far surpassed my meager contributions to the whole.

—Kevin M. Hallinan, December 2021

PROLOGUE
NOVEMBER 26, 1976

It was an unusually warm day. Looking back, the balmy sixty-degree temperature was strangely appropriate for both New York City and the nation, as the year up until that point had already been a heated time.

In fact, America's Bicentennial year was the worst on record for crime in the Big Apple, with felonies up an alarming 13 percent and nearly two thousand serious offenses committed every day. Those grim numbers amounted to an astounding rate of seventy-five criminal acts per hour.

What few recall is that this was also a deadly decade of militant bombings across the nation. Incredibly, during just an eighteen-month span from 1971 to '72, FBI statistics revealed "more than 2,500 domestic bombings...with virtually no solved crimes and barely any significant prosecutions."[1] Nearly a dozen radical groups took the credit for the incidents, and while some of the devices were supplied by domestic organizations, others exhibited ideological and funding ties connecting them to shadowy foreign actors.

It was just the beginning...

By the middle of the decade, such attacks became so common in the city that during one post-bombing interview, a woman responded to a *New York Post* reporter by asking, "Oh, another bombing? Who

---

[1] Alterman, Eric. "Remembering the Left-Wing Terrorism of the 1970s." *The Nation*, April 14, 2015.

is it this time?"[2] As to the cause of such civil unrest, there were many, and, like solemn drumbeats, most will echo throughout the following pages—perhaps revealing a picture eerily relevant to today.

As for me, by November 1976, I had been employed by the New York Police Department for fourteen years, which, for some, could be considered a long stretch. Promotions had been pretty hard to come by, and, when they did arrive, changes were usually based on what the department needed, and not the cop's chosen career path. From beat cop to squad car and now detective sergeant, I'd always taken what was given. While maybe I hadn't gotten quite as far as I wanted, I was always ready and willing to step up to the moment, even if it wasn't entirely the one I'd wished for.

On November 26, 1976, that sort of wish nearly got me killed.

***

With the dull fog of the previous day's Thanksgiving feast still clouding my brain and slowing my body, I maneuvered the Bruckner Expressway from Manhattan to the South Bronx. Fresh from delivering a downtown presentation on "Police and the Media," there I was, dressed in a brand-new suit and headed to the formidable 8th Homicide Squad as one of three detective sergeants on the roster.

Housed in the 43rd Precinct, 8th Homicide was no joke. While the area around the precinct was a mixed bag, the 8th Homicide Zone, which also included the nearby 41st and 45th Precincts, usually ranked near the top in murders each year. Drug and mob-related killings were common in the area, and bodies were often dropped into the nearby Bronx River or hastily tossed over the side of the Bruckner Expressway. As one of the 4-3 detectives later described it to me, these were "routine South Bronx jobs."

My detective sergeant post was a mix of managerial and investigative duties, so while I was often out on calls and looking into cases,

---

[2]   Burrough, Bryan. "The Bombing of America That We Forgot." *Time*, September 20, 2016.

OVER THE WALL

it was also my responsibility to allocate resources and make sure that the squad's detective units were properly staffed and supported. Also, I'd been four years riding a desk, and I knew that before I could be a more-active cop again, I'd need time to get my edge back.

Cops got rusty pretty fast when chained to desks and, as many street cops would attest, a rusty cop could be a dangerous and unwelcome partner. Yet there I was, rusty and eager...and about to crash somebody else's party.

The recently completed red brick 43rd Precinct building sat at the corner of Fteley and Story Avenues and, after spending much of my career inside rickety and shopworn facilities from Brooklyn to Harlem, the 4-3 looked like a brave new future. Inside however, a more familiar reality awaited, with organized chaos, a haze of cigarette smoke, and stacks of paperwork.

As I approached the 8th Homicide room, frantic detectives and frazzled cops crisscrossed in a buzzsaw of grim and determined police activity. Something big was up in the inner sanctum of one of New York's finest, battle-tested detective units, an elite group known as Team C. After an early morning shootout, the entire precinct was all-hands-on-deck.

Six or so Team C detectives caught my eye as I entered the fray. The room responded to them in silent choreography, and as these elite detectives prepared to move out, I decided to tag along.

Let me set the stage.

***

Earlier that morning, members of Team C had tracked a homicide suspect named Manuel Rivera, or "Nector" to his alleged home on nearby Bronx River Avenue. An informant had fingered Nector for the late spring murder of a drug dealer named Rafael Guzman.

Simple enough.

For all Team C knew, they were investigating a homicide case, though they understood all too well that their suspect was known to interact with drug dealers. Hoping for the element of surprise, Team

C arrived at the 4-3 in the wee hours of morning. There they grabbed shotguns and bulletproof vests for a surprise 5:00 a.m. raid. When Team C arrived at Nector's apartment, however, there was no sign of the suspect, so they decided to remain staked-out in surveillance vans down the street.

The vigil dragged into the early afternoon when a car arrived carrying Nector and another known male. Rather than entering the two-story brick building, though, the pair seemed to get spooked and hastily took off, still in the car.

The sudden change of plans prompted Team C to split up. Part of the surveillance team left in pursuit, while others stayed behind to check Nector's first-floor apartment. Once inside, Team C detectives discovered a woman and a baby and—after a quick, cursory search of the premises—hit some alarmingly dangerous pay dirt. There, carefully tucked into a hall closet was a large trunk containing three kilograms of Mexican rock heroin, a score that in 1976 dollars comprised a street bonanza worth at least a million dollars.

Needing a proper search warrant to secure the find, two members of Team C left for the 4-3, leaving a patrolman outside to guard the location. It seemed secure enough, except the building holding Nector's place was actually an entire drug family's safe house, and there were spotters watching from adjacent rooftops.

All hell was about to break loose.

***

While speeding down the Sheridan Expressway toward Brooklyn, Team C detectives Ron Marsenison and John Meda made their move and pulled Nector and his partner over. Just as the two Team C detectives climbed out of their vehicle, however, Nector and his associate drew their guns and opened fire.

In the sudden barrage, Marsenison and Meda dove for cover, which allowed the two suspects to quickly speed off. A treacherous high-speed chase ensued, with the two vehicles weaving in and out of traffic and slamming into each other. Dozens of bullets were exchanged, and the interior of the NYPD vehicle was choked with the blue haze off spent gunpowder. The Team C guys finally managed to force Nector's car to crash into a center divider. Still firing off shots, the suspects jumped over a guardrail, falling to the street below.

Once the mayhem subsided, what did the hardened Team C cops do? Marsenison and Meda dusted themselves off, got back in their vehicle, called in, and returned to the precinct—where they joined their 8th Homicide teammates and headed back to the safe house to make certain it was secured.

Hoping to do whatever I could to help, I followed Marsenison and Meda, along with fellow detectives Charlie Summers and Jack McCann, to a squad car and squeezed into the back. Mind you, I didn't know any of these guys, and to them, I likely looked like some guy fresh from the brass looking to pee in their pool. Nobody really spoke to me on the way to Bronx River Avenue and that was okay. I was there to observe.

Well, at least that was my plan.

THE 138TH STREET WAR

Unbeknownst to me entirely—and mostly to Team C—what would become a back-and-forth series of gang and drug-related kidnappings and murders had begun early that spring. It was in fact, the brutal opening act of a deadly three-gang war for control of the South Bronx's thirty-million-dollar heroin market. The conflict would become so widespread and so violent that it would be christened the 138th Street War.

Over a two-year span, three gangs—the Teenager-Ramins, Renegade-Colons, and Julitos—abducted and murdered each other's couriers and soldiers. Twenty-seven people in all were brutally executed, some cut up alive by executioners using electric chainsaws, their body parts dumped in cardboard boxes. On one occasion, the victims were discovered by playing school children.[3]

One or more of the rival gangs had taken to masquerading as police officers to gain access to drug establishments, or to facilitate the kidnapping of competitive gang members, the easier to rob them of money or drugs, or simply to execute them. This turned cops into gang targets.

***

We arrived at the safe house, also known as a "taxpayer" building, and climbed out of the squad car, I tried my best to keep my distance from

---

[3] O'Kane, James. *Wicked Deeds, Murder in America*. Piscataway, New Jersey: Transaction Publishers, 2005.

the men of Team C. I didn't need to be told what to do, and either moved at their speed or got left behind. On the way inside, years of police habit had me taking quick note of the scene. The well-worn red-brick, multifamily unit was set on a trash-strewn corner of Bronx River Avenue. The distance from the street and uneven roof facade made it appear every bit the defensive yet formidable outpost it was.

I couldn't look long though. Team C was in high gear.

The slim and imposing Ron Marsenison was the operational leader of Team C. He was a detective first-grade, which gave him both the experience and rank to be point man on the street. This allowed Team C's ranking officer, Sergeant Al Howard, to keep a more distant, organizational, and hands-off approach. Marsenison stalked the area outside that safe house like a big cat, grim, hungry, and on edge. He was impeccably dressed, laser focused, and barely shot me a glance.

I noticed Detective Charlie Summers next. He had the air of a professional about him and quickly set about thoroughly assessing the scene. Detective Richie Paul also carried himself with polish and presence though he, too, barely gave me a glance. These guys were locked in.

The most welcoming of the group was the youngest, Detective Jack McCann, who at first blush seemed the least by the book. With a styled mustache, big sideburns, and long hair brushing over his collar, McCann was quick with a joke and struck me as the team diplomat and glue. He was the only one who spoke to me that day.

Detective Tom Davis, whom I met later at the station, was a good-looking, friendly, red-headed mountain of a man the rest of the team had dubbed "Father Tom." A streetwise cop, he was good with people, a skill that enhanced the team's ability to gain information in the South Bronx community. There were other great team members, too, but as some rotated in and out, I had yet to meet them.

As a front-line squad, Team C operated much like their counterparts at the Drug Enforcement Administration; Bureau of Alcohol, Tobacco, and Firearms; and FBI. They did their homework. Even before I arrived at the 4-3, they'd already made some calls and checked me out, likely deciding that I was a desk jockey, a rusty cop, a potential liability.

Thankfully, McCann and I had a mutual friend, an off-duty cop who had been shot while moonlighting as a cabbie—a case I'd doggedly pursued as a Harlem detective many years before. That told McCann I had chops, and as Team C became more aware of my career and work as a detective, they loosened up to the new guy.

***

As I stood in the apartment, still more observing perhaps than assessing, a debate broke out regarding who would stay behind while the rest of the team went for a search warrant. Knowing how the lowest job on the totem pole that day was babysitting duty, I spoke up.

"I can stay."

Suggestions and plans flew around me almost as if I wasn't there. Then the room went quiet as it registered what I had said, and the guys warmed to the idea of not tying up their own resources. After all, how dangerous could it be? There was a police officer and radio car out front so, in theory, nobody was going to slip in behind me. It was a job that needed doing and I was there to help, so a deal was struck and I was left to stand watch over heroin stash, woman, and baby.

As I locked the door, the circumstances began to sink in.

Am I ready for this? I wondered.

It seemed simple enough. The apartment was pretty spartan, with a few sticks of furniture here and there. None of it mattered—my world was focused on the closet and that big, black trunk, and I kept my head on a swivel.

The smallish Hispanic woman was cradling the toddler in her arms. Either a gang member, gang member's wife, or apartment owner coerced into running a safe house, she locked eyes with me and shot me a look that said if her eyes were guns, I'd have been dead where I stood.

Knowing from experience that the first few minutes were key in establishing dominance, I became determined to give my host the notion that I was watching her closely, baby or no baby. No bullshit or funny business would be tolerated.

She tested me right away, repeatedly moving toward the slightly open closet, each time forcing me to warn her away. At one point, I even had to take a step toward her to cut off her movement, after which she glared at me, cursed under her breath, and stayed put. I felt certain that if it weren't for the baby, she might have resisted with more force.

In reality, she was stalling.

***

When the Team C guys rushed out as quickly as they had arrived, the spotters on the roof of the River Avenue building thought the apartment might have been emptied, but they had to be sure. An anonymous call had been placed to 911 with a 10-13—an emergency call for assistance—usually, the grim news of an officer down. This pulled the police officer outside the building back to his cruiser and away from the scene.

Meanwhile Jack McCann and the rest of Team C were headed to the district attorney's office to obtain the needed search warrant, but when the 10-13 call blared from the radio, the guys suddenly realized they'd been had.

"Holy shit!" Jack recalled shouting to his partners. "We gotta get back to the apartment! We lost the fucking patrol car!"

***

The apartment remained quiet, peaceful even.

The woman had backed away from the closet and become strangely docile. Figuring that my stay was going to take some time, I picked up the apartment phone—this was long before cell phones—called the squad administrative assistant, and asked her to call my wife, Joan, and let her know that I was going to be awhile.

A few minutes later, there was a firm knock at the door, and the woman with the baby shot me a smug look. Even so I figured it was the warrant arriving, but as I slowly looked through the peep hole, I couldn't see anyone or anything. That was when I proved just how rusty I was, as I impulsively opened the door.

It all happened pretty fast after that.

The hulking shape of a man appeared.

Behind him, I spotted another unknown male as he darted past and up the stairs toward the roof. That was of lesser concern as I had a more immediate task before me.

There stood what I can only describe as a human cobra, with long black hair that flowed out in a curly pyramid of tangles. While he was barely six foot, this guy's head was massive and his shoulders seemed impossibly wide. What looked like a sixty-two-inch torso tapered down to a strangely narrow thirty-three, so he appeared as a giant "V," some kind of strange, comic book character.

The cobra knew instantly that I was a cop, but as he never expected me to be there—let alone answer the door—he was momentarily caught off guard. What he was thinking I can only guess, though his first words partly betrayed him.

"Where is my friend?" he demanded in Spanish, referring I guess to Nector. I chose not to say anything and, instead of going for my gun, went for my shield, hoping to stall him for a few precious moments while the cavalry returned. I still had no idea about the 10-13, nor the whereabouts of Team C or the patrolman outside.

The stakes had inched dangerously close to life and death.

In the tense moment, I shot a glance toward the woman. She had slipped just out of sight in the direction of the closet door. The cobra's eyes darted, as well, and I realized I'd bought some precious time. Perhaps with it, an opening.

He's wondering if there are other police in the apartment with me, I thought silently as I continued to pull out my shield. The chain seemed to go on forever, like a magician's silk scarf.

The woman reappeared, and I shot her a stern look. That look might have saved my life, as I could instantly see the concern in the cobra's eyes. In that moment of doubt I put my hand on the man's chest and pushed. It was like trying to move Superman or a statue, but with no other option, I just pushed harder and shoved him back into the hall. He actually seemed shocked that I'd tried at all, and maybe that too gave him pause. Perhaps I was a more worthy adversary than my tailored suit and magical shield chain.

The advantage was short-lived.

As I continued to push him into the hall, the cobra's jacket fell open, revealing the butt end of a gun carefully tucked into his waistband. He was packing a Smith and Wesson snub-nose .38, a Detective Special—the very same gun I had. It was unnerving.

Could that have come from a dead cop? If I went for my own gun, he would certainly draw his. *Now what?*

We stood there in a stare-down, then I started to move step-by-step toward the building's front door, which now seemed miles away. I'll never know why or how, but the cobra matched me step for step, glaring at me the whole time. It was as if we were dancing a strange sideways cha-cha, one that seemed destined to end in gun smoke and bullets once the music stopped. What was at the end of the hall, it was anybody's guess. I hoped for the cops; him surely, for his friends.

There we were, barely two feet apart and slowly, agonizingly edging down the hallway toward the front door, both holding our hands inches from our firearms.

We got to the end of the hall, and I felt for the doorknob, never for a second taking my eyes off of the cobra's. Slowly, I curled my fingers around the tarnished metal knob and turned it.

The damn thing came off in my hand.

I didn't even react—I couldn't—so I just dropped the knob there like it was supposed to happen. I needed to buy more time, so I indicated with a head tilt that we were going to retrace our dance back to the apartment. Amazingly, the cobra complied, and it seemed like it took an hour as we inched our way back to the apartment...

My dance partner was Jaime Villa, known on the street as Teenager—one of the two leaders of the Teenager-Ramins drug gang. For years Teenager had been plotting his rise through the drug ranks of New York, going so far as to become a martial arts black belt and New York State Champion. He then joined the Army and become a Green Beret, all part of a plan that included romancing and marrying a US Army general's daughter in order to set himself up for trips to the South Pacific, where he built a heroin ring that spanned from Asia to Los Angeles and New York.

Months later when I testified against Villa in a grand jury, we estimated that he had killed maybe six people. The number was closer to thirty, including his first killing at age twelve. Later, after Teenager became a major drug trafficker, he carried two silver-plated .45s and had no compunction about using them.

Case in point, after a Los Angeles court hearing didn't go his way, Villa determined that his attorney had betrayed him. Later that day, he accompanied the man on a drive, and upon reaching a secluded stretch of California's Pacific Coast Highway, Teenager put several bullets into his lawyer's head. Some of them passed through the dashboard and into the engine block. With the vehicle disabled, Teenager had no choice but to take off on foot and down the highway, all the while, licking his dead lawyer's blood from his hands.

That dance, the two of us a foot apart with our backs against the walls of that narrow hallway passage, took me back to another set of walls from my early police training…

THE KIND OF GUY I WAS

PART ONE

THE KIND OF GUY I WAS

◢ FACING THE WALL

The six- and eight-foot walls seemed to stare back at me—walls that required a full-on sprint and jump just for the height, momentum, and leverage to get over them.

They were just two of the formidable obstacles awaiting all recruits at the famous Delehanty Institute in New York. Founded over a pool hall in 1915 by Michael J. Delehanty, the now defunct institute once held classes for firemen, police officers, and other city services employees, and was deemed so effective that the program was responsible for 90 percent of city policemen and 80 percent of its firemen.[4]

The institute's studies included in-depth courses in criminal law, interpersonal relations, and group supervision. It was incredibly progressive for the times, and about much more than getting participants physically fit for police work. In fact, the program focused on producing recruits polished enough to be both effective cops and adept city ambassadors. To help bring these lofty goals home, the institute's main instructor was our guide and prototype, a legendary New York City cop named Henry Mulhern.

Larger than life, with a low booming voice and imposing demeanor, Mulhern was a wealth of advice and experience. Standing six foot three inches, with a wide jaw and full head of grayish-black hair that hung dramatically over big piercing eyes, he was famous for a catch phrase that became our mantra.

"If you will it, it shall be done!"

---

[4] "M. J. Delehanty Headed Institute; Founder of School for Civil Service Candidate Dies." *New York Times*, April 13, 1964.

Mulhern spoke in detail about the use of deadly force and what we all had to consider before taking a life. For hopeful recruits coming from day jobs, often tired and bored, Mulhern, grabbed our attention and held it. Coming from my own hardscrabble background—a life lived mostly in search of fun, sports, adventure, and girls—this was about as inspired as I'd been.

In many ways, Henry Mulhern reminded me of my parents, first-generation immigrants who always presented a passionate mixture of strength, dedication, and guidance. Several times at Delehanty, while listening to Mulhern speak, I found myself thinking of all the things my mother and father had gone through, the opportunities they worked to provide, and the many life lessons they bestowed.

***

I had a pretty common childhood for the New York of the late '40s and '50s. My first few years were spent on Powell Avenue, in one of the city's often-romanticized regional neighborhoods where life seemed very secure and tight-knit. A short five-block stretch of road between Virginia and Zerega Avenues at the border of Castle Hill, Powell was that American Dream Irish-German neighborhood of old movies and TV shows.

Later though, as postwar dreams faded and money got tighter, the Hallinan family was uprooted to the melting pot of the South Bronx where several ethnicities came together in a shared economic struggle.

It was on Cypress Avenue where I received my true education in diversity not always a smooth transition. Team sports certainly helped—especially baseball—as kids from all backgrounds, Irish Catholic, Jewish, Italian, and Hispanic could get together on the common ground of competition, to challenge other clubs and neighborhoods and, sometimes after the game, with knuckles instead of gloves, balls, and bats.

Long before our teen years, my brother Tom and I experienced the police as embodied by the beat cops on our street, most notably a guy named Eddie Horan. Eddie and his brother were good friends to our family, and Tom and I knew Eddie as a caring community presence, a man who commanded authority respect and, perhaps most of all, fairness. Still, the idea of being a cop never occurred to the brothers Hallinan until after high school. We were just too preoccupied with the adventure of being teens.

We also had our childhood shattered by tragedy after cancer took my mom just before my fifteenth birthday. Mom's untimely death left widower Michael Hallinan to look after his brood of three, and the man never blinked or wavered. With threat of his kids being put in a foster home, Dad plowed through two jobs and a raging ulcer just to keep my sister Margaret, brother Tom, and me close. I think the deepest marks my father left on me were his outlook on life and views of others, concepts that provided me the openness to accept help and take responsibility for my actions. In my case, however, it would take quite a few years for the second part of those lessons to sink in.

When I close my eyes, I can still see my dad's gentle smile and the sparkle of his eyes through his horn-rimmed glasses. The look often came over the top of a favorite book or newspaper. Dad favored local politics, the Holy Bible, and a certain book on parliamentary procedure called *Robert's Rules of Order*. I instantly thought the book was stodgy, though later I realized it was less about politics and more about civil discourse and human relations.

Turned out that my dad was pretty worldly. I can also recall how each and every night he took to his knees in gratitude and prayed to God to keep us all safe. Michael Hallinan's foundation was built upon God, family, and education.

My mother, Nora Cannon, complemented her husband perfectly. Both were self-made, and both arrived at America's shores from towns in the same Irish county, as if they were destined to meet and marry, even if it took a couple thousand miles to bring them together. Where Michael Hallinan was more laid back and whimsical, the five-foot-three-inch Nora was a force of nature.

A striking and engaging natural beauty, Mom could unleash a squall or two when properly provoked. As with most stay-home moms of the '40s and '50s, Nora was thrust into the role of family general, though not without a neighborhood army to help. Like many moms of the city's postwar era, she was part of a human surveillance network that existed long before technology took on that role. Therefore, my early lessons in home rule included the evasive maneuvers of using rooftops and fire escapes to sneak out and go on adventures that would make Batman proud.

Mom was the family detective long before my younger brother Tom and I got our gold shields.

Like most postwar city kids, I was a big fan of street sports, played soldier in the parks, and hung out in the neighborhood businesses that back then were at the ground floor of most apartment buildings. Being the middle child was both good and bad for me. It provided me a strange leeway in life as my older sister—Margaret, or Marg, as we called her—was most often thrust into the unenviable role of being both the lookout for Mom and the cover for Tom and me when she graciously afforded us some space.

I was often able to slip through the cracks.

Tom was definitely Nora's boy, which set the stage for an early competition between us that continued into our careers. Whether sports, boxing, or bragging rights, Tom and I were at each other from early on, with me often coming in second. He was the better student, sometimes the better athlete, and certainly—when the time came—the better cop.

I wasn't exactly the academic sort; there was just so much life to live and so many adventures to chase. At one point, things got so bad that my father and I were told by Brother Burton, the local high school principal, that it might be best if I found a trade.

Me? I couldn't even bang a nail.

Thinking some study could solve everything, my dad promptly rushed out and bought me a brand-new desk and humped it up five flights to our apartment.

It did not have the desired effect.

Instead, baseball became my passion, and after we had moved to Cypress Avenue, a makeshift outfield wall up at a tennis court-turned-diamond became my main measuring stick for success. We dubbed the area "Cowboy Land" for the western games we played there, and hitting a baseball over that wall became my goal—especially after my very first Yankees game when "Yankee Clipper" Joe DiMaggio deposited one into the stadium's famous bleachers.

Cowboy Land in many ways presented my first real wall, and I recall it as perhaps one of the toughest of them all.

***

After escaping high school, I floated from job to job. There was a draft scare, a stint in the National Guard, and time served with the US Army & Air Force Exchange Service, where I was tasked with procuring and coordinating food and equipment for PXs and BXs located in different locations throughout the military world. At one point, I was slated to be sent to an Arctic base but managed to make myself too useful to transfer. The exchange was where I learned the value of horse trading and politics, two skills that would serve me well in the NYPD and beyond.

What I didn't learn, however, was common sense.

Determined to zoom through life, fueled by teen dreams and a childhood I suppose was partly cut short by my mother's premature death, I spent a chunk of my first real salary on a sporty used car and entertaining as many young ladies as I could make time for. That first car, a total impulse buy, quickly mocked my recklessness by dropping a transmission. Regardless, it did not slow me down with the girlfriends.

Fortunately, among my many teen romances was a girl by the name of Joan Gunning.

Joan lived in the building diagonally across from ours on Cypress Avenue, and she caught my eye early on. Blonde and sassy, Joan was the leader of her pack. What she saw in a pimply-faced, skinny kid, I may never know. For some reason that only Joan could understand, no matter how hard I ran, Joan kept up. In fact, I met her one day while the neighborhood boys were trying to figure out who could run the fastest on the block. Joan joined the race and finished second to me.

She was the most beautiful girl on the block, and yet I kept on running…right into the arms of any pretty girl who would have me. Fortunately, Joan was persistent and a far better undercover operative than I would ever be, at one point skillfully absconding with my little black book just long enough to change all the phone numbers, effectively cutting me off from my list of casual girlfriends.

After I got my second car, this time a brand-new white-and-gray Ford Fairlane 500, I outfitted it with loud Hollywood mufflers, rear fender skirts, and spinner wheels. I proceeded to run red lights, drag race, and nearly kill Joan and me on the Bruckner Expressway.

Maybe as a clever form of family "policing," my father got me thinking about the NYPD, potentially a good career with a pension. Having no other concrete plan, I figured "why not?" and took the entrance exam. Then as a backup precaution, and with Brother Burton still in mind, I took the fire department exam, too.

While awaiting the results, I took a job as a proofreader for McGraw Hill Publishing, and it was there that I got perhaps the best lesson of all, one delivered in such a way that would make Michael Hallinan truly proud. It came from a book called *The Kind of Guy I Am*. Penned by Robert McAllister and Floyd Miller, the gripping biography chronicled the riveting life of McAllister, an honest NY beat cop who, during the Prohibition era, swam through a sea of organized crime and rich and powerful politicians on the take.

The cover leapt out at me, showing a cop in uniform, surrounded by shadows and danger. The tense adventure painted both a chillingly real and inspiring journey amidst the violence and desperation of the Depression. Down to every dangerous detail, McAllister captured thrilling and hair-trigger face-to-face battles with city corruption so entrenched that it spread from powerful gangsters to politicians and even inside McAllister's own precinct.

Determined to dispense justice and steer clear of bribes and influence, this lone, honest cop was framed for crimes he didn't commit. His reputation was smashed so badly, in fact, that he had to endure a month in the city's infamous and dangerous Central Booking facility called "The Tombs." There McAllister was forced to fend off repeated attempts on his life before managing to reclaim both his job and reputation.

McAllister's adventure reminded me of the neighborhood beat cops my brother Tom and I looked up to as kids, and while men like Eddie Horan had been seen through a child's eyes, McAllister vividly depicted the harsher realities of a cop's life.

By contrast, I realized, all my life I'd reflexively moved away from responsibility. Reading that book, I suddenly found myself wanting to do more and to have my life mean something.

But what exactly? Can I even cut it as a cop?

There was chance it would be a moot point. Before the Police Department even considered hiring a new recruit, they performed a thorough investigation. That meant my grades, my teenage fights, my running red lights, my drag racing, and my other youthful "misadventures." After weeks of interviewing friends and neighbors, a sergeant from the 46th Precinct summoned me for a series of weekly in-person chats during which I had to endure a veritable litany of my lapses in judgment.

"I've talked with so many people about you," he said. "I have to tell you, there wasn't one person—from the storekeepers and neighborhood guys, the people you wouldn't even think of—that didn't have something to say."

Uh-oh. If that wasn't a setup for a fall, what was? Then it came, the shoe drop. He sat back and barely blinked.

"I think you should reconsider being a police officer."

Brother Burton strikes again?

While the sergeant never got specific, I sensed from his words that this was different. He was worried that I was maybe too innocent, too nice for the harder edges of the job, the places Robert McAllister had to maneuver. Like McAllister, could I resist strong-arming? Would I survive extortion and bribery? This seasoned 4-6 sergeant was suggesting that maybe I wasn't the kind of guy I needed to be. It stung.

Still, I told him I was determined to stay the course, and I guess that impressed him, because I hung around several more months until I got the nod.

Then, it suddenly all got very real.

While Robert McAllister's gripping book foreshadowed the perils of the job ahead, holding that first police shield and gun in my hand was a game-changer.

EYES ON THE STARS

By July 1961, I had been married to Joan for over a year and, with our first child on the way, was directed to report to the police academy to begin a three-month stint. Before my initiation, I was directed to NYC Police Headquarters for my shield and my gun.

It was a formative moment, especially after entering the historic Police Building at 240 Centre Street in lower Manhattan and finding myself standing before the memorial to fallen officers. Another wall, only this one with hundreds of names and numbers on it, officers killed in the line of duty.

Still, my new policeman's shield was comforting in some ways. It suggested a brotherhood and was a real and tangible symbol of my accomplishment in getting this far. It also meant I had gained some trust from the city. The gun I received, on the other hand, was an instant and weighty reminder of the responsibility that came with my new line of work. Just holding it pulled my mind back to Delehanty and Henry Mulhern's words about taking a life.

What really drove home the stakes of the job was a second trip to that memorial of fallen officers. This time, one name caught my eye, a name that had been most recently added—Patrolman Francis Xavier Walsh, shield number 22349. End of watch September 4, 1960.

Unbeknownst to me at the time, Walsh and I had both attended Rice High School in Harlem, yet somehow it still felt as if I'd followed him onto the force. The young officer was killed trying to stop an armed robbery at a liquor store on 8th Avenue, not far from my childhood home. He was just twenty-nine.[5] While I never knew him, I met Francis Walsh at the memorial wall that day, and he walked with me for the rest of my career.

My first assignment was walking the beat of Manhattan's 20th Precinct, the very same first assignment as my police inspiration, Robert McAllister.

Located just off the Hudson River and in the city's posh Upper West Side, the 2-0 in 1961 boasted a smorgasbord of police experience. There were luminaries and celebrities at every turn—folks like Yankees legend Babe Ruth, who had an apartment between 71st and 72nd Streets.

Only a few blocks north, though, sat the infamous Endicott Hotel, which was at times the epicenter for the city's drug and prostitution trade. With dive bars, drug dens, whorehouses, famous people, and posh nightspots all within a few blocks of one another, I was able to bounce through a humanity that transcended cultures and incomes—a great environment for a young officer to gain both experience and perspective.

There are a few important stories that stand out from my time in the 2-0, and they bring an important added dimension, not just to my personal journey but to the tapestry of experience needed to be a balanced and effective policeman. To begin with, I was "baptized" on what was known as the "Holiday Post"—one which took place during the holidays. The advantageous timing provided both a slow break-in for a new cop and more coverage and resources for crowded, holiday shopping areas.

Walking a beat also gave me a lot of time to think, make friends, learn by experience, and understand the neighborhood. It could be wonderfully personal at times, though it could be equally isolating, exemplified perhaps by my fellow men in blue who had the privilege of riding in one of the precinct's relatively few patrol cars.

5   Lombardi, Frank. "Street's New Name in Slain Cop's Honor." *New York Daily News*, May 12, 1996.

A foot patrolman was basically invisible to a patrol car. On the odd occasions where I would interact with them, the car guys were usually looking for somebody to babysit a DOA or an emotionally disturbed subject. I understood. These guys usually had a much more dangerous job than I did. Still, trouble had a knack for finding the beat cop.

Remember, there were no cell phones and no radios for foot patrol in 1961, only call boxes and the occasional payphone, so it quickly dawned on me that if I went into a tenement to investigate a fight, burglary, or armed assault, I essentially disappeared. I might go missing for a least an hour—if not longer—before the station would get around to sending a car to look for me.

Thankfully, being a beat cop also came with a unique and enlightening benefit. The people on my patrol got used seeing me there—both the troublemakers and those who genuinely needed help. My regular presence made it harder for criminals to act on impulse, while bringing other residents' comfort and a sense of security.

I knew I'd arrived as a beat cop when phone calls stopped going to the 20th Precinct and, instead, people looked for me on patrol. In the process I made my first arrest and learned about two important elements of law enforcement.

Politics, and the identity of Mr. Green.

***

I had just left the precinct one afternoon when I observed a phalanx of cops rushing past in pursuit of a suspect. I fancied myself to be a pretty fast runner, so off I went to join in the chase.

I knew I was fast, but somehow I caught and overtook all of my fellow men in blue and made the collar. *Gee,* I thought, *I'm pretty good at this police stuff.* Then, I found out that my running speed outpaced my intellectual ability.

My fellow cops had let me make the arrest, knowing that the likely result was that I'd be pinned to a courtroom bench for the next several days. It was a policeman's rite of passage, in a sense—the endless hours waiting for defense counsel to show up and judges to set cases. And the time waiting allowed me to study for promotions, so I guess my early police career was almost as much bailiff as cop.

Even so, the endless process was known as "waiting for Mister Green," which many rookies mistook for the name of a lawyer. It really meant waiting for the defense lawyer to get paid to show up.

***

One absolutely freezing night only a few days before the end of the year, I was walking my beat when a guy ran over to me to report smoke filling the hall in a rooming house at 80th and Amsterdam. By the time I got there, I didn't have to go inside to see the problem. A twisted snake of black and gray soot was uncoiling from a second-floor window. As people evacuated, I directed some bystanders to call the fire department, then tugged the collar of my overcoat tight and went inside to get a closer look.

Up on the second floor, I pounded on the apartment door and called inside. There was no response, and my pulse and blood pressure rose with the heat and urgency. I backed up a couple steps, kicked the door open, and charged in. What I missed in the rush of bravado and adrenaline was the door swinging back behind me and shutting.

Meanwhile directly in front of me, a huge column of flame was reaching up from a mattress and licking at the ceiling and walls. Not yet feeling the full force of the heat, I did a quick search, and thankfully nobody was home. I relaxed a moment and then got the brilliant idea of putting the mattress out on my own. Score one for NY's Bravest and, I guess, for a question I must have missed on the fire test. Turned out, a beat cop beating and turning an old mattress only spreads the fire. After just a few seconds, the apartment was filled with flame and smoke, and I was choking.

Discretion being the better part of valor, I turned back for the door but found that when it had slammed shut, the cracked door frame had shifted and stuck the door in place. With no real leverage and just a door handle to pull on, I couldn't get out. In seconds, I was nearly overcome, and I thought about jumping out the window. I also thought about dying. The moment I took to think sealed my fate and seconds later, I was struggling just to see and breathe. Suddenly, the door exploded off the hinges as axe-wielding firemen burst in. Calmly and without a word, the lead man assessed the situation in a nanosecond, grabbed the mattress, and heaved it out the window to the street below. Problem solved.

The firemen then turned to me rather indifferently and pointed me for the door. "Nice job," I think one half joked. It was a mix of sarcasm and a hint of appreciation for my bravery I guess. It was another quick lesson in planning and assessment. Any dumb mistake, it sank into my head, could absolutely get me killed. My overcoat stank like smoke for the next week, and while I carefully downplayed the incident to Joan, I told brother Tom all about it.

***

While learning the lessons of a young patrolman, I discovered that there were wonderful mentors who could help me along the way. Officer Tom Gannon for one. Gannon was highly decorated and one of the most well-respected cops in the 2-0, but he was in his thirties and should have been in the Detective Bureau instead of out walking a beat. Word was that he was active in the Army Reserve, and the department never wasted a higher position on a guy they might lose.

Regardless, Gannon never wavered, never complained, and for some reason he took me under his wing. The friendship and ready guidance he offered made a real difference. It began with chatting as we left the station house, mostly helpful information about the post I would be working on any given shift. He was my first real role model on the force—extremely polished, carrying himself with dignity, and he always showed respect to anybody he met on the street.

It was a lesson by example.

Gannon also taught me that I shouldn't just look at those I arrested as criminals. They were, after all, human beings trying to survive, and in doing so had committed "criminal acts." It was a critical distinction for a young man, carrying a shield and gun, to remember.

This is the kind of guy I want to be, I thought. He made people—good and bad alike—feel safer, a powerful example that was critical to this former teen troublemaker.

Gannon's advice would prove especially critical the night I had my first run-in with the dreaded Internal Affairs.

***

It was a brutally cold night, one filled with crusty, treacherous, and dirty snow, the kind you could feel slicing through your shoes even as its crunch told the entire street you were coming.

There was also a light mist of sleet falling that night. It made my overcoat—known in police lingo as the "horse-blanket"—damp and partly frozen. Trying to stay warm by movement, I happened down West End Avenue to a poorly lit section, the kind of foreboding spot that cops called a mugger's paradise. Keeping my head on a swivel, I spotted an older man in a doorway across the way. I'd seen him before and we'd exchanged greetings, but that night he had more to say.

"Hey, young man," he called out in a thick Irish brogue. "Get yourself warm a moment." He waved his arms as I slowed. "Come on then. You'll catch your death."

I knew him as a local building super and figured a moment to get warm would be okay, so I followed him down to the basement near the boiler to grab a few minutes of heat. In the cozy confines, we chatted about the neighborhood and about our shared Irish roots until the time drew close for my call-in to the precinct. Just as I retrieved my coat and hat and readied to leave, I heard the tell-tale blast of air that announced the removal of a bottle cap.

"Here, have a beer," the man said with a twinkle in his eye as he pressed a cold Ballentine Ale into my hand. I didn't want to drink on the job but figured, *what harm could a few sips do?* A moment later, I was up the elevator and back on the beat, no harm no foul. Then, not wanting to seem rude, I went back to the building and, after spending some time discussing daily events and my new line of work, I thanked the super for his kindness and ducked back outside, thinking all was well.

It was a quiet night, after all.

Returning to foot patrol, I went toward the call box and glanced back down the street. A car caught my eye. It was parked across from the building, and inside I spotted the shape of a man, strangely sitting in the passenger seat. He seemed just to be waiting there in the darkness and, stranger still, the engine was off. That meant no heat. It didn't add up.

Growing suspicious, I carefully crossed the street out of sight of the man and slowly walked down the sidewalk toward the passenger side. Once there, I took out my nightstick and tapped on the glass. Through the partly frosted windows, I could see that the guy inside was wearing a suit and hat more suited for the daytime. He had a hard face, and as I leaned closer he looked at me sternly and then silently rolled down the window.

Still he just stared.

"May I ask what it is that you are doing here?" I waited.

Without a word, he opened the door, stepped out and showed me his captain's shield. Instantly, the few sips of beer I had just enjoyed started to leap from my stomach.

"I'm Captain Rockwell with Internal Affairs," he finally growled. I knew the name. Rockwell was famous for nailing guys with complaints. Suddenly all I could think about was my soon-to-be next career with the fire department. "So, what were you doing in that building?" Rockwell looked straight down his nose at me.

If my time maneuvering around as a teen had taught me anything, it was how to be quick on my feet.

"Super flagged me down to help get an unruly tenant upstairs and put to bed." I said, looking everywhere but back into Rockwell's eyes.

"You came out and made a ring," he said, referring to my trip to the call box. He said it calmly, like he was reading from the newspaper. He was reading me with far greater interest. "Did you tell the sergeant?" He waited for me to look at him.

"No."

"Then you went back in, why?"

I don't know what came over me. Maybe, it was just gallows humor, like a last joke before an execution. All I could do was shrug.

"To make sure he stayed."

Rockwell stared at me so long that I felt like I was already sliding down that fire pole, but then a hint of a smile creased the gruff investigator's mask and his demeanor changed.

"I'll give you credit," he said. "You came after me. You observed me."

Rockwell certainly knew my story was off, but maybe he was suddenly more appreciative of my skills. Maybe he made a moment's assessment of my future worth to law enforcement and let me slide.

"This one's on me," he said as he turned back for the car door. "Have a good night."

After my run-in with Rockwell, I quickly sought out Tom Gannon, hoping that my ability to spot the guy would garner me some points. Instead, it got me a well-deserved earful as my mentor took me to task for providing Rockwell the opportunity to write me up. He reminded me what such a complaint could do to a police career. It stung for sure, but as usual, Gannon gave me food for thought, and the lesson never left me.

Carry yourself as an example, at all times.

***

In the early 1960s, each precinct only had four or so patrol cars or "sector cars," so getting into them was an extremely competitive affair. If you were lucky, you started out as a fill-in when space appeared. It was called "getting a seat." The coveted car detail meant that you'd go where the action was, and, most important in winter, you'd be warm and dry. It also meant a blur of partners, some great and others not so much. In fact, each of us was taught early to be wary of whom we might be partnered with during roll call. It was my first exposure to the notion that some cops were burned-out and, sadly, that others could actually be liabilities.

18

Fortunately, I got very lucky with my initial radio car assignments, including Officer Frank DeRosa. He taught me where to position the car when stopped for various types of calls, what to look out for, how not to get trapped or boxed in. DeRosa could look out the window and point out a guy who was sizing up a business or a mark, then direct me where to move to observe or contain him if we had to apprehend.

A few choice words from Frank often sent guys packing and averted a crime altogether. When I asked him why not wait for the arrest, he taught me about prevention—about not letting things get that far just for the sake of a collar.

"We're here to prevent as much as protect," he reminded me. "Not to issue summonses and make arrests after the fact."

Another of my great sector car experiences came alongside Jerry Giorgio, a smooth operator who was every bit as polished and on the ball as Frank DeRosa and Tom Gannon. Unlike Gannon and DeRosa, however, Giorgio had the air of a detective about him. Little did I know that he would go on to have one of the more distinguished careers in the NYPD. So well-known, in fact, that he was later credited with inspiring the Jerry Orbach character of Lennie Briscoe in the TV hit *Law & Order*.[6]

After a blur of cars and partners, I had the good fortune of landing in a car with the six-foot-two, two-hundred-ten-pound form of Heinrich "Hank" Buck, shield number 695. Hank had manned a patrol adjacent to mine and with his physical stature, blond hair, and striking German scowl, he was hard to miss.

Buck projected a disciplined and military bearing, one that had been honed by six months in the US Marine Corps Reserves. Surprisingly, he knew a lot about me—my arrests and even the time I single-handedly delivered a baby. My life wasn't that interesting, nor was it department news. Like previous mentors, Hank was adamant

6   Tracey, Thomas, and Parascandola, Rocco. "Retired NYPD Detective Jerry Giorgio Dies—Known for Work on Baby Hope Case." *New York Daily News*, September 28, 2018.

that a cop's image and professionalism were two of his most important assets. People on the street responded best to respect and the projection of fairness and authority.

There was an added early benefit of our partnership, too—Hank's shield number, 695. With mine a distant 19157, people on our patrol always took his number first, as it was easier to remember. This was good and bad depending on the situation at hand. If somebody wanted to complain, it'd be Hank's shield they'd recall, but the same held true for good news or positive reports to the precinct.

We mostly got positive reviews, though, and when hit with the odd complaint, Hank would direct people to me, saying, "My assistant will take your report." For both our sakes, he hoped they wouldn't remember my number. Meanwhile, my brother Tom was surpassing me. Not only had he followed me into the department, but he'd taken on tougher and more dangerous assignments, including getting "the seat" before I did.

The times Hank Buck and I got the coveted sector car assignments, we quickly noticed how much more difficult it was to observe the city from a vehicle. To think we always looked up to these guys. In reality, the confines of the car put you at a cold distance from the community. Speed and responsiveness came at the cost of quality time. The beat had required us to be a mix of investigator and counselor. The sector car made us little more than first responders.

Yet I couldn't dwell on the particulars and challenges of the discovery. There were other more pressing matters to which I had to respond...

***

I recall the early morning hours of March 29, 1962, as raw and miserable, a bitter swirl of rain, wind, and snow that whipped the tolerable thirty-degree temperature down toward the frigid teens.

Pregnant from the previous July, my wife, Joan, was due at any moment, yet there I was back on foot patrol and walking Central Park West by the Museum of Natural History. At maybe 3:15 a.m., I stopped at the corner of 79th Street to make my third call-in of the shift when the sergeant gave me a message, almost as an afterthought.

"Oh, by the way, your wife called a couple hours ago—she was on her way to the hospital."

I hailed the first cab I could find and rushed back to the precinct. When I barged in to tell the sergeant I was leaving, he looked at me like, *"What the hell are you doing here?"* I didn't even return the look, nor did I care what it meant for my job.

"My wife's giving birth," I yelled on the way out. There were no "Congratulations," or "Is everything okay?" I think a suspect or two—those waiting to be booked or questioned—might have offered their support.

I didn't care if I got fired. I wasn't going miss the birth of my first child and, still in uniform, raced into the hospital with such purpose that the whole hospital staff backed away, likely convinced I was there to arrest somebody.

Next thing I knew, the beautiful Joanne Hallinan was looking up at me through newborn eyes, and my life was forever changed. Holding that tiny human life in my arms, the true scope of my responsibilities hit me.

Then, I had to use my gun...

***

April 22, just about a month after Joanne was born, I wanted to do something special for Joan's and my first anniversary. As luck would have it, I got assigned to Radio City Music Hall as part of the NYPD detail for the star-studded premiere of the film *To Kill a Mockingbird*. I recall it as another miserable, rainy, and raw night.

After the show, our commander informed me that Radio City had provided each officer two free passes for a future showing. I decided to take Joan to dinner and an anniversary show, only with me playing the hero this time.

As I headed home and just off the West Side Highway, a disheveled man pulled alongside me in a shiny new auto, asking if I wanted to buy a bumper jack. I was totally taken by surprise.

"A jack?" I think I mumbled.

"Yessir, three dollars," he replied with a nod.

I just shook my head and said, "No thank you."

Then, the light changed and the guy drove away at high speed, straight down Broadway, pulling into a gas station on 225th St.

It's every young patrolman's dream to eventually make detective, and I wasn't doing a very good job of it. I simply watched that new car go down the street, and thought about the guy's state of dress and actions. Then, it finally hit me.

"Why the heck was this guy selling a jack?"

Had he stolen the car?

Selling it one part at a time seemed pretty poorly planned. After this *"ah ha!"* moment, I pulled into the station and parked a short distance away.

Sure enough, my "suspect" got out of his car, all six-foot-four and rail-thin one hundred seventy-five pounds of him. I'll give him credit. He was persistent, going straight to the station attendant and trying to sell him the jack. After a few moments and out of luck, the guy headed back to his car, and as he returned, I exited my vehicle and identified myself as a police officer. I then walked him over to a nearby phone booth so I could check in with the NYPD Lost Property Unit.

As I made the call, I realized that not only were my detective skills lacking, but my police procedure as well. Just as my fingers slipped into the old rotary dial-wheel of the payphone, the guy jumped back in the car and sped off. I had failed at the simple task of taking the car keys.

I ran screaming for him to stop, and the bad situation got worse as the guy pulled a high speed U-turn and came barreling back and straight for me. Finally my training kicked in, and I pulled my snub-nose service revolver and took aim. Only problem was that I'd never fired it anywhere outside the pistol range. I pumped a warning shot into the car door, and I guess I wounded the machine.

Car and driver then rammed into the support beams of the overhead Metro North Railroad tracks, and I ended up pulling the guy out. We struggled there until two NYPD Emergency Services officers pulled up.

"What you got kid?"

"I think he stole this car."

The officers looked over the wrecked vehicle, the lone bullet hole in the door, then looked at each other. It must have seemed to them I'd had quite an adventure. They radioed Lost Property for me, and, sure enough, the car had been reported stolen from Queens just an hour earlier.

With two passes to Radio City Music Hall in my pocket and Joan at home dressed for an anniversary dinner, the only show awaiting me was a double-billing—at the 34th Precinct and then night court. A date with Mr. Green. As she had done so many times already, Joan took my duties in stride and ended up coming to night court to watch me work or, perhaps more accurately, to wait.

Obviously, I needed to get her out more.

***

A Sector Car assignment provided one of the first great "Forrest Gump" moments of my career, a chance meeting with my astronaut hero, John Glenn. Glenn for those who don't recall, was the second American in space and the first to orbit the planet in his *Freedom 7* Mercury space capsule. After he splashed down, NY held a ticker tape parade in his honor. During the parade, Glenn commented that he'd love to ride along with some cops, and the department decided to grant his wish.

That night started routinely enough as both Hank and I came to the station house for the 4:00 p.m. to 12:00 a.m. shift. During roll call, two of our fellow cops—Beatty and Kerrigan—were summoned to our captain's office. This usually meant one of two things: a special assignment or discipline. After a few moments, we all heard a commotion coming from the office, followed by laughter and lively chatter. Then, the door flew open and out stepped Captain McCarthy, Kerrigan, Beatty, and astronaut John Glenn!

In seconds the whole precinct was abuzz and as Glenn moved through the ranks, exchanging handshakes and small talk, McCarthy singled out Hank Buck and me.

"While you're out there tonight," he said with a smirk, "you guys stay close to Beatty and Kerrigan, in case backup is needed." We were the new guys in the sector game, but were going to shadow one of the country's biggest heroes.

Later that night, backup was indeed needed when Beatty, Kerrigan, Glenn, Buck, and Hallinan all showed up at the same burglary call. Once the interviews were done and paperwork was in the offing, Beatty and Kerrigan needed to head back to the station. The man from space wanted nothing of it, and quickly eyed Hank and me, asking if he could continue his tour with us. My partner and I exchanged a surreptitious nod of agreement before taking the Mercury 7 astronaut off our colleagues' hands. Next thing you know, the national hero was in the back of our car and back on patrol.

Hank and Glenn hit it off quickly, with Hank a Marine reserve and Glenn a former US Marine pilot. Glenn and I bonded over baseball, and the astronaut let us know that during the Korean War, none other than baseball legend "Splendid Splinter" Ted Williams was his wingman.

For the next couple of hours, Buck, Glenn, and I chased down burglary calls and even a couple of suspects, at one point across some rooftops where somewhere over a ledge I realized that we might accidentally send a national treasure to an ignominious kind of splashdown.

Glenn didn't care. He was all in, and the night was just getting started as our next call took us to a domestic dispute. There we walked in on a three-hundred-pound wife pointing a knife at her equally large husband who, for his own part in this passion play, was taking swings with a large frying pan. John Glenn loved every second of it and even tried to help talk the couple down, a totally surreal scene with knife flashing, pan swinging, and Hank and me struggling to get the "happy" couple separated. Once they were under control, the couple began directing their complaints to Glenn, calling him "detective." The astronaut just looked at us with a shrug and half-smile, and at that moment, I saw over his shoulder that the couple had taped a color magazine photo of Glenn himself on their wall. There was a big roach crawling over it, and I don't think the bug recognized him either! I tried hard not to laugh.

To my surprise, John Glenn later memorialized the event in his own memoir, only from a very different perspective. "Hallinan tapped me and pointed out a photograph of me from one of the newspapers, tacked to the kitchen wall...when I noticed that the tack that held the picture to the wall was placed through my head.

"Here was a place that I was definitely not a hero, and I realized that the space program, for all its Cold War import and future scientific benefits, and for all the excitement it generated in many quarters, remained remote from people whose hard-pressed lives didn't allow them to appreciate it."[7] John Glenn would have made an excellent detective, and showed why he had such a meaningful career as a public figure and senator.

***

After our successful tours in the sector car, Hank and I were posted to a precinct conditions car, a next-level assignment that had us driving around in an unmarked cruiser, though still in uniform. The plain vehicle gave us the stealth of detectives while maintaining the immediate presence of men in uniform.

The post also came with some added leeway. Rather than just go where we were directed by dispatch, Hank and I were able to monitor calls and take our pick of what was occurring nearby. It allowed us to do more of what we knew, make our schedule somewhat and take the time to respond more fully to members of the community. Conditions car fare didn't disappoint either, with calls ranging from

---

[7] Glenn, John, and Taylor, Nick. *John Glenn: A Memoir*. New York: Bantam Books, 1999, pp. 378–379.

dangerous armed burglaries to the occasionally silly situation, such as female impersonators posing as hookers. As our patrols grew tougher, we embraced the opportunity to do more and dove in head-first.

Meanwhile, the world seemed to grow a little darker and more intense and, despite the hope that the postwar era had brought the city, a slowing economy and Cold War tensions foretold of uncertain times ahead.

◣ BACK DOWN TO EARTH

The year 1962 brought the harrowing Cuban Missile crisis, and then after the 1963 assassination of President John F. Kennedy, the city and country seemed to lose their innocence. Civil Rights next took the spotlight, alongside the growing national discontent over America's involvement in the Vietnam War.

By 1964, everything going on in the country seemed to fuel more anger and unrest at the system. As cops, we were symbols of that very system. It certainly didn't help that a massive influx of drugs and rack-eteering had targeted the inner cities. The massive spikes in crime that accompanied the drug trade required more patrols and arrests. That in turn allowed some with a more activist bent to paint the police department in an ever more adversarial light.

To compound matters, Hank and I—along with most city ser-vices—were frozen in place by a creeping recession. The economic downturn accompanied the flatlining of the city's poorer areas, which, in turn, created an escalation of drug use and trafficking, resulting in still more crime and still more poverty.

Everything seemed to boil over in July 1964 when a desperate and despondent Harlem population lashed out after an off-duty police officer shot and killed a Black teen in Yorkville on the Upper East Side of Manhattan. With the details of the shooting still murky to this day, the anger and protest that followed quickly escalated into riot-ing. At the time, I was just a guy in the department and stationed in another precinct, where I read and heard the versions of the story that were presented on the news. While I don't have any inner wisdom into what exactly occurred, the images of police brutality that filled

TV sets and newspapers added several incendiary degrees of heat to the already-smoldering city.

I will say this—after the rioting began, the press, whether motivated by politics or just profit, did not help the situation. For those of us in the department, their knee-jerk reactions to frame in racially charged absolutes the initial shooting, subsequent riots, and police response seemed extremely irresponsible. We knew for a fact that there were criminal elements involved in the rioting, and these opportunists endangered the community as much as they threatened the police and city.

Yet practically none of this was covered in the press.

Meanwhile, the harsh reality of the riots as we saw them was as sad as it was troubling. One dead, over a hundred injured, and almost five hundred arrested. The property damage was off the charts. Police precincts were damaged, and businesses all over the area were looted, broken, or destroyed outright, most of them owned by Latinos and Blacks. Nobody printed or reported on that aspect, yet we in the NYPD lined up to help put a stop to it. Were there guys with race-related problems in the NYPD? Of course there were, and sadly the NYPD didn't have the monopoly on it. Was that me? I certainly didn't think in that way. It just wasn't how I grew up.

For a cop, seeing color could be a recipe for getting people killed. By 1964 there were more than twelve hundred Black cops in the NYPD, and while this was barely more than 6 percent of the force, the number had been growing since the 1950s.[8]

Sure there were guys uncomfortable with a Black patrol partner, just as there were Black patrolmen who caught an earful for being seen with a white partner. The department to its credit was extremely sensitive to the issue and, after the situation calmed, joined the city government in the hope of refocusing the narrative. After all, New York was the nation's melting pot, so we needed to take the lead.

---

[8] Browne, Arthur. "A History of Blacks in NYPD Blue: It All Started with Samuel Battle." *New York Daily News*, June 11, 2015.

The New York Board of Education came calling with an idea to create a book about Black and white cops on patrol. In fact, a Black patrolman named Josh Harris was teamed with Hank Buck to star in a children's book on racial unity, law, and order. It was a good pairing as Hank and Josh were already good friends—though sadly, it seemed too little, too late. As the small effort was just developing, demonstrations and then riots spread to upstate New York, New Jersey, and Philadelphia.

Let me take a moment here and say that one of the most important aspects of the job of police officer was learning to limit emotional responses, especially anger, frustration, and most of all knee-jerk judgment. Yes, most crime occurred in lower income areas of the precinct, which sadly were the places where a higher percentage of minority populations lived and worked. Some cops came back to the station harboring a growing generality and even resentment for such areas, yet many more went in to these same zones trying to understand and help.

As the national civil rights cause grabbed the headlines and attention, the city where America's most diverse population mostly got along began to fray along racial lines. Indeed, there were so many nights where Hank and I went home emotionally exhausted from the things we saw and the situations we couldn't help or change. At the end of every shift, we took that pain home with us and did our best to process and move past it by the next day's roll call.

When I became a cop, I vowed never to bring the job home with me, but despite my determination to "leave my armor at the bridge," the job was often still lingering with me in the driveway. Thankfully, checking in on my sleeping kids, pulling a blanket up for one, maybe removing a toy from another's unconscious grasp, often brought a final and needed release.

Then a twin-headed beast struck the city in the forms of the Vietnam War and the gruesome murder of the Nation of Islam's Malcolm X. The fiery civil rights leader had "made the police a focus of his demands for a bloody black revolution in American streets and after his assassination…(his) baton was picked up and carried forward

by angry militants such as Stokely Carmichael and H. Rap Brown...
who popularized the term 'Black Power.'"[9] As you can understand,
Malcolm X's death precipitated a steep rise in anti-police violence
and rhetoric. Soon, bombs targeting police officers began showing up
with ominously increasing frequency.

One of my friends in fact—a guy who always went for the duty
of driving sergeants around—left the precinct one morning after roll
call to get a car. As he got to the door, he spotted some kind of package underneath the wheels and, after bending down to investigate,
was blown off his feet and nearly killed. Nobody ever took credit for
the improvised device, but it coincided with the genesis of certain
groups that targeted police in ways that didn't include bribes, extortion, and drugs.

That one explosion became my baptism in antiestablishment and
anti-police activism, and one of its leaders, H. Rap Brown, would be
somebody whose path I would cross later in my career. At the time,
however, all we could do in the department was take our chances and
do our jobs. And while I was blissfully unaware of what was coming,
some of my fellow cops and the FBI knew better. These new bombings weren't just a deadly harbinger of domestic unrest. They signaled
rising international and revolutionary movements that were headed
for our shores.

The pressure was mounting, and at the end of 1965, it got to me...

***

It was an absolutely brutal, cold night when Hank Buck and I stepped
inside a dilapidated brownstone just off 80th Street and across a car-
pet of broken glass. In front of us, the frame of a huge picture window
gaped to the street, jagged shards framing it like teeth.

Huddled in a corner of the room, a frightened mother and
children cowered from the angry and despondent rage of a broken

[9] Borrough, Bryan. *"Today, A Softer Response to Police Violence Than in 1960s and '70s."* Los Angeles Times, May 2, 2015. Web, January 16, 2018.

man before them—a husband, a father. During an argument, he'd smashed out the window, plunging the entire apartment into the icy chill of winter. I'm not sure how to describe what happened next, but suddenly on that night, with my suburban home behind me and my armor firmly in place, the job suddenly became deeply and painfully personal.

It was the closest I came to snapping.

I saw many things as a cop, terrible things and wonderful things, but what did I really do? Sure, I stopped a crime or two, recovered a few stolen trinkets and such, but that night I was reminded of what mattered most. As Hank dealt with the frozen and crying family, I went to talk to the man of the house, but indignant and furious at our presence, he was having nothing to do with me. He remained belligerent and distant, cursing and threatening not only his family, but now Hank and me, too. I don't exactly know what came over me, but I hauled off and slapped him. I slapped him right across the face and made him look at his wife and kids freezing there.

Then I pointed to the window and asked him if that's what he meant to do? Punish them.

"For what? What did they do to you?"

With every step I took, he stepped back from me. Suddenly, I stopped and backed away, too. I'd crossed the line. Before I could apologize, the husband suddenly broke down crying. He rushed for his family and embraced them, choking out an apology. When the police arrived, he thought, it was the beginning of things only getting worse for him. I had just wanted him to snap out of his rage and know things could be better, that *he* could be better.

After his breakdown, he focused and slowly recognized what he'd done and why were really there. We all talked about it. Hank and I then got the building super to come in and board up the window and turn up the heat. I hoped in some way, it all helped, but after the tense scene I was shaken. For the next several days—and apparently to today—it stayed with me. The city I loved and knew was becoming a pressure cooker.

Something was going to have to give.

***

For the next two years, Hank and I saw crime in New York City absolutely soar. Indeed, between 1965 and the early 1990s the crime rate increased nearly every year, with violent crimes and murders more than doubling, while rapes and robberies nearly tripled.[10]

We saw it up close and personal too as one morning Hank I were rolling past a liquor store when I spotted an armed holdup in progress. Without a word to my partner, I reflexively pulled the car over, jumped out, unholstered my service revolver, and entered gun drawn. I found the robber pointing his own gun at the store owner. I felt I had the element of surprise.

"Drop the gun!" I yelled.

Thankfully, our perpetrator was in no mood for a shootout, quickly dropped his weapon on the counter and backed up. Even in the sheer blur of it all, I was reminded of what I had to lose. It was the same exact scenario that had taken the life of Francis Xavier Walsh the year I joined the force. I had three kids at home and knew all too well what it felt like to lose a parent.

At home that night, I sat up thinking back to a late spring day just before my fifteenth birthday when my father returned alone to our Cypress Avenue apartment, face drawn and eyes moist, shakily whispering to his own three children that their mom had six months to live...

What really stuck out to me after recalling my mom's passing was hitting one of my life's biggest walls—not just in the figurative sense but in the literal. A few weeks after Mom passed, I took a bat and ball up to the empty Cowboy Land tennis courts to fungo some balls at that infamous outfield wall. It was less about baseball than it was a

<hr>

[10] Disaster Center. "New York Crime Rates 1960–2019, NYC Crime." www.disastercenter.com.

kind of exorcism, perhaps a defiant declaration that I was not going to let her death take my childhood.

In all the years we played there, I'd never hit one over that wall, and that day I was determined to do it. I remember taking swing after swing, retrieving ball after ball and again taking mighty hack after hack. I did so until my legs and arms were as heavy and as aching as my heart. After twenty or so tries, I managed to hit the barbed wire atop the fence, but the ball defiantly tumbled back. I tried and cried the rest of the afternoon and never came close again.

Long before my Delehanty training, I knew about walls. This was one that I never truly got over. Many more were still ahead.

After the scene in the liquor store, I certainly didn't want to subject my family to that kind of experience, and yet it was an everyday reality for a policeman. Being a patrol cop, on foot on in the car, was not easy on a family. The hours were long, there was a ton of court time and lots of study involved in qualifying for promotions, more money, and perhaps even better hours.

Night court was a curse in time but a blessing in opportunity, allowing Hank Buck and me to bring our books and study materials. Either those walls and hurdles in front of us were going to give eventually or we were.

***

Then, as the city grew ever more dangerous and the country more volatile, a larger storm arrived on the night of April 4, 1968, after James Earl Ray coldly assassinated Dr. Martin Luther King Jr. at the Lorraine Motel in Memphis, Tennessee. Dr. King was pronounced dead at around 7:00 p.m., and by 8:00 Harlem exploded into protests and violence. Being at the border of Harlem, our precinct quickly fell under intense pressure and while the anger and outrage were justified, it seemed to me that the level of violence was not. The nearby 2-5 Precinct, my later home as detective, was undermanned and quickly placed under siege as demonstrations coalesced into marches and marches devolved into rioting and looting.

For the most part and just as tragically as the previous Harlem riot, the vast majority of the business targeted were owned by Harlemites. I became aware of the shooting at around 6:00 p.m., after using the call box at 84th and Columbus. There, I was told to stand by for a pickup to Harlem. Next thing I knew, I was being herded into a paddy wagon and driven up to the 2-5. Once inside the precinct zone, the van stopped at various corners and let guys out for their newly assigned patrol posts.

As 7:00 p.m. approached and the news arrived that King was dead, the assignment became a gauntlet. We had bricks and bottles thrown at us from rooftops and shots were fired in our direction. We struggled to stop looters from smashing store windows and came across other businesses that were already torn apart and burning. Groups of rioters began pulling people from cars and beating them to bloody messes. It became apparent that the vast majority of looters that night were guys already predisposed to trouble, but even as cops doing a job, a lot of us knew it marked the failure of the system and that, for the night, we were the face of it.

That being said, there's a lot that wasn't reported that night, because it didn't sell newspapers. There were dozens—if not hundreds—of people in that very same Harlem community who in the midst of rage and chaos came to our defense, at the risk of their own safety. Mob mentality, though, was and is a powerful force, and many joined the rioting just to belong. The whole night became so permeated with pain, suffering, and terror that many of my fellow officers needed days to recover before they could even speak about what they'd seen and been part of. Still, not one of them wavered in their duty, and nobody, to my knowledge, ever quit or walked away from the job.

Later, as the sun rose and Harlem quieted, many of us were sent back to our command. Only this time, no paddy wagons showed up, no rides. We just got the message, "Return to command." Thus, the previous night's protest marches transformed into a vastly different human gathering, a parade of filthy, smoky, bloodied, and exhausted men in blue, taking to buses and subways where commuters looked at us like refugees. When some of us, myself included, staggered back into the 20th Precinct, nobody said much.

The city and the department were equally numb. I will never forget the bizarre sight of that night of rioting and our place in it. It was our job. It was another milestone and another marker showing that the city and country would never again be the same. To my eyes, the impact of losing Dr. King, just three years after the assassination of Malcolm X, was staggering for the Black community. Hank and I saw it every day on the streets. The '60s undercurrent of antiestablishment and rebellion was mixing with an already smoldering outrage and anger over drugs and poverty. The economic inequality and loss of hope were ready fodder for organized crime, drugs, and militancy.

Then as 1968 rolled toward 1969, thousands of people abandoned the faltering city and began moving to the suburbs. The loss of population left a deepening recession in its wake, one that manifested as a deeper freeze in city services. It was the proverbial vicious circle, with the NYPD in the center. After the random call box booby traps and the explosion outside the 20th, it began to sink in that cops were increasingly the symbols and targets for anger.

Law enforcement fatalities were markedly on the rise, and from the period of 1965 to the mid-1970s, law enforcement deaths rose almost 300 percent.[11]

Cops everywhere were in the crosshairs.

---

[11] Kelly, Eugene. "Killed in the Line of Duty." FactCheck.org., July 13, 2016.

◢ BROOKLYN SOUTH

In December 1968, three US Apollo 8 astronauts became the first humans ever to orbit the Moon. Back on Earth, I felt utterly grounded and began to wonder about my NYPD future.

I'd worked so hard to make detective; Hank too. We had stellar records, and yet we were still out on patrol. As the year came toward a close, we finally got the call that we were being considered for promotion.

We were ecstatic of course, though department politics and fiscal reality would again place a wall in front of us. Meanwhile, my brother Tom zoomed ahead again and took an assignment in what was known as the extremely dangerous "combat car," which in his case included the most dangerous, frontline calls. Though he'd started his career behind me, Tom had already passed me by. He then escalated our childhood competition by volunteering for a temporary assignment driving for the Chief of Detectives Office, where he took every opportunity to sing my praises and even wrangled me several interviews with the Detective Bureau. Each time, the higher-ups were impressed with my record and work, but also each time I was merely told to "keep it up."

I began to lose faith and, frankly, faltered a bit.

Then as spring 1969 approached, Tom's continued efforts got me another interview, only by then my arrest numbers had fallen significantly and acting Chief McLoughlin seized on it, compelling me to explain that no matter how hard I worked, the gold shield appeared to be forever out of my reach. I was nearing the end of my tether.

"Seven years as a police officer," I remember telling him, "seven years of making arrests and spending more time in courts than the lawyers. Maybe I need to move in a different direction." Much to my surprise, the day after that interview, I was transferred to the Brooklyn South detective task force, which was like a detective training program or, more appropriately, a weeding-out process.

The transfer wasn't the sought-after gold shield, mind you, but it was the back door of the bureau. I was in at last and would stay or go of my own merit.

One step at a time.

***

There were twelve to fifteen "white shield" officers who reported to the 78th Precinct and Brooklyn South with me. We all had high arrest numbers and commendations. We were also all awaiting assignment to a permanent position in the Bureau. The only question was, would we all last long enough?

My first patrol was known as the Brooklyn South Nighttime Neighborhood Task Force. Sounds family friendly and important, right?

If Hank and I had seen things sliding downhill in Manhattan, Brooklyn South was a war zone by comparison. In my first few weeks in there, man's inhumanity to man, the sheer violence of it all, made Brooklyn South one of the most eye-opening experiences of my entire career.

Slowly though, Brooklyn became a blessing and a school that taught me what I needed to become a full-fledged cop and solid detective. It was like being tossed into a fire but as with steel, tempered and sharpened to a fine edge. My fellow white shields and I were partnered two or three to a car, sent into high-crime areas, and in just our first few days on the job people were shot, stabbed, robbed on street corners, and beaten half to death. There were drug overdoses, drive-by shootings, and brawls. Many of the cases we encountered resulted in gun possession arrests. Violent street crimes and robberies were nightly and numerous.

It was like being tossed into a wood-chipper.

The best thing that could happen was to find a great partner with whom you could trust your life, and for me that critical teammate was fellow white shield detective Tom Mullane. About six-foot-one and a little hefty, Mullane's personality was equally large. In a way he reminded me of Hank, and that was a godsend.

A bonus of working with Mullane was that he lived up in Rockland County like I did, so we took turns driving into the city. His brother Jerry was a first-grade detective, and his other brother Dan was second grade. All that detecting in the family gave my new partner a great library of stories and experience from which to draw. Every day when we got over that bridge into Brooklyn, we were already working—often even before roll call as we'd invariably encountered crimes even before we got as far as the station house.

In our first three months alone the crime and violence Mullane and I saw first-hand was more than I'd encountered in my entire career up to that point. Then after we had cut our teeth, our gold shield brothers pulled us into a drug sting operation at a dark and dingy Brooklyn bar. It was a first for me.

The 7-8 detectives had staked out the place for two nights and had a loose description of a heroin dealer who had been using the location as his primary place of business. The guy was known to be armed and dangerous, but we needed a guy inside to make a buy, in order to take him down. I looked young enough to fit the part, so I volunteered. It was exciting, and I thought it would be a great opportunity.

Instead, it placed me in way over my head.

That bar was a choke point if ever there was one—only one way in and out. The front door. To make maneuvering even more difficult, the cramped interior was smoke filled, sweaty, and narrow.

Our dealer had been spotted from a rooftop across the way, so the description was sketchy. I went in and had to do my best to check out everybody without being "made"—identified. The whole place would be crawling with weapons, felons, and ex-cons, and the uneasiness I felt was amplified the moment I entered, when a dozen pairs of eyes fell upon me.

We had two cars of detectives stationed outside, but they were down the block. If any rescue was needed, it would take many precious seconds to arrive.

By the time I was halfway down the bar, I was sweating and certain I'd been made. Then, I saw our guy. Finding him calmed me a moment, as it gave me a target to focus on, but something about me must have tweaked his radar. He jumped up from his chair and tried to throw off his jacket. Expecting a shootout, I instinctively began to reach for my gun, but the guy was more interested in shedding evidence. Once that jacket came loose, glassine envelopes of heroin flew all over the bar and floor.

A half a dozen other guys jumped up, and the rest of the bar followed. The guy ran; other guys got in my way; people reached into jackets and behind their backs. Others took off for the front door. Still more went for the free drugs. Guns and knives were coming out. Not knowing what else to do, I identified myself as a police officer and raced to tackle the dealer. It was all instinct and training.

Thankfully, we had a spotter with eyes on the window and when he saw the commotion, he sent in the cavalry. Just as all hell was breaking loose, the bar door burst open and a flood of detectives rushed in. I was lucky somebody was watching closely, or it might have been my last call.

◣ MAKING THE GRADE

After just four months, Brooklyn South had changed me dramatically and, regardless of my short time there, the 7-8 was an important experience, one where I finally caught a glimpse of the kind of guy I had to be. It was April 1969 when I got the order to report to the Chief of Detectives Office. I'd been waiting eight years to make detective and here it was…well, sort of.

Dressed in my best, or as I called it "my Sunday go to meetin' clothes," I strolled into Police Headquarters ready for a new chapter. Inside the chief's office however, the story was far more familiar. After a few minutes of waiting in the cramped space, the Chief entered, made a few blasé opening remarks and reminded us that we were now on the path to the coveted "gold shield."

Let me explain.

When a cop initially got assigned to the Detective Bureau, he or she continued to use their silver or "white shield." It was like a probationary period, though taking place on the street, and often a cause for derision. Seasoned criminals and street-savvy New Yorkers alike scoffed at the silver shield, saying things like, "I'll wait for a *real* detective," or "Is there somebody in charge I can talk to?"

Even so, it was a step in the right direction. After I'd received my promotion, the chief's aide began calling out names and squads.

"Hallinan," he droned. "Two-five Squad." Just like that, it was back to Harlem near where I went to school.

Located at 126th Street just off Lexington Avenue, the 2-5 Precinct building looked like it had been built around 1900 and then torn down, but hadn't been told to fall.

Inside, filthy green paint peeled off walls that were pitted and gouged as if they had been used for artillery practice. The air smelled like smoke and urine. From behind a towering entrance desk, an indifferent desk officer didn't notice my level of spit and polish as I flashed my "white shield" and didn't give me so much as a glance as I asked for the Detective Squad.

"Second floor," he growled before dismissively waving me toward a set of rickety stairs.

When I got to the second-floor squad room, I saw the familiar small green gate that kept visitors at bay. To my right was a long bench that was overflowing with local citizens and maybe a few perps awaiting attention. It was April but felt like a July in Hell, so those locals were sweating, unhappy, and jammed together so tightly that they seemed to merge into one damp mass.

There was only one detective in the room—Tom Bowes, a stocky, well-dressed type in his mid-forties with receding blonde hair. He was hunting and pecking on an old Royal typewriter and barely twitched as I approached. When he glanced up at me and noticed my new suit and well-used black briefcase, the sight stopped him in mid-peck. Obviously mistaking me for somebody important, he quickly rose to his feet.

"Yessir, what do you need?" He looked worried, likely thinking somebody had come from downtown or maybe even Internal Affairs.

"Excuse me." I was as polite as possible. "Is the lieutenant here? Al LaPerch?" Beyond Bowes, there was a clear view into LaPerch's office, and I could see the lieutenant's feet up on his desk. He was leaned way back, a newspaper blocking his face.

Bowes nodded to me and then went into LaPerch's office. From outside, all I could make out was mumbling as he spoke. LaPerch, however, thundered.

"Well, find out who the fuck he is, and what the hell he wants… and get out of my office!"

Bowes returned and, with a heaving sigh, looked me up and down.

"Excuse me." He narrowed his eyes. "But who should I say is calling?"

"I'm police officer Kevin Hallinan," I produced my white shield, and suddenly Bowes's entire demeanor flipped to the same stoic indifference that had come from the desk officer downstairs. He just turned away.

"Take a seat."

With that, I had to squeeze myself onto that sweaty bench and swat flies for the next fifteen minutes.

***

Finally I made it into the lieutenant's office. LaPerch silently motioned for me to take a seat, and for the next several minutes I was forced to stare at the soles of his O'Sullivan shoes. When my new commanding officer finally spoke, he did so through the still-raised newspaper.

"Give me a second. I need to check the Yankees box score from yesterday." It took a few more minutes for the newspaper to come down, revealing a short, stocky man with a steely face framed under curly dark-brown hair with wisps of gray across the temples. LaPerch was built like a football player and exuded quiet—if not tired—authority. After eyeing me a beat, he sat up straight and exhaled.

"What can I do for you, kid?" Despite his initial gruffness, my new CO quickly relaxed, joked with me for a bit, and then called Tom Bowes back in. He assigned us as partners, and, just like that, I was a detective in the 2-5, having passed the first test of my resolve.

The precinct included nearby Pleasant Avenue, a famed locale that stretched a mere six blocks from 114th to 120th Streets, and later was described by *New York Times* reporters Corey Kilgannon and

Vincent Mallozzi as "one of the most famous gangland stretches in mob history...."[12]

Whatever the darker details of Pleasant Avenue were at the time, the detectives assigned there seemed as tight-lipped as the crews they were tasked to take down. By contrast, some of the other 2-5 detective teams were pretty much "get through the day" kinds of guys and plied their trade with little planning and less teamwork.

Regardless, I was happy to be on board and on the way to another adventure.

***

The next year, 1970, was a big year for organized crime in New York and the growing corruption in the department that coincided with it. The decay in the department became a major topic among the good cops, and a kind of split developed between those cops and others who were burned out, extorted, or simply weak of character.

Complicating matters, the unrest was kept mostly under wraps, well-hidden behind the so-called "blue wall of silence." That wall and the shadows beyond it were going to provide my next major tests.

My 2-5 career took place during the time when Frank Serpico was working behind the scenes as the NYPD's most famous whistleblower and just as the massive and famous corruption investigation, the Knapp Commission, was descending on the NYPD. Unbeknownst to all of us in the precinct, one of our own was wearing a wire, and the entire department was under intense scrutiny.

In truth, most of the detectives assigned to the 2-5 were good men who cared about their work despite the working conditions. A few, however, appeared to have a very specific agenda. They were excellent investigators, mind you, men with considerable experience, but they were insular and exclusionary. Even so, their connections sometimes gave them access to information no other cops could acquire. These

---

[12] Kilgannon, Corey, and Mallozzi, Vincent M. "On Pleasant Avenue, a Mobbed Up History Is Hard to Live Down." *New York Times*, January 5, 2001.

men clearly had, shall we say, an "interesting" working relationship with the natives of Pleasant Avenue.

It was explained to me that such "proximity" was a benefit to the squad, if used discreetly, and I came to understand the nuance. In fact, back at the 2-0 with my first partner and great friend Hank Buck, we'd go a little easy on certain guys we snagged for minor stuff if they helped us with information on bigger fish. It was all part of the job.

Taking bribes and letting the big fish go, however, wasn't our style. Therefore, if the 20th Precinct could be a dangerous chess game, the South Bronx and Pleasant Avenue were more like Russian Roulette.

Straightaway at the 2-5, I began noticing a certain cop hanging around the squad room, a guy named John Roff. He walked around with unusual swagger for a uniformed patrolman and would eye me from time to time. It just didn't ring right. Why Roff lingered and why he paid me any mind made little sense. As a white shield, I usually got about as much attention as the precinct flies.

Mind you, Roff wasn't particularly intimidating. Maybe about five-foot-ten and a chunky one hundred ninety pounds, round head and face, but he seemed to be taking it all in, especially me. On the rare occasions we did engage, he rarely looked me in the eye, yet he always seemed to have an opinion of my work—most of it, pretty dismissive.

Otherwise, the 2-5 Squad was a pretty tough post with plenty of action. The place had its share of armed robberies and assaults, plus a fair collection of drug deals, numbers rackets, and turf crimes. Stuff I'd seen during my tough apprenticeship in the violent confines of Brooklyn South.

Nearby Pleasant Avenue, however, was another animal entirely. The mob enclave was a multitentacled beast that reached through all categories of criminal activities via money, influence, and violence. Those tentacles not only wrapped around the cash flow of the South Bronx, the city, and the rest of the country, but they ran through the very heart of the 2-5.

To further complicate things, budding activists and openly anti-police groups were making a home in the 1970 South Bronx, most notably, Oakland's Black Panther Party. While creating positive programs to fight poverty, they also contained militant elements that directly targeted police for assassination. By 1969, Panther Party members on both coasts had clashed with the law on several occasions, at times resulting in woundings and fatalities on both sides. Though I was blissfully unaware of this at the time, the Panthers and several affiliated groups would circle my life and career in the decades ahead.

Outside of Tom Bowes, my first couple of partners at the 2-5 were the sharply dressed Al Drafts and the less-flashy Detective Louis Rice Sr. Al had this pencil-thin mustache that gave him the rakish aura of a classic gumshoe straight out of a 1940s detective yarn. By contrast, the methodical and seasoned Rice was more contemporary and by the book. I learned from both and, as had become my usual practice via my religious father, found the nearest church and offered a few prayers for guidance and protection from a higher authority.

I was certainly going to need it.

***

My break-in to the 2-5 happened fast, too. One spring Sunday morning, Tom Bowes and I got a call about a dead guy on the street, throat slashed. It was just a couple blocks from the precinct so we arrived while the body was still warm and the blood undried.

The victim was an African American male, maybe thirty-five, and was found lying on his side, sprawled out as if he'd dropped dead while running. After looking over the scene, Detective Bowes went over to a stationed uniformed officer as I scoured the area.

Only a few feet away from the body, I spotted a bright crimson pool of blood and walked over to it. There, I noticed a trail of more blood, leading off. Bowes and the other guy were deep in conversation and waiting for the medical examiner, so I just kept following the trail, and it led me to a building across the street.

Wouldn't you know it, but that blood trail went straight into the front hall where another large puddle was. It then continued up the stairs and right to the door of an apartment. It was surreal, like being led to the crime by the victim's own past as written in blood.

Bang! Bang! I knocked hard on the apartment door, took out my shield and announced that I was a police officer. Not knowing what to expect, I got my pistol ready as the door opened and I was confronted by a very angry woman who at a full five-foot-ten, with a hefty build and blazing daggers in her eyes, never for a second shied away from my presence. I asked if she knew about the man we'd found, and got an earful.

"I know all about that motherfucker." She backed me into the hall. "I killed him twice!"

Now that the confession was quickly out of the way, I hoped for an equally uneventful arrest.

"Ma'am," I said politely. "I'm going to have to ask you to come downstairs with me."

"Why? Where is that motherfucker?" She looked over my shoulder like she wanted more of this guy.

Without further explanation, I had the woman follow me back to the street where I called for my partner.

"Hey, Tom! Can you come over here a sec?"

Bowes just shrugged at me with a silent *"Why?"*

"Because I think we got our perp." Bowes's eyes widened, and he turned. He was the one "catching" that day, meaning the arrest and paperwork were his. So he wasn't happy that his "white shield" partner had so quickly solved the crime.

The year was just getting started.

WRITING ON THE WALL

That spring, political agendas and activism saw a steep rise in New York City and across the country. Along with the more famous Black Panthers, a Puerto Rican separatist group called the Young Lords joined the party, and they made their home in the 2-5 Precinct.

The Lords sported bright pink berets and patterned themselves somewhat on the Panther's example, seeking a similar "equal but separate" agenda, only for Puerto Ricans at home and abroad. In early 1970, the growing tensions between law enforcement and the Young Lords boiled over and incidents between police and Lords members saw a drastic increase.

As with the Panthers, on one hand there were members of the Lords who truly cared about the poverty and the struggle both for Puerto Rico and New York's Puerto Rican residents. Many of the Young Lords' membership in fact, collected food for the hungry and one time, helped clean up during a NYC garbage strike. That being said, some members of the group also collected money from store-owners in Spanish Harlem and claimed it was "for the community." Instead, we noticed some of that cash funneling into party coffers and pockets as funding for criminal activities.

Often, store owners weren't "asked" so much as payment was demanded. To those retailers, the Lords were nothing more than shake-down artists who hid their activities inside a church on 110th Street.

It was always a red flag when a group put itself into a church or place of worship, as it appeared to be the perfect move to avoid prying eyes and ears. It was a deadly dichotomy I'd see and get to know in the years ahead with several domestic and international militant groups.

I experienced it up close and personal one spring morning when I decided to follow up on a communication I'd received. Allegedly, drugs were being sold in the hallway of 69 East 111th Street. It was Holy Thursday, in fact, March 26, 1970, when I grabbed Tom Bowes to do a drive-by of the building in question. The idea was to take a look at the area before moving in to investigate, but as we cruised past number 69, the front entrance was open and just inside was this guy, his back to me and facing another guy farther inside the hallway.

Something seemed off. The way the bodies were positioned and the arms moving, it looked like some kind of exchange was taking place. With our car rolling slow, I threw open the passenger door and jumped out to get a closer look.

As soon as my feet hit the pavement, the guy with his back to me felt the presence, spun, saw me, and flew out of the building and down the sidewalk. I let him go. He was the buyer. The guy left behind immediately started throwing things everywhere and backing up. It was like raining confetti at a parade. I quickly blocked the door and gave him a shove. There on the floor under me, I spotted a couple dozen glassine envelopes of either cocaine or heroin.

Flashing my shield, I gathered up the evidence, grabbed my guy, and pulled him to the street. When Tom Bowes saw the arrest in progress, he too jumped from the car and met us at the curb. Then as I focused on my partner's arrival, something else caught my eye. People. Lots of people, all rushing down the street and coalescing into one roaring human mass. My stomach sank. Many in the crowd were sporting those telltale pink berets of the Young Lords.

In seconds, the crowd was upon us shouting, "*Pig*," and so on, so I grabbed my suspect close and reached for my gun, knowing that it might be used against me. The crowd swallowed us anyway, and in the mayhem a huge guy swung a two-by-four down on Tom Bowes's head. In a splash of blood, my partner dropped like a sack, and as he hit the ground, I pulled the suspect closer and swung my pistol.

The crowd didn't care; they just pushed harder, kicking and swinging, though mostly pummeling my suspected drug seller senseless! With Bowes down and my guy about to fall, I was dead meat.

Time slowed as my eyes found a fiery young woman in the crowd, her eyes on me and ablaze.

"Kill the pig!" she shouted as she pointed me out. Then, just as the crowd surged again, I heard a commotion coming down the street beyond. Lucky for Bowes and me, a group of firemen had been just up the block on inspection duty. When they saw the whole thing go down, they came running down the block with hooks and axes in hand, looking every bit the part of a phalanx of Roman soldiers.

The Young Lords spied the charge, backed down, and dispersed.

I ended up with a few painful bumps and scrapes, but poor Tom Bowes had to be rushed to the hospital. Thankfully, his head proved every bit as hard as that two-by-four, or he might have died that day.

Following the incident, I wanted that female ringleader, but nobody would give her up. Then I realized that I had a different woman to deal with, my wife, Joan. The entire incident made the television news, and I was publicly identified as one of the officers involved in the violent skirmish. As soon as I got to my desk at the 2-5, I quickly called home to let my wife know I was okay.

***

The next day we staked out a Young Lords rally, but there was no sign of the woman in question. A day later, though, we found her hanging outside a Harlem storefront and arrested her on the spot.

Face-to-face again, she was even more fiery than before. Her name was Mirtha Gonzalez and, according to 2-5 detectives familiar with the Lords, she was a leader of the group, their "minister of information," in fact.

Back at the station house, Gonzalez singled me out as the main offender in the entire incident and cried police overreach, a legal tactic I'd find militant political groups using for many years to come. We fingerprinted Mirtha, and she was eventually released. However, I would have to meet her several times after in court over the assault charges. I was respectful toward her, but we never spoke. Then, on one of our last court meetings, Gonzalez and I exited the courthouse together and took the same elevator. Once we hit the street, she caught my eye, came over, and half smiled.

"You should leave the police," she said as if suddenly concerned for my safety. "Something bad could go down." It was, in a real sense, my baptism with political militancy.

***

As this book examines the growing complexities of law enforcement in the city and country, let me provide some additional background on the Young Lords.

In 1960 the group initially focused on the tax-fueled gentrification that was driving the poorer Latino residents out of areas in favor of middle-class development. As the Lords movement grew from that cause, a newly emerging leadership shaped it into a political movement that decried American treatment of Latino immigrants, at the same time demanding independence for Puerto Rico.

As the organization grew, chapters of the Young Lords—patterned after the structure of the Black Panthers—took hold in several other cities including the heavily Hispanic Lower East Side and East Harlem neighborhoods of Manhattan. To exacerbate the challenges we faced, in 1969 the FBI used an older, anti-communist program called COINTELPRO against groups like the Lords and Panthers. COINTELPRO was established in the 1950s as a way to keep tabs on the activities of the American Communist Party but quickly expanded in more a problematic direction.

These groups were incredibly well organized and educated. The Young Lords for example, employed meticulous strategy, a good intelligence apparatus, and excellent training. They were also organized across various cities and affiliated with other more heavily armed and dangerous groups like the Panthers.

At the time I wondered just what was in store for us. I wouldn't have to wonder long though—it was coming like the tumult of late fall as it gave way to the biting chill of winter.

One cold night, Tom Bowes and I responded to a robbery at an area bar. It was an easy beginning to the shift as the suspect was kind enough to grab a beer after his theft, which provided us a clean and ready set of fingerprints. We had barely finished up though when we got the dreaded call.

"*10-13. Officer shot.*"

In a blur, we rushed to the scene and found a fellow cop wounded and under emergency care. He had been off duty and driving a cab for needed extra cash. It was a common refrain, and, unfortunately for us all, the shooting unfolded so quickly that the wounded officer barely recalled the details of his attacker.

It didn't matter. Robbing a guy was one thing, pumping a bullet into him was another matter, and I promised the officer—who I'd later learn was a close friend of Team C's Jack McCann—that I was prepared to shake every tree in the city and stick with the case until it was solved. To prove my resolve, I made a point of visiting him in the hospital every day to update him on every step being taken. I did, however, manage to joke that he wasn't very important, since all they'd assigned him was a white shield detective.

I hit the streets and picked up on the local chatter as word got out that some known guy had shot a cop. After the story made the papers, more guys were suddenly willing to talk. Each source led me to another, and I got a description.

Weeks later, I finally got a tip on where to find a match, and sure enough, I found the shooter. My doggedness not only led to justice but also helped me cement valuable relationships with 8th Homicide. The police world was that small and that interconnected.

***

One of my more rewarding—though troubling—early 2-5 cases dealt with a young man named Abraham Rivera, a sick soul who lured kids off the street and into the vestibules of neighborhood buildings, where he pulled them under the stairs to sodomize them.

Rivera's most recent victim had been a young African American boy. Sex crime cases were something that every detective in the department took very seriously, even with the fragmented teams at the 2-5. Guys closed ranks for these crimes, especially where minors were involved, so I had plenty of support.

I certainly needed it.

After some initial dead leads and rough going, I turned to the guys in uniform—guys I was closer to in practical experience and street time. Like with my years on the beat, the patrol guys were enmeshed in the community and, in changing times, were fast becoming an overlooked investigative resource. One of them recalled a young man from the area who, a couple of years before, had hung around kids. Unfortunately, all the officer had was a general area to check, a vague description of a small corner house, and an even vaguer description.

It wasn't much, but it was a start. I went back to the family of the victim to see if there were any more details that might help. That entailed revisiting the assault with the young boy, which proved one of the toughest moments in my young career. Looking into the eyes of this family, one that had been so egregiously violated, became extremely personal. Sadly, the young victim really couldn't help much with a description, but he did recall one critical item, a maroon shirt.

Armed with that bit of evidence, I went back to the precinct and pored through the sexual assault reports. To my amazement, I found a disturbing pattern.

There were other sexual assaults, all involving young boys and all around the same area. A couple of the victims noted a maroon pull-over worn by the attacker. I began knocking on doors and was steered to a second-floor apartment of a small building at 119th Street.

Could I finally get this menace off the streets?

This was Abraham Rivera's door, and after getting past his wary mother I spotted the telltale red pullover hanging over a chair in the bedroom. Within minutes, the predator was under arrest and headed back to a 2-5 holding cell.

The extent of Rivera's depravity and the fact that he'd gotten away with it for so long had been deeply frustrating to the men of the 2-5. I felt it, as well, but now it was up to Leslie Crocker Snyder of the Manhattan District Attorney's office to begin to build a case.

A petite blonde who, though small of stature, was tackling sex crimes citywide. Assistant District Attorney Snyder would later help the DA's office and the NYPD to form the country's first Sex Crimes Bureau—the beginnings of what you know today as the SVU, or the Special Victims Unit.[13] For me, Snyder was great friend and tireless prosecutorial partner, and she was extremely supportive of my investigation into Abraham Rivera.

Sadly, it wasn't the end of the Rivera family drama, and only a few years later he was back on the street. I found this out after ADA Snyder called to let me know she was prosecuting Rivera's brother-in-law for manslaughter. He had caught Abraham assaulting one of his own kids and in as fit of fury, had thrown him off a roof.

As strange as it may sound, between all the grim and tense situations and the parade of grinding and emotional cases, by December 1969, I was finally settling in and beginning to feel like I'd found a home as a detective. I can only explain it as hitting some kind of purposeful stride, during which the more tenuous aspects of the career vanished into the sheer human service of it. Appropriately, this was also when I got the coveted gold shield and a pay raise for which I'd worked so hard. It was Christmas week, and my brother Tom was so happy about it, he accompanied me to the Chief of Detectives Office. It was truly a great feeling to go home that night and share the news with my long-suffering wife, Joan, that Detective Kevin M. Hallinan had finally arrived. The bump in pay certainly made for a good Christmas, though Hank Buck and I still spent our free time studying for that next level—in my case sergeant—and maybe a shot

---

[13] Molloy, Jenna. "Snyder Fought Crime from an Early Age." *New York Daily News*, April 26, 2009.

at a supervisory role, something that might eventually bring me a bit more time at home.

***

The new year brought the beginning of an epic slide for the city and country, including an almost yearly escalation in crime and an explosive rise in anti-American militancy. Fortunately not all criminals, no matter how desperate or depraved, felt a policeman's life was expendable.

One night after work, fellow detective and friend Mike Cassel walked into a nearby parking garage to retrieve his car, when three armed men grabbed him at gunpoint. After a quick search, they found his gun and shield. Part in fear and part in hate, they drove him to his knees and prepared to execute him on the spot. Mike later recalled what he overheard while looking down at the cold concrete floor and thinking about his home and family.

"I'm gonna kill this motherfucking cop," Cassel heard a disembodied voice say from above a pair of worn shoes. "He's gonna be a witness."

After several tense moments and some back-and-forth between his attackers, Mike heard the stunning interference by one of the thieves, who convinced his friends to let Detective Cassel live. Mike never forgot it.

Later, after the three assailants were caught and Cassel was called in to testify about what had happened, Mike returned the favor. On the stand, Detective Cassel explained to the judge how this one robber had spared his life and asked that he receive leniency.

Early 1970 also marked a major flashpoint in the massive investigation of police corruption that would ignite into the notorious Knapp Commission. It was—and is to this day—the biggest scandal in the history of the NYPD. Spearheaded by Frank Serpico and Lieutenant David Durk, a secret undercover investigation began in the spring of 1970 and went live in June. Not long afterwards, Frank Serpico himself, accompanied by a deputy inspector, came into the 2-5 under the pretext of needing a desk to type some reports. They were in street clothes, which made it seem even more out of place. What they were doing exactly was anybody's guess, but it stuck with me, especially after the Knapp Commission became public knowledge.

Good cops, bad ones, Pleasant Avenue, factions, friends, and foes aside, the Knapp Commission went on with little notice from the detectives in the 2-5 Squad.

We already had our hands full...

COMPLAINT NUMBER 9443

On August 17, 1970, I began my shift trapped downtown in at the 100 Center Street courthouse, hoping to get a backlog of cases heard. Finally at 2:00 p.m. I was ready to make the twenty-mile drive home. Before heading to the George Washington Bridge, I decided to check back into the precinct.

When I arrived, Detective Sergeants Al Robinson and Freddie Watts asked if I'd mind coming back that night to help out. The squad was shorthanded.

"Go home," they said, "grab a meal or nap, then come back and catch up with the action."

So after a quick dinner and that nap, I was back at the 2-5 and, by 2:00 a.m. on August 18, could be found sitting in the Squad Room doing some paperwork and fighting to stay awake. The lull didn't last long.

The weeds of crime always seemed to grow better in the heat of summer, and I recall that night as especially hot and sticky. Just before 3:00 a.m., a call came in that a couple of patrolmen were at 117th Street and 1st Avenue and requesting a detective on scene. All I got was the code for a shooting and possible DOA—dead on arrival, so off I went to investigate with two other detectives. It was my turn to catch—be the officer of record.

The 117th Street address meant the crime scene was just off the notorious mob haven of Pleasant Avenue and the location did not disappoint. When I arrived, two uniformed officers were standing over an ominous pool of blood near a sewer grate, where a body had fallen. From what we could ascertain, after being shot, the victim had

5 6

staggered directly under a lamppost and died. The yellow sodium lighting turned the still-wet blood a sickly shade of crimson.

Strangely, the only witnesses were two NYPD patrolmen from my own precinct, Paddy McCooey and Edward McTigue. The officers we found on the scene said the two had left with the victim and gone to Metropolitan Hospital.

At Metropolitan I found McCooey and McTigue milling about the emergency room, and they hardly gave me a second look as I introduced myself. It was strange, like they were just killing time, inconvenienced even. McCooey was your prototypical Irish cop, medium build, brownish-gray hair and thick brogue, though he may as well have been mute that morning. Rather than respond to my questions, he deferred entirely to his taller, fitter, though no more talkative Ed McTigue.

It was not an auspicious beginning.

I started with little else to go on but a name, Desiderio Caban, and the rather disinterested report that he was dead on arrival. When I asked the two men how they came upon the victim, McTigue said that he and McCooey were on patrol and stopped at the nearby Delightful Coffee Shop on 116th Street. Now, it was routine for patrol cops to have the passenger get the coffee while the driver stayed in the vehicle with the engine running. McCooey said he was seated in the car when he heard shots fired and spotted a vehicle as it came out of 117th Street, before turning onto 1st Avenue and then right onto 118th Street.

McCooey said he floored the patrol car to catch up, but it kept hesitating and knocking. That delay, he said, allowed the suspected shooter's car to escape. That checked out for me. It wasn't uncommon for our old patrol cars, left idling for hours, engines full of carbon buildup, to stall when quickly floored. It prompted some guys to make their first trip of the day to the West Side Highway or FDR Drive, where they could race their cars to blast the carbon out.

Once he got the car moving, McCooey said, he circled the block once before coming back to check on Caban. That was it. With little else to go on, I tracked down the attending physician, and he directed me behind a curtain, where I found the kid's sheet-covered body.

Looking at a corpse can be like looking at the shadow of a former life, one that you hope contains all the things that a detective can use to reconstruct the past and solve a crime. Seeing the victim of violence is vastly different from a death from natural causes or, say, a quick accident. Caban's body was dotted with swollen and ugly holes, and the browning and thickening blood was all over his clothing. An expression of fear was frozen on his face. I never forgot it.

Caban had been wearing brown shoes, a white shirt, T-shirt, blue pants, black belt, and gray-blue tie. The cut and material of the clothing betrayed some level of income and attention to style so, to me, this was no junkie or street punk. Caban looked like he had been doing pretty well.

Going through his effects, I learned that Caban lived on East 117th Street, and that meant that he was killed right near his home. People in the area should know him, meaning some may have recognized him earlier in the night.

Who was Desiderio Caban?

Did he have a record?

How did he get himself shot?

Whether arising from a street dispute or something premeditated, whoever did it sure took off fast enough. All I could do was gather up evidence from the hospital, bullet fragments, and head back to the 2-5.

***

As the sunrise approached, I sat typing out my report on one of our ancient typewriters, maybe even the very same Royal model that I first spotted Tom Bowes using. I had already made my calls to ballistics and to other support personnel but at 5:00 a.m. it was going to take some time to marshal departmental resources. Later, as the sun began to peek over the horizon, I made a quick call to the chief of detectives and provided all available information for when the press came calling.

This was a first time for me as a gold shield and a drive-by, a strange mix of exciting and sad, all distilled down into a grim determination and the hope I might provide Desiderio Caban some lasting justice and peace.

At around 9:00 a.m., my occasional squad foil John Roff walked in and approached me. I could tell from the moment he entered that he knew all about the case and was taking the opportunity to get on mine, so to speak. He sauntered over like a Broadway star on stage and hovered as I pecked away on the old Royal.

"You're the new boy wonder," he said. "The crime stopper, the hero." Roff then groaned as he leaned against the back of a chair, placing himself right in my line of sight shooting me a cold glance and a smirk. "So, hot shot," he sneered. "You gonna break this one? The big one? The one that's gonna get you the grade?" he added, referring to a promotion from detective third grade to second.

Here was a uniformed patrolman in the face of a detective and talking to him like he was a precinct clerk. From everything I'd already seen that night—indifference and evasiveness—I was pissed off already, so I stopped typing and shoved my face over the typewriter and closer to Roff's.

"You bet your ass." I stared him down. "I'm gonna break this case."

What happened next chilled me to the bone. Roff's face suddenly turned white, and he stumbled up off the back of the chair and took a step away from me before clumsily backing into the fence around the squad room. Something was very, very wrong. He slid away as fast as he could, turned, and vanished down the stairs.

What the fuck just happened?

***

Later that morning, while driving up the Palisades Parkway and headed for home, I ran everything back through my head—the crime scene, McCooey and McTigue, and Desiderio Caban.

I couldn't shake Roff's reaction, but it was the end of a long double day for me, and I was so beat I convinced myself that I had to be mistaken. I had little knowledge of organized crime except what I'd heard on the street, though I had seen for myself that the Pleasant Avenue crews seemed to dance to a different beat. Maybe that was all of it.

It wasn't.

The Desiderio Caban homicide was the beginning of my education. My direct and indirect introduction to everything the Knapp Commission was investigating.

What I didn't know then, but would hear about much later on, was that John Roff had showed up that night on Pleasant Avenue, well before I got there. He arrived on scene with his patrol partner, Officer John Lagatutta. The way I later heard it, Roff at one point told McCooey to back off and said of the shooter, "*He's good people*," though even to this day, that smacks of hearsay.

***

I was weeks away from finding out that the gunman was a guy named Arnold Squitieri, a significant Genovese crime family soldier and drug supplier. Allegedly, Squitieri was accompanied that night by Alphonse "Funzy" Sisca, his driver and right-hand muscle. Both men would eventually rise to the very top of the Genovese organization in New York.

According to later reports at McCooey and McTigue's 1974 trial for bribery, McCooey wasn't in the coffee shop, but in his patrol car and saw part—if not the whole—of the event. McCooey then chased the car, a gold Cadillac, and pulled it over just a couple blocks away on 117th Street and Pleasant Avenue.

Testimony at the trial revealed that Squitieri got out of the car and told the officer, "Don't worry about it. He's only shot in the arm. Let me go. The boys will take care of you." It was further alleged at the bribery trial that Officer McTigue noted a false license plate number in his police memo book and received a payoff via Officer Roff.

The state prosecutor contended that both officers had "thwarted the detectives' investigation into Mr. Caban's homicide from beginning to end."[14]

Knapp Commission insider Bill Phillips's tell-all book *On the Pad* revealed that Roff's version of the events, even "off the record" and "between friends," had some very telling inconsistencies. Patrolman Roff claimed that the shooting went down over Caban leaning on Squitieri's gold Cadillac while outside a local bar. This was the same chain of events that McCooey had used in court. Squitieri pulled his gun and pumped five shots into the victim.

The tidy story didn't make sense to fellow "on the pad" cop Phillips, who knew more than Roff realized about Desiderio Caban and Arnie Squitieri. Allegedly, Arnie was dealing in heroin, and Caban was selling that night on the street. He tried to hold out on Squitieri for a better profit margin.[15]

Regardless of the particulars, when McCooey stopped Squitieri, it would have been the arrest of the year for him and McTigue, and they let it go for an alleged $2,000 bribe. Much of the details of the payoff came from Roff himself, who with Lagatutta turned state's evidence and testified against the other two. As for Officer John Lagatutta, I wish he had just come to me.

All this information would have come in handy in my investigation. For the moment, though, I was still flying blind.

***

The next day was August 19. I returned to the 2-5 Squad and got a forensics report from Detective Fitzgerald. Caban had been killed with a .32 revolver, and at the time of death had heroin in his system. The report made it look like Caban was likely a junkie shot in a robbery gone bad.

[14] Chambers, Marcia. "Bribe Jury Told of Freed Suspect." *New York Times*, October 6, 1974.
[15] Shecter, Leonard, and Phillips, William. *On the Pad.* New York: Berkeley Publishing Co., 1974, pp. 216–217.

By 2:00 p.m., Cunningham of the ballistics squad reported five bullets in all—four whole and part of a fifth—in Caban's body. More info about Caban started to come in. He was a garment worker downtown and was married to an Olga Perez of Brooklyn. He also had a girlfriend named Theresa on 3rd Avenue. Drugs explained the junkie guess; the garment worker status explained the nice clothes. But while I was busy gathering and analyzing evidence to build a picture, McCooey and McTigue were busy excising any and all mention of Squitieri and his Cadillac from their on-scene police reports.

Bill Phillips was paying close attention to it all.

Unbeknownst to all in the 2-5, Phillips had been ensnared by the Knapp Commission, which may have explained why Frank Serpico had been hanging out in the 2-5 a few weeks earlier. Phillips later testified to the commission that he approached John Roff directly while wearing a wire and casually started joking about how much money John was "making on the street" and while "out on patrol." According to Phillips, Roff laughed it off but indirectly admitted as much.

"You want in?" Roff said.

It wasn't just about the Squitieri case, mind you. There was far more going on inside the pitted green walls. In his book *They Wished They Were Honest: The Knapp Commission and New York City Police Corruption*, Knapp prosecutor Michael Armstrong wrote that Phillips was at the 2-5 primarily to uncover a gambling operation—one that had lieutenants, sergeants, and detectives "on the pad" to protect a local gambling racket.

A "known gambler and organized crime figure named Farby" started complaining to Phillips about squad commander Al LaPerch, who was cutting into the game. Farby mistakenly assumed that Lieutenant LaPerch was looking for more "pad," but the opposite was true. Al was just doing his job and, knowing that the precinct was under the microscope, doing it with even more fervor than before.[16]

---

16 Armstrong, Michael F. Phillips. *They Wished They Were Honest: The Knapp Commission and New York City Police Corruption*. New York: Columbia University Press, 2012, p. 129.

Al LaPerch left the 2-5 not long after Knapp, requesting a transfer to lower Manhattan. It's likely he knew what was swirling around and didn't want his career and reputation ruined.

Much later I learned from friends on the inside that I had been mentioned in Phillips's taped conversations. While I was investigating the Caban killing, Roff took some of the money he'd gotten from Squitieri and waved it in Bill Phillips's face.

Phillips himself had arrested Arnie Squitieri some time before on an assault charge and got paid to let him go. This time Roff bragged that it was his turn.

"I got mine, what did you get?"

Reportedly Phillips then asked about me. "What about that detective? What did he get?"

Roff was said to have replied, "Don't tell that fuck anything. He'll lock us all up."

Go figure.

On August 20 I went to the garment district to inquire about Caban. All I got there was more of what I already knew. He was a fabric cutter just doing a job. It was in police parlance "a dry hole," so I went back up to Pleasant Avenue and began asking around. Again, nobody was talking, and I began to get the sinking feeling that my friends at the precinct were hiding something.

Along the way I developed a system for wrapping my head around a case. Whenever a crime went down and remained unsolved, I liked to go back to scene and, on the very same night of the week and at the same time, get a feel for who might be out and about, and why. The usual night crawlers, the dealers, the hard drinkers, guys who couldn't sleep, and, of course, the delivery guys.

So the following Wednesday at 3:00 a.m., I dragged Tom Bowes to Pleasant Avenue. Wednesday night was garbage pickup, which happened right around the time of the shooting. Sure enough, a truck came through, and Bowes and I stopped it to interview the three-man crew, two Italian guys and a skinny Irish kid. The two Italian guys didn't reveal anything of importance and just shot the shit. For his part, the clearly rattled Irish kid clammed up, and I could see that he was getting looks from the other two.

They were all afraid of something.

Bowes and I noted that Patsy's Restaurant, an area landmark, was within viewing distance of the shooting. Some locals told us that the owner, Pasquale "Patsy" Scognamillo, always sat out front after closing. While the jovial, round-faced, bald, and bespectacled Patsy might have had a front-row seat, he was conspicuously absent that Wednesday. So we decided to have dinner with Patsy a couple of nights later.

Let me tell you, the old man wasn't very happy to see us, and while we paid the bill that night, Patsy made sure he passed the buck.

"I sit out here all da time," he said in his thick Italian accent. "I think I hear some noise that night, but this big a truck, she block-a my face. All I seen is the truck, then the police. They come. That's all I see."

It was back to the Irish kid from the garbage truck, but this time we interviewed him at home, far away from his Italian coworkers. Interviewing that kid on the steps of his apartment, we hit a brick wall. Bowes and I could tell he saw the entire thing, but both the kid and his grim-faced father had nothing to recall. They must have looked at each other more than a dozen times in just thirty seconds, before taking the position that it had been too dark for any details.

I was going to have to shake the hornet's nest of Pleasant Avenue, and while Bowes seemed to suggest how dangerous that activity might be, I was too focused, too determined, and perhaps too naive to care.

NOTHING PLEASANT AND NOTHING DELIGHTFUL

As fall rolled in, I started spending a lot of time on Pleasant Avenue, going to bars and restaurants and asking around, letting people know I was there and that Bowes and I weren't going to stop until we found out what happened.

Of course, our presence and business cards were rarely welcome on Pleasant Avenue. One disinterested local bartender, whose last name was Anzisi, casually glanced at the card I dropped on the bar before coldly brushing us off as nobodies. Other avenue residents and workers could be even less pleasant. It only made us push harder.

I later visited Rao's Restaurant, at the time a noted mob landmark. I busted balls, hoping to get some people rattled, get some offers, maybe get some names. For me to do that, though, I had to piss off a lot of people, meaning some in my own precinct.

By then Roff, McCooey, and McTigue had to have figured they had the whole thing under control, but when I thought back to the night Roff got in my face, it began to dawn on me that he was likely still testing me. To back up that theory, I started noticing that the three of them would talk away from me or glance over and lower their voices when I was too close for comfort.

It made me feel isolated, and it really never dawned on me that I could—even by association—become a target of the Knapp Commission. Then late one night I got a strange anonymous call at the precinct. On the end of the line was a low, cautious voice.

"Hallinan?" the caller half-whispered before taking a couple of cleansing breaths. "Arnie the Animal." The voice lowered more. "He's your man." Just like that, I had a name.

At the Bureau of Criminal Information (BCI) I got a whole file on Arnold Ezekiel Squitieri, along with his many other aliases and nicknames including "Squitty" and "Zeke." Along with Squitieri, the name of Alphonse "Funzy" Sisca came up, too—Squitieri's right hand man. Suddenly, the pieces began to fit, and the picture surely wasn't pretty.

Squitieri was a short-tempered Genovese operative known for his imposing stature, violent temper, deep-set eyes, and big arching brows that made him look like a classic '40s movie wise guy. "Funzy" Sisca, by contrast, was chunky wide, with a kind of a sleepy look, round face under bushy, often messy hair.

Armed with this new information, I went back to my early morning stalking on Pleasant Avenue, making my presence known in and around the mob enclave. Day and night, this went on for several more weeks until early one morning I came across a skinny Puerto Rican kid named Carlos Fernandez. Barely seventeen but old before his years, Fernandez was walking with his even younger girlfriend and their little daughter. He said he lived in the area and, when I pressed him, revealed that he had been out walking at the time of the murder.

Fernandez admitted he hadn't just heard the gunshots that August night, he'd witnessed the entire crime.

We met in secret several times after that night. To keep his identity safe from anyone who might read my reports, I referred to him as "Charlie Brown." He identified photos of Squitieri and placed him in the car at the scene, but when I put the "BOLO," or "be on the lookout," for Arnie, my suspect had already vanished from East Harlem.

To complicate matters somewhat, Fernandez didn't see Alphonse Sisca in the car, but he gave a harrowing description of just how the murder went down. He placed Squitieri inside the car and Caban outside and, after a heated argument, Squitieri got out, gun in hand. At that point, Caban started to move away but before he could get more than a couple of steps, Arnie shot him five times in the back, and Caban fell onto the sewer grate.

Squitieri got back into the car and pulled away.

Painting an ever-darkening picture, Fernandez watched Officer McCooey's car get right onto Squitieri's bumper before both vehicles turned right on 118th Street. McCooey was "spitting close," enough to get a clear make, model, and license plate.

It wasn't a great feeling, knowing I was in far deeper than I could have imagined and that, quite likely, my fellow cops were directly involved. Realization set in that I was going to have go slow, acting almost in secret if I was going to solve this case and maybe even remain aboveground.

Where McCooey feigned ignorance, Fernandez identified a gold, late-model Cadillac. Early in 1971 I requested from the Department of Motor Vehicles info on several of Arnie's family members, and sure enough, a match came back: Marie Giardullo of 1110 Stadium Avenue in the Bronx.

It was tricky, keeping "Charlie Brown" on the periphery to protect my investigation and keep him alive. Fortunately, Fernandez knew the score and from time-to-time would vanish completely. In fact, there was a lull from early winter 1970 until the end of February 1971, but I give the kid a ton of credit. He did the right thing and risked his life with little to gain. He was struggling just to get by in East Harlem, so I gave him a few dollars out of my pocket when I could.

Then, as a deepening bleakness fell over the Caban investigation, I came back to the 2-5 one night and found my case files spread out across my desk. It was a clear message, and looking around, I caught a few glances but no concrete idea as to the culprit. All I could do was gather up my papers, stuff them in a box, and take them home. As each page and photo went into that box, I hoped Fernandez, wherever he was, wasn't headed for a box of his own.

Then, maybe a couple weeks after, I walked into the 2-5 and was told by a passing detective that there were a couple guys in a back room waiting to speak with me. That back room was a clerk's office by day, but by night a refuge for detectives for quiet time or privacy. Many of us considered it our "inner sanctum."

Maybe detectives from another precinct, here with information, I thought. *Maybe FBI agents regarding my organized crime suspects.* I hoped it wasn't Internal Affairs.

I might have been better off if it had been.

Inside the back room, two grim-faced men were waiting, one younger and rounder man standing by the wall and another older but far more menacing seated comfortably at the desk. Right off the bat I recognized the guy who was standing, and what I knew about him wasn't good. I didn't have a name but had seen him around Pleasant Avenue. He was a known drug dealer and wise guy. He was the talkative one, affable even.

His friend was another story. He just sat there like he owned the place, not a care in the world, all business, dark and imposing, with sunken, baleful eyes and a stone-cold and serious demeanor. After an awkward beat, in a voice I can only compare to the famous actor Joe Pesci, the guy standing introduced himself as Gigi and presented his less talkative friend as Vincent.

Admittedly, my knowledge of organized crime was still slim, and unbeknownst to me the man doing the talking wasn't just some local drug dealer, but in fact Louis "Fat Gigi" Inglese, the local Lucchese Family drug trafficker. The men seated was Vincent Rao, owner and namesake of the famous mob hangout and a pretty dangerous guy in his own right.

Rao never took his eyes off me as Gigi talked. It was like a twisted game of good wise guy, bad wise guy. Regardless of the danger I may have been in, the sheer balls of their intrusion prompted a rage to well up inside me. *What the hell was going on in the 2-5?* That back room was hallowed ground, and here were two wise guys and, worse, somebody inside the 2-5 had casually let them in and provided them the run of the place.

After Inglese finished with his pleasantries, I let both men know of my extreme displeasure at their presence, at which point, Rao thrust a finger at me like a gun barrel.

"We just wanna talk to you," he barked, more order than request. He then waited, studied me a beat, and continued, "You're pushing pretty hard on this case, on one of our people."

"Squitieri?" I seethed. "Why don't you make my life easy and bring him in?" As Rao's expression twisted into a glare, "Fat Gigi" leaned his huge frame behind his boss and played peacemaker.

"This can be worked out," he said. "This is not a big problem."

Yeah, I'm thinking there's a kid with five bullet holes in him. No problem!

Then, Inglese uttered the words that finally set me off. "Kid"—he eyed me—"you can make telephone numbers on this case. Just tell us what you want."

It was like a blood-red curtain dropped in front of me, and my mind suddenly raced back to the one or two detectives I saw in the squad office, the guys who knew what was waiting for me that night. That's when I felt those pitted green walls closing in like the sides of a trash compactor. There I stood, right between Pleasant Avenue and the Delightful Coffee shop, and there was nothing pleasant and nothing delightful about it.

"You know what I want?" I thrust my own finger back at Rao. "I want you *OUT* of here!" Then, as Rao shot me daggers and slowly climbed to his feet, I pointed again. "I want Squitieri, and I want Sisca right here in the 2-5, and I want to arrest them myself!"

Seconds later, as the two headed through the squad room gate and toward the stairs, I wondered what den of iniquity I was in. None of the cops met my glare. Rao hit the stairs first. "Fat Gigi" lingered behind, and when I felt he was going too slow for my liking I kicked him straight in the ass and sent him stumbling.

After the two were gone, I was shaken and furious. It was time to put it all together before it unraveled. Sure, it would've been so easy to take that bag of cash, but it was my job to be the cop. Suddenly I felt completely alone, and even going back to work the next day felt like a challenge. The only way I got through it was by the hope and faith that doing the right thing would somehow see me through.

The light was fading.

***

A short time later in May 1971, the Serpico story broke in the news-papers, and while it provided fascinating reading for all involved, the exposé hit me especially hard.

Patrolman Serpico had been shot in the face the previous February during a buy-and-bust drug operation and still carried fragments of the deadly projectile in his head. Even more troubling, there was a question in the department as to whether or not the fellow officers involved at the scene had stood idly by while Serpico took that bullet. I couldn't—or perhaps, wouldn't—believe that myself, even when the Al Pacino movie version of Serpico's story implied as much.

The newspapers sounded the full alarm with *New York Times* reporter Martin Arnold saying of Serpico, "His crusade against cor-ruption made him a hated, hunted man within the department.... So Frank Serpico took to carrying a knapsack with several guns in it—to protect himself, he believed, not from criminals but from fellow policemen...."[17]

I knew all about the blue wall of silence and how it protected cops and created the environment for corruption. No policeman, unless as a last resort, was to betray the badge, but the real issue was one of degrees. I want to say emphatically that I never felt I was in any direct danger from my fellow detectives and patrolmen. Sure, some were "on the pad," but they didn't eat their own.

I put my faith in that.

A 2017 article by the American Civil Liberty Union's Josh Bell drew the same conclusion, and documentary director Antonino D'Ambrosio—who together with Serpico himself, created a film about the famed lawman's career—was quoted as saying, "[T]he graft at the time went into many millions of dollars—it was systemic and endemic. Yet, for quite a while, his partner took Serpico's 'share' of the payoffs

---

[17] Arnold, Martin. "Man in the News." *New York Times*, May 11, 1971.

so Serpico could be left alone to do his job." Tragically, the other offi-cers around him eventually found this arrangement unacceptable and became increasingly suspicious about Serpico. This pushed him to act because it literally became a matter of life and death.[18]

That's how I saw it. Both for right and wrong, cops stuck with cops. Maybe I was blissfully ignorant or just too preoccupied. Arnie Squitieri and Alfonse Sisca and their organized crime connections were my main concern. What else could I do? I just gathered my evi-dence, slowly built my case, and did my job.

***

After the Serpico story hit, everything took a darker turn, especially when one loner type nicknamed "Tex" came to find me one day.

The well-regarded Tex was a first grader, a top cop who liked to wear cowboy boots and a big belt, hence the nickname. I barely knew him and he barely spoke to anybody, but only a few days after I res-cued my files from the precinct, Tex pulled me into the same back room where I'd faced down Rao and Inglese, and shut the door.

"You better be careful, Hallinan." He lowered his voice. "You're playing with some bad people." He studied my reaction and contin-ued. "You're a good guy, and I don't wanna see you get hurt."

"Tex, I'm a cop," I said, "with a shield and a gun. I'm the good guy."

Tex looked away a moment, then turned to lock eyes with me. "They take down good guys sometimes." He waited for me to blink. "You're in deep water; this can go sideways."

I thought long and hard about what Tex said to me that night. I was conflicted. Here was a guy named Tex telling me I was becoming the Lone Ranger. The strange symbolism was profoundly unsettling.

---

[18] Bell, Josh. "Never Run When You're Right: The Real Story of NYPD Whistleblower Frank Serpico." American Civil Liberties Union, November 23, 2017.

***

By the summer of '71 the already stale and dank atmosphere of the 2-5 took on a stench of decay as word began to creep through the cracks that multiple forces were closing in on the precinct. This wasn't just the guys from Internal Affairs, this was the Knapp Commission itself, with the poised hammer of the press and the public theatrics hovering just behind.

Perhaps more troubling and just before this shoe fell, I ran into a detective from the 2-0. This particular detective was assigned to Internal Affairs and revealed that they were looking into the Pleasant Avenue shooting but were hesitant about approaching me.

Why? I wondered. *Do they think I was part of it?*

The detective knew me well from our time at the 2-0 and assured me he knew that both my former partner Hank Buck and I were "straight business." Still, I wanted IAD to call me and asked him to let them know that I'd be happy to help. I'm sure he'd vouched for me to them, but I couldn't shake the feeling that Internal Affairs had me in their crosshairs.

True to that, the rapidly falling dominoes quickly pinned. I had never reported that "Fat Gigi" Inglese and Vincent Rao had come to the precinct, let alone that they'd talked with me in the back office. It was like a perfect setup as others in my own department reported that "mob guys" had "come to see Hallinan" that night. If appearances could kill, I was a dead man walking, as the Squitieri case had already shriveled into the dreaded dry hole.

Charlie Brown was gone, and the silence was deafening. Silence from the mob was one thing—usually a harbinger of violent acts to come—but silence from Internal Affairs? That usually meant the hammer could be falling.

Then I caught a real break when Arnold Squitieri's sister walked into a midtown bank where a relative of mine was working. She was there to purchase a savings bond for a christening, and when my relative saw the name "Squitieri" being put onto the bond, she small-talked the sister about the party. The celebration was being held in

Englewood Cliffs, New Jersey, near one of Squitieri's homes—a home that was across the street from one of Alphonse Sisca's addresses.

The neighborhood was known as a mini sanctuary of sorts, where mob families could watch and signal each other. Thus, a bigger puzzle began to come together of property and assets that were being hidden from the government, so I contacted a friend of mine at the IRS, and we decided to go celebrate a christening.

Neither Squitieri and Sisca were anywhere to be found, but a more far-reaching net was cast, for tax fraud.

The next break came when the gold Cadillac turned up—well, parts of it. It had been cut up and dumped. Still we were able to trace it to the Stadium Avenue apartment house where it was registered to Squitieri's family member, Marie Giardullo. There was no reason for a warrant, so we decided to try something termed a "pretext call." The idea was to call in another incident at the same scene, in this case, a report of "shots fired." It was a good way to get the "cavalry" to a spot and maybe get a reaction or careless move from a suspect on the lam or in hiding.

The street quickly filled with NYPD cars, lights flashing, and sure enough a guy who looked just like Squitieri stuck his head out of a fifth-floor window.

"There he is!" I shouted. "That's him!"

Then we waited, hoping for a reaction. Nearly an hour later, a guy matching Squitieri's description came out, and we realized that we'd been had. Either Arnie had lost a few years and about a foot of height while on the lam or we had the wrong guy. Turned out it was his nephew, the spitting image of Uncle Arnie and—get this—he was a former police cadet.

We politely asked him if he'd mind coming to the precinct to talk about his uncle, and when he agreed we put him in a car and gave him a lift.

Our pretext call did not sit as well with the family. After we brought the kid back to the precinct, Squitieri's father appeared and made quite a scene. From the back office, Al LaPerch and I heard him screaming.

"That Irish cock suck." He meant me. "If I had a machine gun, I'd shoot him like a dog." On that comment, I decided to come out and say hello.

"Very nice to meet you, sir," I said as I held out my hand. My greeting was not returned.

The case went silent again after that.

Now what?

◢ THE 4-6

As August arrived, I caught a few precious breaths of fresher air, especially after receiving the news that not only had I passed the sergeant's test for which I'd studied so long and hard, I was being promoted.

The only hitch was that the promotion required a transfer back to the Police Academy for eight weeks of training in leadership and delegating. Looking back, I wonder whether or not the timing was meant to get me out of harm's way or maybe even to get me away from the case.

Strangely, after testifying for the Knapp Commission, Frank Serpico was given his gold shield and promoted—in a sense, pushed away from the action. Maybe good cops were being shifted away from bad situations. I don't know. Regardless, I *did* know that my time at the 2-5 was coming to an end, and while it seemed a fresh start, the fingerprints of the Internal Affairs Division and the Knapp Commission were there waiting for me.

On the very first day, all the prospective sergeants were put into a room and told that we would all go through full background checks, and the academy brass warned that at least one of us wouldn't make it through the wringer.

Which wringer? I wondered.

Interestingly, just after my return to the academy, a "wanted for questioning" went out on Squitieri and Sisca, but they remained ghosts and over the next eight weeks of my training, the investigation faded. "Charlie Brown" Fernandez was still missing, and Desiderio Caban was *not* resting in peace.

By October and accompanied by great media fanfare, the Knapp Commission hearings went on television, and I made a point of viewing at every opportunity. I wasn't, of course, shocked to see that a principal witness at the proceedings was none other than Bill Phillips from my own 2-5 Precinct. Realizing Bill had been wearing a wire gave me some comfort in terms of the Pleasant Avenue cops and what they may or may not have said to him in private. At the time I recall being concerned with my fellow cops and also being bitterly disappointed that my own squad was being held up to public ridicule.

It was, of course, far more upsetting to know that much of the scrutiny was deserved. While I was fully supportive of the Knapp Commission, I remember wishing that there were more such commissions to deal with other city and state agencies that I knew were guilty of some of the same offenses.

Economic reality set in, and by fall the commission staff had been slashed. By the time the public hearings began, many of the members had been working over a month without pay.[19]

Regardless, the unresolved Squitieri case remained with me as I entered my next assignment as patrol sergeant at the 46th Precinct in the Bronx—not exactly the greener pastures I thought it might be. Instead, at times it felt more like joining a frat house.

The 4-6 was a checkered affair of both great and not-so-great cops, and the post got me thinking of all the fellow men and women in blue I'd known and worked with. Those who were too solitary, those who led, those who followed, and those who broke. Interestingly, the 4-6 was home to the first NYPD sergeant who had interviewed me for the department in 1960, the cop who wasn't sure if I had the goods for the job.

After some friendly police "hazing," with my 4-6 staff running me ragged by requesting my presence at every crime scene, a few of the cracks began to show. I'd seen it all before, good guys doing extra work, with the less capable or unmotivated officers in over their

[19] Davidson, Barbara. "The Knapp Commission Didn't Know It Couldn't Be Done." *New York Times*, January 9, 1972. Web, April 19, 2018.

heads or simply coasting. Some were burned out from the intensity of police work.

Mind you, the 4-6 was still a fine precinct working an extremely volatile and difficult area, but it reminded me in a sense of the 2-5, only the factions were more the result of burn rate and attrition. I want to be clear here. My job at the 4-6 was to inspire by going the extra mile, but like anywhere else in life, some got jaded and some got soft. It was a common refrain in a massive bureaucracy that had to constantly react to crime stats, politics, resource and budget crunches.

There were plenty of standout people in the 4-6, too, perhaps none bigger than Desk Sergeant Frank Biehler, whom I met one afternoon after I came to relieve him from his shift. Round face, sparkling eyes, and an easy smile, Biehler was that kind of guy, a great mix of dry wit and friendly sarcasm. He was about to make lieutenant, too, and embark on a memorable career in law enforcement that would include a post as a deputy chief.

The night we met, Biehler quickly stepped out to greet me and asked if I was Tom Hallinan's brother. My reputation—or rather as was often the case, my brother's reputation—had preceded me. After I admitted to my illustrious sibling, Frank lit up and revealed that he'd worked with Tom at the 30th and hailed him as an outstanding police officer. Naturally, I kidded about my younger brother being a year behind me on the force yet beating me into the Detective Bureau by almost three years, to which Frank chuckled that it must have been fun having a brother to compete with on the job. The thing about my career up until that point—and the 2-5 in particular—was that most of my competition was really between me and the shadow of the guy I had been, the guy others often figured me for.

Just as it had come for Robert McAllister though, the time was rapidly approaching where I'd have to find out for myself, just the kind of guy I really was.

PART TWO

THE KIND OF GUY I HAD TO BECOME

FLIES ON THE WALL

With Brooklyn South more than a year in my rear-view mirror and the Squitieri investigation stalled, trouble circled back my way.

With the Knapp Commission on TV and an entire police department in both the crosshairs, something had to give. Almost as if on cue, I received a call from a Sergeant Powers and the dreaded Lieutenant Hess of Internal Affairs. With little explanation, I was directed to report to their main office on Schermerhorn Street in Brooklyn.

For my part, I went into the meeting thinking it was my opportunity to finally clear the air. What I *didn't* know was that they were worried about me, the lead detective on the case.

The meeting therefore began very tensely, and I was asked to provide a detailed report of the investigation from day one, after which Hess and Powers peppered me with rapid-fire questions. At one point, it seemed more like I was on a witness stand at a trial than a detective helping with an investigation. The two men not so subtly looked to poke holes in my story, and it turned into the first major test of my reputation and resolve.

Let me tell you, Hess and Powers grilled me in such detail that I thought they were reading from my own notes. Afterwards I felt beat up and exhausted, but also as if I'd passed muster. I hoped that the worst of it was finally over.

It was hubris on my part, as just minutes after the tough interview, Sergeant Powers delivered the news.

"The Rackets Bureau DA wants to talk to you." He said it like he was ordering a takeout meal. I told him I has a shift waiting for me at the 4-6, but Powers simply groused, "We'll cover your 4 to 12."

Minutes later Powers and Lieutenant Hess had me seated like a common perp in the back of their car as they drove me to the Manhattan District Attorney's Office and the Rackets Bureau.

Hess and Powers went in first, and after several minutes summoned me. Both men took seats on each side as a young, ill-tempered assistant DA with an Afro laid into me regarding every detail of the case. My sense of clearing the air rapidly vanished into a dark cloud of uncertainty. After an exhaustive rehashing of my entire previous year, the assistant DA jammed his small frame and big hair into my face.

"Here's what you're going to do," he barked. "You are going to wear a wire and go back to the 2-5 and talk with the police officers there."

I couldn't believe what I was hearing. This guy seemed to be implying that I was another Bill Phillips and needed to do my part to save my own ass for the Knapp Commission. As certain as I had been about my ethics and behavior at the 2-5, I suddenly felt as if I was in a fight for my reputation, regardless of the truth. To say it got my Irish up is an understatement. I was *furious*.

Still, I managed to pull myself back to solemn and determined. What this ADA was implying was reprehensible, but I knew I was in the right.

"Ok, no problem." I looked deep into his eyes. "But before I do it," I added not so coolly, "I want YOU to wear a wire and go out to your lawyer friends and judges and talk to them too about the same things. Then, we can compare notes."

The room fell silent.

I stood up.

The entire time I kept my eyes on the assistant DA. In essence, I was expressing my own concern for how far the corruption might go—maybe even as far as this guy's hairdresser and beyond. I also was raising the specter that maybe some people in the system were trying to pin it all on the 2-5 Precinct and in doing so end any deeper investigation. Playing this card might get me in the most trouble yet, but I wasn't budging. A few beats passed as the wheels turned in the ADA's head. Finally, he blinked.

"We're done," he announced to the room. I then snuck a peek at the others. Lieutenant Hess's eyes betrayed a hint of being impressed.

I was out from under the microscope, or so I thought. It wasn't over by a long shot. IAD, the Rackets Bureau, and the Knapp Commission had overlapping but potentially competitive agendas. All they had to do was talk. If they'd compared notes, I might not have been placed in this position in the first place.

Days after the IAD and Rackets Bureau meetings, I was pulled back to the 2-5 squad for a meeting with some of the department brass, including the borough commander, the assistant chief of detectives, and Herman Kluge, the new squad commander. The whole meeting turned into a replay of the previous meetings, only far more positive. After hearing my blow-by-blow, handshakes followed, and I overheard Herman Kluge say something to the others.

"That Hallinan pisses ice water."

Thank God that's over, I thought.

Of course, it wasn't.

***

Come November, I got some eye-opening news courtesy of Bill Phillips from the 2-5 Precinct and Knapp Commission. Apparently, during his undercover work at the 2-5 squad, Phillips recorded conversations involving Squitieri, Desiderio Caban, and officers McCooey, McTigue, Roff, and Lagatutta, information that found its way into the newspapers.

With the case going cold, department brass hadn't given the Caban homicide much attention. The Knapp Commission was selling papers, and the *New York Times* suddenly felt the case was worthy of the front page, and a barrage of new headlines ignited a fire. As a result, by November I was assigned back to the 2-5 squad to restart the Squitieri investigation and was given a new boss—Tom Gleason.

Gleason was a deputy inspector, which signaled just how serious the department brass was taking the case. He was a smallish man, much older than me, and sported a full head of silver hair. He was an outstanding detective whom I enjoyed working alongside, and his determination to bring the case to a close was both uplifting and reassuring. Looking back on it now, it carried an aura of irony. They'd done the same for Frank Serpico when he went undercover.

Regardless, Gleason and I again started shaking the trees on Pleasant Avenue, looking for any way to put the pressure back on Squitieri and his network of accomplices and protectors.

By January, a grand jury was called in relation to the Squitieri case, and it brought the grim reality that some of my fellow 2-5 police officers might be prosecuted. The evening of January 11, I got summoned yet again to the Rackets Bureau, but this time to see another assistant district attorney named McManus. Once again it was political tennis, with me as the ball, and I started to again wonder what exactly these guys thought I was doing.

While Hess and Powers were tough, McManus was a boxer, relentlessly jabbing at me for several hours about every report and every event of the Squitieri case. He wanted to know why I was even there at the 2-5 Precinct to "catch" on the night Desiderio Caban was killed and why I had left the scene to go to the hospital.

What the hell is going on? I thought. It seemed like I'd passed through this crucible. Was the Rackets Bureau still concerned that I had some involvement?

Once again it made me furious. The whole line of questioning seemed to be transitioning from investigation to inference. Indeed, after I went home to Joan that night, I was exhausted and needed to sleep on it. I had hit the wall, bigger and higher it seemed than any wall before. Still somehow I figured I'd get over it. Sure enough, by the next morning, I convinced myself that I'd read too much into everything and relaxed. But just like the first wall at Delehanty, there was another one waiting just behind.

THE GOOD GUYS

The next morning, I ran through my usual routine—gathered my shield and gear, kissed the kids and Joan, and got ready for work. Then the phone rang, and it was Sergeant Powers.

"I need you to report to ADA Conboy's office this morning," he said.

Here we go again, I thought. ADA Ken Conboy was chief of the Rackets Bureau, was already a big deal in the city, and was famed DA Frank Hogan's instrument of punishment in the NYPD. A slim six-foot-one-inch tall, Conboy cut an imposing figure, and while I didn't know where the brass thought I fit into this puzzle, I already knew Conboy was furious about the sell-out detectives in the department. He was charging any dirty cop he could find with obstruction of government administration.

I calmed down by convincing myself that maybe Conboy just needed some more information, based on what I'd given McManus.

"Okay. I'll stop by the 2-5 and pick up my DD5s and paperwork," I replied, eying Joan as I did so. Her presence was reassuring, but the response was unnerving.

"No. Come direct to the DA's office." For all that Joan's presence had done, the tone set me off again.

An hour later I walked into Ken Conboy's office and found him waiting with Powers. They were both standing.

"You're going before the grand jury this morning," Conboy barked. "Let's go."

What was happening? "Let's go" was all I got.

Why weren't they telling me what lay ahead?

It only got worse when we walked to the elevator to head up to the grand jury room. As the elevator doors opened, there were McCooey, McTigue, and Roff. One by one they eyed me before hanging their heads or looking away. It was like the scene in a movie, when the main character is about to fall and everybody seems to know it but him.

Was I being dumped into the same barrel?

Outside the grand jury room, McTigue, McCooey, and Roff all elected not to testify. That, of course, left me as the main witness, so I braced for what was about to go down.

For what seemed like two long hours, multiple people grilled me. When I figured things were winding down, they trotted out an older Italian prosecutor named Alfred J. Scotti, who was one of Frank Hogan's chief assistants. Scotti lit into me like I was Public Enemy Number One. *What did I have to do*, I wondered, *to do my job without being implicated along with the rest?*

After the ordeal was over, I resigned myself to the fact that whatever came next was going to come regardless of what I thought. I had nothing more to give. Outside in the hall, I finally caught a break in the guise of Ken Conboy, who approached solemnly.

"Let's go back to my office." Then, he suddenly stuck out his hand and smiled. "Let's go to work."

My head was spinning.

They had been testing me.

***

Maybe two days later, all the press and the coming trial finally yielded some results too—or maybe, looking back on it, some of it was being orchestrated by Arnie's legal team to arrange the softest landing possible. Maybe they knew about my crucible with IAD and thought they somehow could taint my reputation. Regardless of the reasoning, they were about to make a show of it.

I was in the 2-5, still licking my wounds and trying to make sense of it all, when the phone rang. One of the 2-5 detectives took the call and turned to me with a dead serious expression.

"It's Arnie Squitieri on the line."

I thought the guys were playing a joke on me, so I picked up the receiver and bellowed to the whole squad.

"Oh? he's on the phone? So is missing Judge Carter," a reference to a Prohibition-era Supreme Court justice who vanished during a breaking scandal. Then, I slammed the phone back into the cradle.

The dire look I got from the detective quickly hammered home what I'd just done. It had, in fact, been Squitieri and his lawyer, Gino E. Gallina. I was tired; I was angry and put out. That didn't excuse my lack of discipline, and I was as angry at myself as at anybody. Fortunately, the two called again, and Gallina offered a deal. Arnie would surrender downtown at the courthouse.

The Squitieri camp wanted a media circus to put their own spin on it, but I vetoed that suggestion on the spot. I told Gallina and Squitieri that the 2-5 was the only place I'd accept a surrender. A close approximation of my exact words would be, "No way. You come to the precinct and get booked and printed just like everybody else."

The next morning, both Squitieri and Sisca appeared at the station house, accompanied by Gallina, and not without some theatrics. They arrived in this big, gaudy pink Cadillac limo, one that had previously belonged to a drug dealer who was now in jail. The sheer balls of these guys—especially Gallina who had begun his career on the district attorney side, and in Frank Hogan's office no less. By 1975, Gallina had been implicated in drug money schemes and had become the defense attorney for the American Gangster, Frank Lucas.

A couple years later in 1977, he pissed off one of his clients enough to end up dead on a Greenwich Village street with seven bullets pumped into his body.

Up to that point I had never met Arnold Squitieri in person, and only knew him from descriptions and his unfriendly-looking mug shot from a previous assault. I have to say that he was bigger and more menacing than I'd imagined. He stood about six-one, and tipped the scales at two hundred thirty pounds. His eyes were as dark as the lifeless coal bricks you put in the head of a snowman, and he was colder still.

Arnie knew exactly who I was and how it had come to this. As he entered the precinct, in fact, he eyed me the whole time as if making sure that I knew he was sizing me up. After all the crap his case had put me through, I fingerprinted him personally. Then as was customary for an arresting officer with a suspect in cuffs, I brought him to the washroom to stand by as he scrubbed the ink from his fingertips. I couldn't help it, though; I had to say something—the way he eyed me in the mirror, the smug way he looked.

"Two years, Arnie…" I commented as idle conversation.

Squitieri barely flinched and simply looked down at his hands, but I could see the anger as it rose from the pit of his stomach to his face. He then softly nodded and then met my gaze in the mirror.

"Fuck you."

I smiled at him and thought to myself, *He's right.* So, I said it out loud.

"Yeah, fuck me."

Arnie blinked. No one appeared to care about Desiderio Caban or if his murder went unsolved. That's when I shared what I thought was my leverage over Squitieri and guys like him.

"You're right, Arnie." I slowly nodded. "Fuck me. I'm the one that cared."

Squitieri huffed the comment away and dried his hands. Then, he smirked at me, raising one of his big bushy eyebrows. He didn't say anything else, but his expression screamed. It was a knowing look from a gangster, one who'd said I'd never quite be the same, that just like Robert McAllister, my life would be changed forever.

The Squitieri case had hit me where it hurt me the most, my fellow officers, the ones I trusted with my own life. The Knapp Commission was great reading and television, but Bill Phillips, McCooey, Roff, McTigue, the whole lot, right there and all around me, that was humbling. They'd let the mob into the precinct. They were behind my back at every turn and watching over my shoulder every bit as much as Internal Affairs. It was every bit as dangerous and dirty as *The Kind of Guy I Am*, and the eerie similarities between that book and my life had just taken a chilling new turn. After McAllister came into the 2-0, his next big assignment was at the 2-5, as a sergeant. His was my life now, too, and mine was far from over.

***

Only a few days later on January 17, it came out that Gino Gallina had hired two ex-NYPD detectives named Zincan and Dunleavy, and they came forward to claim that they'd found a "witness" who alleged he was pressured by cops to finger Squitieri. That, of course, pointed the finger at me, because the witness they brought forward was Carlos Fernandez, my "Charlie Brown."

The "honorable" Gino Gallina had his "official" story worked out too, claiming in a press conference that Squitieri had called him a couple months after the Caban murder, asking for advice, saying he had nothing to do with it and could Gallina investigate.

Is there no end to this? I wondered.

Next thing I knew, it was alleged that a detective had paid off Charlie Brown to finger Squitieri, and that detective was me. This for the few food bucks I'd given a homeless kid fearing for this life, just so he could survive. Now the rest of the pieces fell into place. It explained the Internal Affairs investigation and being asked to wear a wire. It also explained the timing and style behind Arnie surrendering.

Thankfully it was the mob playbook, and my superiors knew it was. The tax charge was going to stick regardless, and IA laughed off any inferences of misconduct on my part.

***

After the dust settled, I was sent back to the 46th Precinct and back to my post as patrol sergeant. From then on, the investigation into the Desiderio Caban murder again lost steam. Sure, I'd still work on the case from the fringe, but I was ready to at least give my family a break from it all. I just had to keep moving and so did the department.

I chalked it all up to sharing the load and some of the battle fatigue I saw in Brooklyn South. Some precincts were pretty easy; others were like being thrown to the wolves. The battle fatigue and outside pressure were immense, the hours oppressive, upward mobility and pay stalled by budget and competition. Maybe at some point, cops figured *what the hell, I'm stuck, why not make something extra of it?* It was disheartening that guys fell. I had made it through, though, as did brother Tom. Hank Buck and so many more cops I knew and worked with had come through it with their integrity intact.

They never gave me a medal or a commendation for the Squitieri case. I only got suspicions and gray hairs. Case in point was Officer John Lagatutta. Eventually he did the right thing and testified at the trial of McCooey and McTigue, but again, he never came to me. He only cooperated when he realized he was in a no-win situation. Lagatutta ended up with a full head of white hair.

Desiderio Caban was dead.

We were supposed to be the good guys.

***

When I got back to the 4-6 and Frank Biehler, the cracks I'd seen became much clearer to me, and I began to look differently at the whole department. It was no longer precincts and divisions, it was a larger and single entity under attack and under pressure, like a body with organs that when failing or distressed, insidiously and silently affected other parts. If the Knapp Commission was a department colonoscopy, no follow-up occurred to check the department's heart.

Big organizations, after all, tended to have problems fixed but seldom the causes. Where Arnie Squitieri had pegged my life for misery and NYPD investigators had warned that I wasn't ready for more shadowy aspects of the job, Frank Biehler at the 4-6 had pegged me as the kind of guy the department needed.

Knowing—or at least believing—that I was a lot like my brother, Biehler saw that I was fed up and needed some air, some sense that honor and duty counted in the bigger picture. Brother Tom, it seems, had influenced my career path yet again, and one night after getting back into the swing, I relieved Biehler at the sergeant's desk. Yet for some reason, he lingered over some paperwork.

"You're an ambitious guy," he joked dryly as he shuffled a stack. "Maybe you'll do this." He pushed a couple of the papers toward me and looked up. "You're a man of the world now," he prodded. "You've been around."

Although I worried that he was just messing with me, the papers he pushed in my direction already had my name and number on them. It was a Department Personnel Order seeking candidates for a Middle Management Exchange Program—a federal program, actually, one sponsored by the Department of Justice. The post involved sending a cop to one of twelve cities to share experience and expertise, and acceptance required chosen applicants to spend three months in the assigned city.

There were two additional requirements. The first was a stellar record, and the second a written proposal to the police commissioner giving the cop's views on big issues facing the department. Well, I had the record and the time served, but would the department appreciate what I had to say?

Frank Biehler believed in my ability to make something of it, and I was honored and humbled, so decided to give it a go. It was extraordinarily rare, however, someone from a patrol precinct would be considered for such a special assignment, so I wanted to make it count.

Just the fact that Biehler had handed me the personnel order got me thinking of my responsibilities to the department and New York City. Much in the same way that senior cops would take notable busts or shove paper work on the younger guys, orders like these were usually cherry-picked long before they made it down to the guys in the trenches. After what I'd seen and witnessed from the 2-0 beat, through Brooklyn South, the 2-5, and now the 4-6, I hoped to provide some insight on how to proactively protect cops on the job and, in the process, end up with better cops.

What immediately hit me was that the NYPD had no rotations, meaning cops stationed at various precincts often stayed for extremely long tours. It was partly the department's fault that the lack of rotation could leave some cops in meat grinder precincts that could take their edge, sanity, or judgment.

To be fair, short money and the Knapp Commission had most of the department on fire brigade duty, so a broader view was difficult to achieve. Maybe it was perfect timing for my message, and I firmly believed that moving guys around, sharing the experiences and responsibilities of the job, would make for a tighter-knit, more professional, and more accountable NYPD.

I also wanted to make sure that I honored the man that had shared the opportunity with me. So I wrote my paper and titled it "Sharing the Load," and off it went with my record and résumé. After that, it was back to work to further my experience.

Frank Biehler had other plans.

***

True to his word, he put me in as his replacement on the Anti-Crime Unit at the 4-6.

The new gig was like my brother Tom assigned to the combat car.

The guys in the Anti-Crime Unit were the go-getters of the precinct. I had the good fortune to work alongside Precinct Commander John F. Skelly. The former World War II naval air corpsman liked being in the action, and the unit was all of that and more. To fill his specialized ranks and requirements, John hand-picked crew of ten dedicated and fearless guys. The NYPD wasn't always preemptive, but this unit was very much ahead of its time.

The whole idea of an anti-crime unit was to look into reports of unsolved cases or look for patterns and do our best to catch perpetrators if possible, *before* the act. We had great success catching sexual predators and destroying a ring of home invaders who preyed upon the area's elderly. Getting out in front of crime was a new experience for me. It was highly rewarding work and had me thinking long and hard about what policing was all about.

A lot is debated today about surveillance and profiling. That's not what we did. We went after known issues and conditions, and nothing quite matched the satisfaction of preventing innocent people from becoming victims. John Skelly passed away in 2015, but I want to point out here in his honor that his welcoming me to the unit and the things I learned there were as critical and important as any part of my law enforcement career.

Frank Biehler wasn't exactly done with me, either. Just a couple of months into my anti-crime tenure, I got the call to interview for the Middle Management Exchange Program toward which Biehler himself had pointed me. There were ten or twelve cities on the list, and by March my name came up somewhere in the first two or three. I think Cleveland and San Francisco went first. Then, I got the call to pack my bags for New Orleans.

My paper on "Sharing the Load" had received considerable attention.

HARD TIMES IN THE BIG EASY

My New Orleans experience began in March 1972, over a hastily setup lunch with my new exchange program partners, Lieutenant Dick Olpe and Captain Terry McKeon. Both were considerably more experienced than I, and both outranked me. Still, they couldn't have been nicer and immediately insisted that we address each other on a first-name basis and not use our ranks.

Dick Olpe was a top investigator, a true hustler whose future stops would include the coveted position of deputy inspector. He was the perfect balance of tough and fair, a guy who once he found you capable piled more and more responsibility on you while encouraging you to fly on your own.

Terry McKeon, by contrast, had spent a bit more time in the day-to-day grind of the NYPD and we quickly hit it off via our mutual time spent in the trenches. Our trio made for a good combination of experiences and personalities, yet as we prepped for our trip south, the question remained—would we mesh under the pressure of this high-profile assignment, and might we clash with our New Orleans counterparts?

We stepped off the plane ready to work and determined to show our hosts that the NYPD had selected the right guys. The New Orleans police officers who met us were professional, friendly, and gracious hosts, whisking us to a fantastic introductory lunch at the famous Brennan's in the city's historic French Quarter. I couldn't help but wonder where our New Orleans counterparts would be wined and dined by grizzled NYPD veterans and joked to my partners that they'd likely get a hamburger on the run.

After lunch, our welcoming committee introduced us to Department Superintendent Clarence B. Giarrusso and his deputy, Luis J. Sirgo, who briefed us as to the department's profile and most pressing issues. Superintendent Giarrusso was a kind and soft-spoken man but an imposing law enforcement figure just the same. Built like a stocky prizefighter, Giarrusso was a World War II vet who was front and center in the city's growing tangle of rising crime, drug trafficking, and civil rights unrest.

It all seemed to center around a greater conflict, as New Orleans was becoming a notorious and controversial battle ground against the local Black Panthers movement. Just two years prior to our visit, in fact, the Black Panthers had set up a headquarters in the low-income Desire Public Housing Complex. Giarrusso had been in charge during a tense standoff between that group and the cops.[20]

Whatever your views on the '60s and '70s Black Panther Party, which I freely admit did at times institute programs to help the community, their radical anti-police and anti-government stances invited both a violent and criminal element to join them. One such affiliated arm, the militant Black Liberation Army was by 1972 well known for targeting police officers nationwide, and violently so. It was this volatile mix of agendas that helped create an atmosphere of antagonism that often permeated the entire city of New Orleans.

Prior to the incident at Desire, two separate shootouts had taken place in the complex, both after police faced off with known Panthers who were sought in connection with earlier crimes. The tense and racially charged situations escalated to the point where Giarrusso sent in more than 250 New Orleans cops, a helicopter, and a police tank. It became a hair-trigger crisis, and the entire city of New Orleans prepared for bloodshed.

Thankfully, after some intense back-and-forth negotiations, the explosive situation was defused without incident. Afterwards, however, fingers still pointed.

---

[20] Shea, Dan. "N.O. Police Chief in Turbulent 1970s Dies." *Times-Picayune*, November 4, 1970.

The police narrative implied that with the threat of force, cooler heads had prevailed. The Panther story was very different, with party leadership claiming that children from the Desire Complex had faced down the police as they moved in, forcing an over-the-top law enforcement to blink. Wherever the truth lay, following the incident there were those who painted the hard-nosed Superintendent Giarrusso as predominantly responsible for the tension.

Many of the issues stretched back to 1965, when the crime-crushed complex, which area residents called the "Dirty-D," been flooded and nearly destroyed by the powerful Hurricane Betsy. Black Panthers and community leaders alike asserted that the District 7 facility had been left to flood on purpose, allocating city resources to save more valuable waterfront land—in their minds, more affluent and predominantly white-owned land. This belief festered for years and only got worse when the Panthers moved their headquarters into the beleaguered complex. They staffed it partly with men suspected of serious crimes, including murder—men who were also alleged to be tied to the Black Liberation Army.

Keep in mind that the Black Panthers, with their complex makeup, operated in an extremely fast-evolving and complex time. Their goals of racial justice were accompanied by the stated warning "by any means necessary." This presented law enforcement with a very difficult and delicate challenge.

That phrase sounds familiar in today's political climate, as well, and it's worth keeping it in mind as some interesting parallels emerge between the Panther movement of the '60s and '70s, and the political movements seen on the news today.

In her 2009 book *Showdown in Desire: The Black Panthers Take a Stand in New Orleans*, author Orissa Arend noted that at a Black Panthers reunion held in 2003, both the Panthers and Superintendent Giarrusso were commended for the peaceful resolution to the crisis.

Time, I suppose, had mellowed some of the participants, but it also left others too angry to attend.[21]

No doubt Giarrusso was tough as nails and certainly heavy-handed, but many other nuances were in play on the ground in New Orleans. In fact, Giarrusso had surrounded himself with some pretty progressive people, his own deputy superintendent Lou Sirgo for one.

Louis J. Sirgo was an important figure in New Orleans and bears special mention in this book. Why? Because from what I could see, the man's approach to crime very closely echoed my own experiences as a beat cop, patrolman, and detective in New York City. Sirgo often stressed the economics of crime and how there was only so much that a police officer or department could do without being directly involved in partnership with the community itself.

Orissa Arend's book and indeed many of the Panthers of the era eventually came to agree with this idea and, in that regard alone, Sirgo seemed about as forward-thinking and preemptive a cop as I would ever come across.

He was so much more than that.

Prior to my time in New Orleans, Deputy Superintendent Sirgo had given many local speeches on the subject of police and African American relations, citing the betterment of urban conditions and opportunity for minorities as the only real solutions to inner city crime. He knew that cops were well-prepared to act and respond but not particularly prepared for the social and economic elements that caused urban crime in the first place, leading to inequality and a lack of opportunity. Sirgo hoped to change that from the streets to the halls of justice.

A local New Orleans news story from 2003 painted this picture of Sirgo. "A white, 17-year veteran of the NOPD, Sirgo deplored public indifference to poverty, a 'vindictive system' of crime and punishment, and 'the greatest sin of American society—the status of the American Negro.' He decried 'slum' housing as well as educational

---

[21] Arend, Orissa. *Showdown in Desire: The Black Panthers Take a Stand in New Orleans.* Fayetteville, AR: University of Arkansas Press, 2009, pp. 205–208.

and social inequities, which he said increased the power of anarchists and the appeal of breakfast programs in the Desire Housing Project sponsored by the Black Panther Party. If there were no 'Desires,' there would be no Panthers."[22]

Lou Sirgo was a man far ahead of his time, and I found his views both refreshing and educational.

***

After that initial lunch, our gracious hosts dropped us at our hotel, a local Howard Johnson's, where that night, Olpe, McKeon, and I held an initial strategy session about how best to mesh with our "Big Easy" counterparts. We wanted our study and exchange to be as expansive and inclusive as possible, so we decided that on our first working day, each of us would select a unit of the NOPD and spend four days or evenings working with that particular group.

On the fifth day, we would return to headquarters and ask questions in preparation for our first report back to the NYPD. The particulars of our assignment required us to prepare a detailed set of conclusions for the Department of Justice, who wanted our time in New Orleans to have a positive impact on our home force.

I have to say that the men and women of the NOPD were outstanding, taking us inside their department and revealing very openly what they saw to be their strengths and weaknesses.

Our prearranged Howard Johnson's accommodation was on Loyola Avenue across from City Hall and, frankly, was a bit of a dump on its best day. The NYPD certainly wasn't splurging on our behalf. Once checked in, I quickly found a stashed whiskey bottle under my bed, and the whole hotel reeked of smoke and other far-less-savory scents.

Dick Olpe went into action and found us new accommodations at the landmark Richelieu Hotel on Chartres Street, right in the heart

---

[22] Johnson, Allen Jr. "The Heroes of Howard Johnson's." BestofNewOrleans. com, January 7, 2003.

of the French Quarter and just a couple of blocks from the notorious Bourbon Street nightlife. I don't know what local magic he employed, but we ended up in suites with kitchens and sitting rooms, and all at motel prices. Our NOPD counterparts were thoroughly amused by our New York haggling. They provided us with three unmarked cars in which to get around town and department credit cards for gas.

Feeling as if we'd already caught a nice break, we turned in all the credit cards and two of the three cars, deciding to "share the load" and pay for our own fuel.

We were assigned to New Orleans Police Headquarters, which was across the street from the city jail, and from those barred windows—which made for an interesting commute as every morning—we'd get an earful of abuse. In New York, detectives enjoyed a certain amount of undercover anonymity. In New Orleans, the cops were right there on display for the criminals to see. It made for a kind of reverse morning "lineup" every time they went in to work!

My first official New Orleans patrol was alongside lifelong city native Sergeant Rene DeCokess. A trim and handsome thirtysomething cop of medium build, Rene was closer to my age and pay grade, so we had a lot to talk about. I also had the opportunity to show off a few of the city skills I'd picked up from cops like Frank De Rosa and Jack Skelly.

Our very first foray took us through the French Quarter, which to me, seemed more like a movie set than an area of the city. It was bright, colorful, crowded and even in the off-season, festive. Also, with the time of year, Bourbon Street was far less sultry than Hollywood often portrayed. Even so, the NYPD contingent would be sweating soon enough.

Not long into my ride with DeCokess, I observed a man walking toward us down the block. I was certain he had a concealed firearm, so I mentioned this to DeCokess and got a strange look in return, as if I was perpetrating some strange mind-reading parlor trick.

Still, I had my NOPD partner curious, so Rene stopped the car, got out, and he asked the man to raise his hands. I was unarmed and there to observe but got out of the car anyway in order to give the potentially dangerous man the impression that there were two armed officers to deal with. To Rene's shock, the man did indeed have a concealed gun. It was tucked into his belt and right where I thought it would be. I had scored my first points in New Orleans and, hopefully, made the NY boys in blue look good.

***

That morning patrol was the first of many for me over the next three months, and all were with field units, including vice, detective, narcotics, and patrol. It was like being an exchange student at a new school, and the lessons and techniques shared were great for cops and departments alike.

As I noted, a major aspect of our exchange program assignment was to capture all our experiences on paper, and since my "Sharing the Load" paper had garnered some attention, Olpe and McKinnon quickly tabbed me as the "writer" of the group. Personally, I think they were all too happy to saddle me at the typewriter every night, though both did help a lot with the writing.

During these writing sessions, Dick Olpe asked me a lot of questions about my career. He focused in on my time during the Knapp Commission and with Bill Phillips, Arnie Squitieri, and the men of the 2-5 squad. Through Robert Daley, who was a deputy commissioner in the NYPD at the time, Dick Olpe was friends with Michael Korda, the fiery wunderkind editor at Simon & Schuster. Olpe thought the Squitieri tale was ripe for novelization. I thanked him for both the interest and encouragement but responded that I had "too much scar tissue," and seeing how the blue wall broke down wasn't something I was ready to talk about.

Not yet.

Happily, it wasn't all typewriters and questions. Dick Olpe was a foodie and had found a comprehensive pocket guide to the French Quarter's food and nightlife. *The Underground Gourmet—New Orleans* had us out most every night, taking in local shows, jazz venues, and restaurants. We became regulars at the famous Pat O'Brien's. We also became jazz enthusiasts and food critics.

My "Big Easy" education only had just begun.

***

A stint with the NOPD Urban Squad gave me an insider's view on just how serious the department was about repairing community relations in the wake of the incident at the Desire Complex. The husky and warm Sergeant Johnny Miller commanded the squad, and his main focus was that very complex. We traveled to the Desire site several times during the day and evening, and I saw how hard Sergeant Miller and his men worked to make things better. It meant going far beyond the role of cop.

For example, sanitation collection in the complex had been a long-standing problem, and it was the first area that the Urban Squad focused on. The NOPD sought and gained cooperation from the city's services to increase sanitation pickups, a gesture followed by increased communication between residents and the police. Aside from politics, the Panthers and their position on cops had put a lot of the residents in danger, sometimes reducing them to political game pieces. While the cops' help was welcomed by many of the residents, it created a struggle for influence as some in the complex didn't know which side to trust.

During our time in New Orleans, services such as street lighting, building repairs, and emergency services all were addressed. As this happened, some in the Panther contingent stirred fear and worked to convince tenants that they were being duped.

New Orleans offered the same dizzying complexity as New York City, and even more nuance. After spending a week with the Urban Squad, the "Big Apple" came calling when I received an urgent call from Sergeant Miller who requested my presence forthwith at headquarters. An officer who was noted to have a photographic memory had come into the station that morning to report on a man he spotted on a local bus. He believed he had seen the face before, distributed on a nationwide most wanted list. We checked, and sure enough he was right. It was Herman Bell, a Black Panther and Black Liberation Army member, who was wanted for gunning down two NYPD cops.

The BLA was particularly troubling as a militant wing of the Panthers movement. Not to oversimplify, it's notable that parts of the BLA had been known participants in bank robberies and multiple illicit money-making schemes, the proceeds of which were partly used to fund a clandestine program of police assassinations.[23]

While there is still debate today as to the depth of those plans and whether or not they only were carried out by fragments of a larger BLA movement, the killings of the two NYPD cops spoke volumes. As visiting cops, Olpe, McKeon, and I weren't supposed to get involved, but Herman Bell had attacked our own, and the details of the murders were particularly horrific. Just the previous May, Officer Joseph Piagentini and his partner, Officer Waverly Jones, had been lured by a bogus 911 call to an ambush by Bell and an accomplice, Anthony Bottom.

Witnesses reported that a wounded Piagentini begged Bell for his life, asking for mercy for the sake of his wife and two young daughters. Instead, a remorseless Bell executed the officer with his own police revolver, firing every bullet until the gun was empty.[24]

A truly puzzling part of the BLA story was that at the time, with all that was happening in the city and the department, it was hard for the department to wrap their heads around the notion of a BLA hit squad being so well organized. There was even doubt as to the existence of the BLA as an organized entity, though the FBI was investigating via their regrettably problematic COINTELPRO operation. Still, two officers were dead by execution, so it wasn't particularly difficult for Olpe, McKeon, and me to convince our New Orleans partners to let

---

[23] Murphy, Mary. "Targeted for Their Uniform." WPIX-TV New York, December 20, 2014.
[24] Cohen, Shawn. "How Infamous Cop-Killer Herman Bell Convinced Parole Board He Should Be a Free Man." *New York Post*, April 11, 2018.

us ride that bus a couple of days at the same times as the sighting, just on the off chance that Bell might show up again.

While our suspect never appeared, the New Orleans cop with the photographic memory was spot on. NOPD detectives continued to keep watch and eventually caught and arrested our fugitive.

While parts of the BLA story were just beginning to emerge, the seeds of the complex challenges ahead were taking root all over. Something extremely dangerous was coming together just under the surface of American society, and tools—both legal and technological—were coming on line that would prove highly effective in the years ahead. Two legislative acts in particular were intended to help prosecute organized crime enterprises and political groups bent on violence.

The first was the Racketeer Influenced and Corrupt Organizations Act (RICO), which was passed on October 15, 1970. The next was the follow-up Title III Wiretap Authority. RICO allowed cops and FBI to tie cases together as part of an "organized crime" enterprise. It was a game changer for law enforcement, as no longer could the mob hide behind legitimate businesses, and no longer could mob bosses claim that just because their orders were carried out by others, they were removed from the crimes committed.

Title III allowed for better infiltration and tracking of organized crime groups and violent political groups like the Weather Underground, Black Panthers, BLA, and the Puerto Rico Separatist group FALN, or *Fuerzas Armadas de Liberación Nacional*. These groups were increasingly networked and had from the start been grown and cultivated like vines. They were also attuned to new techniques and tactics, and used the media, the law, and emerging technology to strike at corporate targets, authorities, financial institutions, communications, and transportation.

This is of particular significance here as these political groups were far more organized and embedded than we could possibly have imagined. Some were tied to foreign players and ideologies. All were on track to become the face of crime in America and the world ahead for years to come. Those in law enforcement were headed straight for it. The only question was, would we be ready?

***

The chief of detectives in New Orleans was a man named Henry Morris, and he personally invited me to learn about an extremely successful NOPD anti-burglary program known as Operation Fence. Coordinated by the smart and affable New Orleans Sergeant Jules Killelea, this ingenious sting operation was one of the most creative and effective law enforcement ideas I came across in my career.

Operation Fence involved encouraging local thieves to unknowingly dump their merchandize back into the hands of police department personnel posing as fences, and handing themselves over in the process. Chief Morris enlisted police officers who posed as criminals and set up locations where the best of burglars believed they could unload stolen property for top cash. At the facility, the unknowing perpetrators were videotaped making confessions as they bragged about their work and take.

At NOPD Headquarters, I viewed the videos of the operation and interviewed the officers. Better still, I was allowed to be present when the officers conducting the operation invited their "customers" to a party to celebrate their criminal success. I couldn't think of better party favors for these thieves than a pair of handcuffs and a booking slip.

The innovative program recovered a lot of stolen property and allowed the NOPD to proactively remove a large number of burglars from the street. I wrote up the program in great detail and hoped it would make a similar difference in the Big Apple.

As the three-month New Orleans trip came to a close, I managed to get Joan and the kids down to New Orleans. Terry and Dick followed suit with their own families, and it made the last week a perfect ending of sumptuous meals, eye-opening sights, and family bonding.

Before we officially left the city, the New Orleans Police Department held a news conference during which they presented us with honorary NOPD police shields signifying each of our ranks, along with an official police card giving us an honorary commission in the NOPD. From that time on, New Orleans would forever hold a special place in the hearts of three New York police officers.

PART THREE

THE INSIDE GUY

THE PUZZLE PALACE

After returning to New York and reporting on New Orleans, my star seemed suddenly on the rise. While I figured I'd be back to the 4-6 Precinct and my duty as patrol sergeant, the powers that be had other plans and assigned me instead to Police Headquarters, or what rank-and-file officers often dubbed "the Puzzle Palace"—a not-so-complimentary moniker that referred to the steady stream of bureaucratic edicts and reorganizations that often made little sense to men on the street.

Specifically, I was to report to the Planning Division full time. Problem was, I considered myself a street cop and preferred my ears to the ground and eyes on the city. Yet as Frank Biehler had fore-shadowed and as Dick Olpe and Terry McKeon helped to groom, I was already becoming deeply enmeshed in the bigger picture of the department.

Initially, I resisted the new move until I gained some assurances that I'd be back on patrol within a couple of years, fully relenting only after being offered a post in the Chief of Detectives Office and in their Planning and Research Program.

My initial Chief of Detectives Office interview was done by Lieutenant and soon-to-be Commander John Culley, a known department mover and shaker. Like Frank Biehler, Cully quickly pegged me as ready for a new chapter, and while I wasn't all that thrilled by the idea of being pulled off the street, working with John offered invaluable access to department hierarchy and advance planning. That vantage point gave me hope that I could be part of bigger and better things for both department and city.

To that very point, Culley himself would soon be part of expansive department reports on sharing the load, as well as better investigative procedures and police-community relations. Culley also helped usher in the arrival of revolutionary hostage negotiation tools and counter-terrorism initiatives.

For example, after the infamous Munich incident at the 1972 Summer Olympics Games, one in which eleven Israeli athletes were murdered by members of the Palestinian Black September Organization, Culley was enlisted to help the NYPD create protocols for potential hostage scenarios in the city. The expansive report, "Defusing Human Bombs—Hostage Negotiations," written with hostage negotiators like Bobby Loudon and citing the groundbreaking work of men like Frank Bolz, is still used today.[25]

My final interview before joining the COD was with the highly respected Chief of Detectives Louis C. Cottell, a man who demanded high standards and accepted no excuses. Cottell and Culley were long-time collaborators who, in 1971, along with another "boat rocker," Chief of Patrol Donald Cawley, were on the radar of new Police Commissioner Patrick V. Murphy. At the time, Culley was working a Brooklyn plainclothes organized crime post, and the unit was under the command of future commissioner Donald Cawley. The unit became so successful, it was expanded and re-designated as the City Wide Anti-Crime Section.[26]

With my new assignment I certainly stepped into something, including the potential stigma of "going to the other side." Joining the Chief of Detectives Office meant I was now distanced from the rank and file, a community that for a decade I had relied on as a critical support system and streetwise network. Was it going to be possible

---

[25] Louden, R. J. *Local Law Enforcement Hostage/Crisis Negotiation*. Amsterdam, Netherlands: IOS Press, 2007, p. 171.

[26] "The Origin of the Street Crime Unit." The Squad Room. Brooklynnorth. blogspot.com, December 14, 2009.

to maintain that connection going forward, or was the Puzzle Palace going to pull me away forever?

**

For some time, the local WCBS television news department in New York had been asking Chief Cottell to help them with a police-oriented show. The idea was "hatched" rather appropriately by CBS News Executive Producer Tony Hatch. During the interviews for this book Hatch revealed that he'd tried for some time to get Cottell and Commissioner Murphy to go for the idea, based partly on a news segment he'd seen in Britain called *Police Five*.

In the UK show, local police would present open cases for the public to help solve, inviting viewers at home to send their own criminal sightings and identify issues for the authorities to address. The idea of inviting involvement from the community was right up my alley. It harkened back to both the advantages of the beat and the amazing community outreach I'd seen in New Orleans.

Tony Hatch and I were instant kindred spirits.

One thing I remember about getting the TV assignment was the funny way I was chosen. As Culley and I sat with Chief Cottell and discussed the pitch from WCBS, the chief suddenly looked me over and made an offhand comment.

"Well, he does look good in a suit. Let's send him."

Next thing I knew, I was headed to WCBS News headquarters on West 57th Street, hustled through reception, and led to a conference room where News Director Ed Joyce, Tony Hatch, and legendary reporter and former NYPD cop Chris Borgen were waiting.

Hatch's international experience showed right away. He was a slick combination of newsman and statesman, and put me instantly at ease. With his dark, wispy hair and glasses, Hatch presented an aura of polish and worldliness. I figured myself to be just a representative of the COD, but time would reveal that I was about to begin a far bigger journey with the network.

Tony Hatch wasn't one to shy away from doing the right thing. While a reporter in Israel, Hatch and CBS senior reporter Larry Pomeroy got hold of Air Force film of Israeli jets hitting Egyptian posts across the Gulf of Suez. The film was acquired through proper channels, but the Israelis didn't care. A hundred civilians were killed in the airstrike, a tragedy that officials did not want to get out. The Israeli government quickly cracked down and revoked Tony's press credentials. He claimed censorship, and CBS brass backed him up, but as far as Israel was concerned CBS news was placed on lockdown, so Hatch returned to the States. There he climbed to the role of executive producer for WCBS News.[27]

As a fellow cop, I quickly took to Chris Borgen, who was a former detective in the narcotics division. It's funny looking back, but as much as I was intrigued by the opportunity to partner with the media, I could see in Borgen's eyes that he was chomping at the bit to be more of a cop again. It made us a perfect fit, and not only did Tony Hatch orchestrate it, he reveled in it as he excitedly talked about the potential show and the difference he hoped to make with it.

After a nearly two-hour discussion, a format for the series was agreed upon, along with the name, *Police File*. The show would appear three times a week as a segment of the 6:00 p.m. and 11:00 p.m. news. The choice of cases would be mine, after which I'd work directly with Borgen and a film crew as we covered the crime scenes and interviewed witnesses. The only hitch came from Chief Cottell and Commissioner Cawley.

Enter the bureaucracy.

It would take well into the next year to completely sell the plan to department brass, but what eventually got it done was the public service aspect.

In our meetings with the department, Tony Hatch stressed this new merging of community, law enforcement, and network—all to be captured, developed, and empowered by the show, a television first.

---

[27] Mideast/Fighting/CBS Reporter, #205418. TV News. www.vanderbilt.edu.

"We're all public servants," I recall him asserting, "and people on the street need to understand the grind and the time and risk involved in the police officer's job. When a wife says good-bye in the morning, she doesn't actually know if she'll see her husband again that night." As a former detective, Borgen carried significant weight with the department, and slowly the potential of it all sank in.

In the meantime, I was plenty busy with a barrage of activities of my own, including setting up a meeting with Lieutenant Frank Herron, the head of the Burglar Analysis Unit. The unit was another example of the NYPD working after the fact, and I wanted to bring a real proactive solution in the guise of a New York spin on New Orleans's Operation Fence. I explained the plan in detail, Herron took it under advisement, and all went quiet.

Sometime later, the plan magically appeared as if the department had come up with it—and with Herron at the head, no less. This was fine with me, as the right thing got done. Every person in law enforcement and politics should ask themselves the question, *"What matters more to you, getting the credit for something good or making sure what's good gets done?"*

I always tried to choose the latter.

***

It didn't take long for me to miss the adventure of the street. There certainly had been a lot to miss.

One notable string of crimes came courtesy of the infamous Weather Underground Organization, which, from its genesis in the 1960s, had grown from a small university protest movement into a large network that shared an agenda and capability akin to that of the Black Panthers. Like the Panthers, the Weather Underground Organization was antiwar yet paradoxically at war with the American government. Despite the similarities between the "Weathermen" and the Panthers, the two groups diverged in two significant areas.

The Underground was vastly white and middle class, which afforded them the stealthy capability of better blending into the system, sometimes on behalf of both organizations. Conversely, the predominantly African American Panthers took refuge mostly in poor areas, partly because it provided security but also as bias and racism were their main rallying points.

Another critical difference between the Weathermen and the Panthers was their choice of weaponry. Instead of using guns to enforce their agenda, the Weather Underground preferred bombs. From 1969 through 1974, they bombed multiple targets across America including NYPD Headquarters, the US State Department, the Pentagon, and the US Capitol Building.

You read that right. In 1974, the US Capitol Building was bombed. *Vanity Fair* scribe Bryan Burrough, who wrote *Days of Rage*, one of the seminal works on domestic terrorism and militant violence, more recently penned a piece for *Time* magazine that captured the political violence and bombing craze of the period.

In the *Time* article, Burrough focused on the 1970s—a time in our history that many of us do not recall, a time when college campuses across the country, emboldened by talk of revolution and injustice, turned to antiwar and anti-government demonstrations that became increasingly violent, something that many may find resonates with present society and current events.

In 1970 alone, more than three-hundred bombs were planted in the New York City area. Think about that for a moment—that's nearly one a day.

"Alarmed by a series of Weatherman attacks, [then President Richard] Nixon told [then FBI Director] J. Edgar Hoover...that 'revolutionary terror' represented the single greatest threat to American society," Burrough wrote. "As paranoid as Nixon could be, it was hard to argue with his line of thinking: Bombing attacks were growing by the day...by 1971 protest bombings had spread across the country. In a single eighteen-month period during 1971 and 1972 the FBI counted an amazing 2,500 bombings on American soil, almost five a day."[28]

---

[28] Burrough, Bryan. "The Bombings of America That We Forgot." *Time*, September 20, 2016.

From my new post, I could more easily see the writing on the wall, even if I couldn't yet decode the language. All the pieces and players of today's complex geopolitical and economic world were coming together. Battles over control of resources, rising terrorism, activist groups, ideological conflict, religion, political corruption, and the shifting of power from the Cold War to the far more volatile energy and ideological wars to come. Perhaps what fueled this most of all was the rapidly accelerating rise of technology and the proliferation of a mass media that was increasingly beholding to ratings and profit over information and education.

The 1970s also saw the birth of computers and the creation of the first cell phone, pretty much the technological genesis of our modern world. Even as government and law enforcement maneuvered to prepare for the future and for the worst, we were still mostly in reaction mode, still picking up pieces from the Knapp Commission and trying to catch up to criminal enterprises.

Then, just as I focused fully on what lay ahead, some of my recent New Orleans past came back when on January 7, Black Panther member and self-proclaimed BLA sympathizer Mark James Robert Essex opened fire on New Orleans Police from the very Howard Johnson's Motel where Dick Olpe, Terry McKeon, and I had initially been housed.

Already wanted for a New Year's Eve ambush that had left two NOPD officers dead, Essex brought a sniper rifle to the hotel and set up a nest. In the eleven-hour standoff that followed the first shots, eight people were wounded and seven killed, including three officers. Deputy Superintendent Lou Sirgo was among the fatalities. What a tragedy. Not only had Sirgo become a personal friend, but he was also a man who had pledged his life and career to fix race relations from the police side. He died at the hands of the very Black Panther movement that he tried to understand and render unnecessary.

Upon hearing of the terrible incident and later learning of Deputy Superintendent Sirgo's killing, Dick Olpe, Terry McKeon, and I were on the phone and talking about paying our respects. I recommended petitioning the police commissioner to allow us to show our support at the memorial service for the fallen officers. Within a week, the department sent us back to New Orleans where we appeared in full dress uniform at the somber service for the fallen and the devastated families left behind.

The New Orleans shootout was a gruesome harbinger of what lay ahead. Before the memorial, in fact, and just as Olpe, McKeon, and I flew south, the BLA struck in the Brownsville section of Brooklyn. There, four known members of the Panther-affiliated organization ambushed two NYPD cops, riddling their patrol car with automatic weapons fire. Luckily, the two 73rd Precinct patrolmen—brothers Vincent and Carlo Imperato—survived despite the blazing hail of twenty-three rounds.

The next day, the New York papers called the attack, "The latest in a series of surprise and ambush assaults on policemen in the city."[29] The three Black Panthers involved were JoAnne Chesimard's brother-in-law Zayd Shakur and two accomplices, Kearny and Fred Hilton. Chesimard, who will appear several times in this book, was later identified as the assumed head of the BLA organization and was alleged to have helped track and select the BLA's police targets in New York City.

The case took the BLA from merely an alleged and possible Panther assassination organization to front page news. After the shooting, then Mayor John V. Lindsay responded to Police Commissioner Patrick V. Murphy's call for action. According to *Days of Rage* by Bryan Burrough, the attempted execution of the Imperato brothers—coming not long after the murders of Officers Piagentini and Jones—set off a sequence of events that led Chief Cottell and John Culley to reorganize the department. They started with the detective squads, a few of which were part of the stalled investigations into what then clearly became identified as BLA-led crimes.

---

[29] Fried, Joseph P. "Two Patrolmen Who Are Brothers, Shot in Brownsville Attack." *New York Times*, January 26, 1973.

There were eight separate units investigating the BLA, and even after two more cops were targeted by Chesimard and her group, none were sharing information.[30]

Slowly it began to emerge that the BLA acted on both coasts, as well as in St Louis, Chicago, and New Orleans, and partook in police targeting, drug dealings, and bank robberies, culminating in an April robbery of a Northern Boulevard bank in Queens.

According to Bryan Burrough, when Donald F. Cawley became the police commissioner in May 1973, he had marching orders to go after the BLA and passed those directives on to Chief Louis Cottell, issuing the emphatic command, "Get the bastards...and Louie, think big." Cottell did indeed think big, bringing several people to bear on the problem including John Culley and twenty-seven-year veteran Deputy Chief Harold Schryver, who took command of the Major Case Unit.

As a result, all the city's detective squads working on the BLA case were consolidated—and that was just the beginning of sweeping changes.[31] Once the department was allowed to take the BLA seriously, the picture that emerged was truly chilling. The BLA unit was confirmed to be tied to the Panthers, who had legitimized themselves through books, public programs, student and university affiliations, and speaking tours.

The BLA by comparison, maneuvered more like the homegrown terror cells of today, using small and well-insulated units, highly trained to take down as many as possible when cornered. The BLA also relied on their nebulous connection to the Panthers, one that was easily blurred by spinning the press coverage toward cries of racism and unfair police targeting.

In *Circle of Six*, Randy Jurgensen's riveting book on the infamous 1972 police officer Philip Cardillo murder, he wrote, "Members of the

[30] Burrough, Bryan. *Days of Rage: America's Radical Underground, the FBI, and the Forgotten Age of Revolutionary Violence*. New York: Penguin Books, reprint 2016, pp. 243–244.
[31] Ibid. p. 245.

BLA were emboldened behind worldwide connections. They could get false documents, money, planning and refuge in Canada, Europe, and Africa."[32] Something about the way these groups were trained and supported certainly suggested they were in contact with other countries, some Marxist in ideology and fiercely anti-America. It would be years before we could uncover the scope. To us in the department, the net result of these groups was deeply personal.

***

Forty-six NYPD officers in all were killed in the line of duty in the 1970s, and forty-one more in the 1980s. Everybody connected to law enforcement knew all about the numbers. What was in the papers at the time though—which is eerily reminiscent of today and palpably foreboding—was a noticeable increase in anti-police sentiment emanating from some of the mainstream press.

Against this flashpoint of history, something else even more personal occurred in the city not long after my return from the New Orleans memorial. There were two families waiting for me, mine and the Genovese crime family. Arnie Squitieri, who had pulled me back to the 2-5, would finally close the book when on March 14, 1973, he pled guilty to first-degree manslaughter. He served only eight years.

Desiderio Caban wasn't exactly resting in peace.

[32] Jurgensen, Randy, and Cea, Robert. *Circle of Six*. New York: Disinformation Books, 2007.

BREAKING THE FOURTH WALL

In May 1973, I witnessed a massive department-wide shakeup, including moves to dismantle the squad structure of the department, meaning the specialized squads for homicide, robbery, and burglary. The goal was to break down the levels and share the load, something I agreed with in principle but not by such a sweeping and heavy hand.

It was also during this buzzsaw of upheaval that I got the nod to return to CBS and begin work on the *Police File* show. In theory, the series was supposed to take up three days of my work week, but it became a full-time job from the start.

For the task at hand I needed a full understanding of any potentially chosen investigation, which required me to fully interview the investigating officer or officers and get the lay of the land as if it were my case. As a representative of the chief of detectives, I also had to be sure that all investigative leads had been followed and that the televising of any particular case didn't compromise anything sensitive.

It would also become my job to be on camera for every 11:00 p.m. segment to go over the calls we received and discuss any leads being pursued by the detectives who had been interviewed during the 6:00 p.m. broadcast. My own camera time aside, one early aspect of *Police File* that I perhaps most enjoyed was the effect it had on my fellow detectives, some of whom were frustrated by cold cases and limited resources.

Suddenly some pretty tired, underappreciated, and jaded men saw new hope for helping long-suffering victims and their families. It was transformative for some, but there was plenty of resistance, too. Police in general—and detectives specifically—felt the cameras could interfere with their work. Regardless, I was determined to make this show succeed and, working closely with ex-detective Chris Borgen, did my best to assure my fellow men in blue that it would tread as lightly as possible. Chris Borgen brought a ton of credibility to that promise and comfort to the guys on the street, far more I'm sure than I did with the guys in the newsroom.

Borgen had never truly stopped being a cop and even after moving to television was called back by the NYPD to help on cases.

During my time on *Police File*, however, I did witness depressing trends in the television news world, some that have only been amplified in the present day. One morning after Tony Hatch pulled me into the assignment editor's meeting, I found to my dismay that a ton of TV news consisted of copying and repeating already known and successful stories from the newspapers. It reminded me in a way of what often didn't cut it in police work—it was reactive instead of proactive. In response Chris Borgen, Tony Hatch, and I agreed that aside from warming the cold cases, proactivity was to be a cornerstone of the show.

From our time as detectives, Borgen and I both knew that people in the community basically looked for two things: what made them feel safer and what distracted them from what made them feel less safe. We provided both, entertainment and purpose, information and participation. I believe that the sense of having some control was a big draw for people who were watching, and it gave them extra security knowing that cops were working for and with them. Also, knowing that their neighbors were looking out for one another provided a greater sense of "community."

It was great for the men in blue, too. Soon after the show went live, we suddenly had detectives coming to us with cases that could use the public's help. It was inspiring.

***

Perhaps the most rewarding initiative under the new COD leadership was the landmark creation of a dedicated unit for sex crimes, cases that had previously been handled by available detectives from the existing burglary and homicide squads. Again Commissioner Don Cawley, who was all about providing better opportunities to women officers and recruits, wanted to make sure that sex assault victims got a far more specialized and effective response from the NYPD. What we today know and celebrate as the Special Victims Unit grew out of early work on the district attorney side from Leslie Crocker Snyder and internal initiatives spearheaded by Chief Cottell, who built the unit around its new commander, Lieutenant Julia Tucker.

Among the unit's revolutionary initiatives was a specialized hotline through which women could report rapes directly to police-women, which got victims to open up more and share critical details that might elude male detectives. Men still had to be involved, and a perfect addition to the new unit was Detective Sergeant Harry O'Reilly, whom I met by chance just after my former squad leader at the 2-5, Al LaPerch, left for a new West Village post. To celebrate, Al held a dinner during which Harry was the standout guest.

Assigned to 6th Detective Squad, O'Reilly was a truly impressive individual—whip smart, "New York" sarcastic, and versed in any subject that came up. Despite his easy way, O'Reilly was a tough and no-bullshit investigator and a self-starter. Before I recruited him, O'Reilly had done stellar work as a narcotics detective, including a selfless and dramatic bust of drug dealers, accomplished off-duty and while riding the subway back from taking college classes in Spanish. O'Reilly was learning the language to better interface with his Hispanic detective partner.

A dedicated officer and family man, Harry wasn't the guy who would come into a unit to look good—he would come to make as much of a difference as humanly possible. I recommended O'Reilly to Chief Cottell and, knowing Harry's stellar record as both man and cop, my boss agreed.

The groundbreaking new Sex Crimes Analysis Unit came into being in November 1973 and took off from there. There's been a lot written—and rightfully so—about NY State District Attorney Robert Morgenthau and Assistant DA Linda Fairstein's tireless and dedicated work creating the Sex Crimes Unit of the Manhattan DA's Office in 1975. What's perhaps not as well known is how their amazing work dovetailed into ours. My sincere hope here is to celebrate and honor the contributions to the critical cause of women's rights and ensure that Commissioner Cawley, Chief Cottell, John Culley, Leslie Crocker Snyder, Julia Tucker, Harry O'Reilly, and others in and outside the NYPD are not forgotten.

In fact, Harry O'Reilly's tireless work and the country's first Sex Crimes Unit transformed sex crime investigations, and Harry, the lone man on the squad, became a nationally known figure. For years after, he toured the US teaching and lecturing on sex crimes investigation. He also went on to help write SVU manuals and procedures for departments nationwide. Harry passed recently, and I want to make sure his many contributions are memorialized.

***

While all this was going on, my brother Tom was again moving ahead of me. He had gone the volatile route of narcotics, bank robberies, and organized crime, then transferred to the newly formed Burglary Larceny Squad and was promoted to detective second grade.

Tom then landed at the Safe and Loft Squad, which dealt with significant heists, mostly banking and trucking due to the often massive amounts of money involved. An extremely dangerous post, it was partner in a sense to the Major Case Squad, which handled kidnappings, hostage situations, bank robberies, art theft, and major truck theft and hijacking.

Safe and Loft was mostly organized crime stuff, so right after I'd gotten out of the 2-5, brother Tom dove headfirst into the same treacherous rapids that I'd just survived. Amazingly, the cases Tom worked also included the BLA attacks on NYPD officers, which tied his work directly to New Orleans sniper Mark Essex and BLA assassin Herman Bell.

Tom was also ahead in the department's overarching direction. His work with the Major Case Squad was often accomplished side by side with counterparts from the FBI, and, because of this, he became another of my many instructors and opened my eyes to the merits of working closer with other intelligence agencies.

This idea, however, presented another potentially rocky yet distinctly needed evolution in law enforcement.

The NYPD rank and file often thought of the FBI as a one-way street. Common opinion was that the Bureau preferred cops in the role of information gathering and support for FBI investigations, and didn't feel the need to share the results. Tom, however, gave me a totally different picture. In Tom's eyes, the FBI was as relentless as he was—not spread onto as many cases, mind you, but laser focused on a few.

Many FBI agents were also far more flexible with NYPD's role in investigations than I'd been led to believe. Tom's partner at Major Case was Detective John Stein, and both Tom and John found great partners in the FBI. They had the same interests, after all, and both groups were absolutely obsessive in solving cases. Tom shared his appreciation of how systematic and detailed the FBI approach was to their investigations. He learned from their techniques and revealed how FBI agents didn't just act on leads, they constantly tried new angles.

When Tom and I got together, the bank robbery stories alone made my head spin. They were particularly educational, as many of these new-wave bank heists were crimes tied to funding for bombings and other activities of groups like the BLA, FALN, and such. Groups I would come to know well.

THE WILD WEST

As the city and country crept toward deepening recession, the changes came fast, furious, and, in many cases, chaotically. For the NYPD, one particular upheaval arrived courtesy of the newly opened Police Headquarters Building at 1 Police Plaza or, as they often call it on your favorite cop shows, "One P.P."

Under construction since 1969, 1 P.P. was hastily opened so Mayor Lindsay could share some of the political credit for it before he left office. To me, Lindsay always fancied himself a JFK type of figure. Unlike my political hero, however, I felt New York's 103rd mayor was far more flash than substance. Many reporters and politicos of the time agreed.

Like Lindsay, 1 Police Plaza wasn't ready for prime time. Even as we moved in, parts of the building lay dust-filled with nonworking elevators and unfinished offices. Sure, I was a kid from the South Bronx and well acclimated to a fifth-floor walkup, but our new Chief of Detectives Offices were on the thirteenth floor! Further complicating matters, the rapidly approaching end of the mayor's term, like any outgoing administration, created a shifting-sands environment as people jockeyed for position relative to an incoming new mayor and his appointments.

It was an extremely bumpy ride.

Then as the calendar ticked toward late summer, a different kind of shakeup occurred when our new *Police File* show hit a troubling snag. We had been filming for two months with no arrests to show for our work. Culley and Cottell remained supportive and patient, and we were certainly getting some good street smarts taught to our viewers, but it started nagging at me. It was as the saying went, "a dry hole."

Tony Hatch and CBS weren't worried. We were still getting good ratings numbers, but I think my fellow men in blue began to feel bad. Soon, various detective friends came to me offering cases that were about to pan out. I flatly refused them. The show needed to work the way it was supposed to and solve the *hard* cases, not showcase the easy pickings. With pressure mounting and no leads coming on our existing cases, we were still getting new crimes reported in by viewers, and this created a backlog.

In response, Chris Borgen and I talked about stepping up our educational angle and decided to do some coverage on street confidence games like three-card monte. We also checked into reports of three women who were ripping off the elderly, covered the con, and then put their pictures on the air.

That night, their attorney called.

The three were in the West Indies but were arriving back in New York the next day for the express purpose of surrendering to us! This could make or break us, so the very next morning, Borgen, the assigned case detectives, a camera crew, and I waited outside the Queens Criminal Court Building. The scene quickly became a CBS circus, yet the courtroom inside remained so eerily quiet that I think the judge started nodding off.

Just as another dry hole beckoned, the three women and their attorney arrived and on camera were placed under arrest. Borgen and I then walked them into the court whereupon the judge, spotting our TV crew, suddenly sat up straight and started shouting directions to the court like the show was all his.

That night, CBS did a special on the news about *Police File*, and when our viewers saw a case actually come to fruition, jaded New Yorkers got a dose of hope. In the days that followed, our hotlines rang off the hook.

Over the next couple of months, we made twelve arrests. I'm proud to report that *Police File* resulted in more than forty arrests and over 1.2 million dollars of recovered property. We solved kidnappings and took down a burglary operation running out of a sanitation company. We were also able to feature some of the great investigators I'd known over the years. You may recall the famous network TV show *America's Most Wanted*, which went on the air in 1988. It, too, was inspired by similar shows in Europe. *Police File*, however, was first on the case in 1973, making Tony Hatch and Chris Borgen true American pioneers in the merging of law enforcement and media.

I also managed to have some fun with the show, at the expense of my fellow NYPD detectives Tom Bowes and Charlie Paioli. One morning on scene with Bowes and Paioli, my father approached, dressed in his Sunday best. Immediately, I spotted my opening.

Aftershocks from the Knapp Commission shake-up still were ongoing, so when I spotted Michael Hallinan coming down the block, I turned to my fellow detectives and groused, "Jeez, just what we need. A shoe-fly." From the crestfallen look on their faces, Bowes and Paioli were hooked, thinking my dad was an inspector from Internal Affairs. This was in front of Chris Borgen and a whole camera crew, mind you, and with the cameras rolling.

Stifling a smile, I turned and walked away to intercept my dad, quickly shook his hand, and announced, "Inspector, it's so nice to see you." Tom and Charlie instantly snapped to attention, and my ham of a father, loving every second of it, played along brilliantly. For his part, my dad looked the two detectives up and down for a couple beats. Then, he rather coldly nodded.

"I see you guys are helping out with the show and the investigations." The two seasoned NYPD detectives bought it, hook, line, and sinker.

***

Fun moments aside, global pressures were escalating, and as the infamous October Oil Crisis hit, everything changed. The oil crunch dealt a crushing economic blow that would remake the entire US auto industry and put the already cash-strapped city and now the country into a geopolitical vise. It was a recipe for even more crime to come.

New York was fast becoming the Wild West, and I was a sheriff.

By January 1974, the city, already suffering under a poor economy, began losing more residents. As the population dropped and businesses moved out, adult entertainment, drugs, and arson moved in. Everybody saw the writing on the wall. After accomplishing what he came in to do in terms of cleaning up the department, Commissioner Donald Cawley retired to the private sector, and Michael J. Codd was named as his successor. Codd ended up presiding over what was to be perhaps the most tumultuous and uncertain time in modern New York's City history.

The gray-haired and tall Commissioner Codd dealt with hair-trigger battles across the city and within the ranks of the NYPD as, during his tenure, both the city and department encountered unprecedented budget cuts. As a result, the department was forced to lay off thousands of personnel, which set Commissioner Codd on a collision course with the police union. The man was controversial to some, but former Commissioner Benjamin Ward said that Codd "led the department during its most severe reduction of resources, especially manpower...his competence in that crisis resulted in a continual, uninterrupted, high-caliber police service to the city."[33]

Mind you, from the trenches and offices of middle management, my colleagues and I only saw the tip of this coming iceberg. While efforts like *Police File* pointed to future possibilities, criminals also seemed to see and use the power of the press. Certainly, activist groups like the Weather Underground, Black Panthers, FALN, and others began to thrive on media coverage and their ability to steer the narrative to spread intimidation and fear.

The trend continues to evolve in the present day, in social media where the spotlight is even more accessible, and where sensationalism has become—to many—a means to an end of its own.

---

[33] James, George. "Michael Codd, Ex Police Commissioner, Dies." *New York Times*, August 30, 1985.

To perhaps drive this point home, in 2018 Mubin Shaikh, a former al-Qaeda recruiter turned counterterrorism expert and consultant stated, "Media gives terrorism a longevity it might not otherwise enjoy. It's the idea of terrorism as theater. When we see these images, we are actually reinforcing the idea that extremist groups understand very well that fear really motivates people and extremist groups know what that fear will do. It works and it's as simple as that, and they know it. It's not the number of people who are killed, it's the number of people who are watching."[34]

***

With so much in flux around the country and world, internal friction reverberated through the department, eventually shaking up the Chief of Detectives Office, too. The first shoe to drop was the departure of John Culley, who was transferred to a Bronx Sex Crimes Unit.

One of the great takeaways of my stint with the COD was meeting and befriending Culley, who was one of my most significant mentors in the department. Before he left, John strongly suggested I round out my career experience with a stint in the FBI National Academy in Quantico. The FBI Police Program, he explained, provided rare insight into the same teamwork and training to which brother Tom had been exposed in both the Bank Task Force and Major Case Squad.

FBI Academy training would also open the door for a career with the Bureau and, at the very least, provide tools to be a far better-prepared detective and police officer. The only problem was they had to accept me.

Culley pressed and said it was my next step.

***

[34] "Mind Control." *In Search Of.* Season 1, episode 7. The History Channel, August 31, 2018.

Beyond the practical lessons gleaned from that time in history, my professional life was transformed by my time in the Chief of Detectives Office. Not only did I get to be a big part of *Police File*, I was particularly gratified by my work with the dedicated team behind the creation of the Sex Crimes Analysis Unit and its new commander, Lieutenant Mary Keefe.

Thanks to the Sex Crimes Unit, the District Attorney's Office, and support throughout the city, conviction rates for rape jumped from 2 percent to more than 60 percent. Harry O'Reilly always said that New York City was the great crime lab, and he was right. He knew intuitively that if what we were doing with Special Victims worked in NY, it should work anywhere.

Chief Cottell got behind the idea, and soon we started giving seminars about sex crimes and our unit in other cities. Women officers came from Europe and around the country to hear and learn. We invited feminists and involved members of the LBGT community, local rape counselors, and nurses. We came together to great effect.

***

My two-year assignment in the Chief of Detectives Office had now stretched to four, and I began researching and planning my next career move, pulled constantly by the desire to be a working detective again.

I literally got dragged back into my former life when a grand jury convened to examine NYPD corruption and impropriety as it related to the Squitieri case. My return to the world of the 2-5 included some very familiar faces as officers Roff, McCooey, and McTigue all were summoned into a police trial room to detail their roles in covering up the murder of Desiderio Caban. Officer John Lagatutta, the man I fruitlessly searched the hospital for that night, was now a star witness against the others.

Ultimately McCooey, McTigue, and Roff would walk and serve no time, though they would be dismissed from the department. Still, it was my job to testify against them, and it was surreal. It was the first time I'd seen these men since the initial grand jury. After I took the stand, I glanced at the defense table hoping for some acknowledgment of their deeds, but none of them would meet my eye.

Rolling the entire Squitieri case over in my mind, their seeming lack of accountability really galled me. They knew they were going to escape serious punishment. Yet while I was disappointed with the result, my long nightmare had finally ended. Another larger nightmare, though, was only just unfolding, courtesy of the aforementioned Puerto Rican Separatist Group, the FALN.

***

In 1974, the FALN officially began targeting NYPD Officers. On December 11, operatives of the group placed an explosive device constructed of dynamite and nails behind the door of an East Harlem tenement, and then summoned police to the scene.

Rookie patrolman Angel Poggi was on his second day of the job and patrolling with Detective Raymond Flynn when a woman phoned in the call. As Flynn went to access the building via the basement, Poggi opened the front door. The explosion hurled him twenty feet down the sidewalk. When he awoke, his face and neck were punctured and shredded by fragments of nail, wood, and glass. His arm was broken, and he was blinded in one eye.

After the explosion, a woman called the Associated Press and claimed credit in the name of the FALN. She directed police to a communiqué left in a midtown phone booth.

We were targets of a terror campaign.[35]

***

As if to pile on to an already beleaguered city, 1975 marked the crushing, drug-fueled reality of the aftermath of war and recession. In a

---

[35] Borrough, Bryan. *Days of Rage: America's Radical Underground, the FBI, and the Forgotten Age of Revolutionary Violence*. New York: Penguin Books reprint, 2016, pp. 318–319.

1970s interview for the PBS news show *Frontline*, former New York DEA Special Agent Robert Stutman explained the situation.

"Crack literally changed the entire face of the city. Street violence had grown. Child abuse had grown hugely. Spousal abuse, too. I had a special crack violence file that I kept to convince the geniuses in Washington who kept telling me it wasn't a problem."[36]

The city was reeling.

By 1975, arson became an epidemic unto its own, and there were an estimated 40,000 prostitutes in New York City. The New York City Planning Commission also estimated the city had about 245 stores with "adult uses," including adult movie theaters, massage parlors, book stores, and peepshows. As this transpired, the NYPD was soon to lay off fifty-thousand employees and during the next five years the police force would shrink by 34 percent, while serious crime increased by 40 percent.[37]

In 1975, terrible headline after terrible headline piled on as bad news became the best news for selling papers to an ever more pinched populace. With all the attention, success, and immediacy of *Police File*, TV news changed in response. After we went off the air, ABC News reshuffled and created the concept of *Eyewitness News*, which had the feel of TV's first foray into reality-style reporting. To some, it was more theatrics than journalism, but ABC seized on the opportunity, bringing in new faces and younger more diverse reporters, among them, the bilingual Geraldo Rivera. To many, it was seen as what was news becoming product.

Then, the product came for me.

Geraldo, who famously broke into the public eye through his 1972 exposé on Staten Island's infamous Willowbrook facility for the mentally disabled, did not impress Tony Hatch or Chris Borgen. They told me how Rivera had come to their table the night of the Emmy Awards and congratulated them as if his blessing meant they'd

[36] Sterbenz, Christina. "New York City Used to Be a Terrifying Place." Business Insider, July 12, 2013.
[37] Ibid.

somehow made it. They considered Geraldo's style more sideshow than news.

On January 24 Geraldo invited me to lunch at the Gingerbread Man by Lincoln Center, and there pitched me his new detective TV show idea.

"I'm the reporter and you're the cop," he began. "We take these cases and solve them."

My question was an obvious one. "What makes you think that NYC detectives are gonna just hand over cases to us?" As I cast a jaundiced eye at Rivera, a commotion rippled through the Gingerbread Man as word spread that a bomb had just exploded at the posh and historic Fraunces Tavern near Wall Street. It was the Puerto Rican Separatist group, the FALN, and they had made the terrible transition from government and police targets to civilians. The dynamite fragmentation bomb killed four and injured forty, and upon hearing of the terrible blast, Geraldo rushed out for the story.

I went back to the NYPD to monitor the aftermath.

Brother Tom and his partners in the FBI were among the first responders. There also was a young Chicago FBI agent named Richard Hahn, who will become more prominent later on in this book.

With all of my activity in the public eye and behind the scenes at the COD, the bombing was a grim reminder of a far bigger and deadlier picture.

***

Not long after the bombing, my new boss, Inspector Robert Johnson, invited me to lunch. I figured a nice steak or something similar, but all Johnson had in mind for nourishment was a hot dog at a local vendor cart. He had more important items on the work-related menu and, right there on the street, informed me that I was going to be the new training officer for the detective bureau.

I was confused. This was an unusual promotion for me as a lieutenant always held the post. Regardless, Johnson assured me that Chief Cottell was in full agreement, so I accepted.

Upon returning to the office, I immediately went down to meet with the training officer, Lieutenant Justin McGarvey, hoping that my appointment wasn't a slap in his face. I wanted to assure him that I wasn't looking to steal his spot. Thankfully, he could not have been nicer and said he was glad to be moving on to a field position.

While I secretly envied that McGarvey was getting back out on the street, I was pleased to have the opportunity to work with detectives in programs designed to increase their effectiveness. I was provided a small but capable staff, and they too had great interest in expanding our programs and finding new direction. We agreed to enhance our course curriculum for the homicide, robbery, burglary, and sex crime seminars.

Hank Buck and I had personally dealt with many burglary cases during our stint in the conditions car. Burglary was such a deeply personal violation, as personal items and mementos of life were taken, usually forever. Sometimes identities and bank accounts followed. To deal head-on with the problem, I began talking with active detectives for sources of preventive knowledge. Was there a real pro out there among the ranks of the convicted, I wondered, a guy who could talk about the crimes from *his* point of view?

Fortune again smiled when I recalled the would-be car thief and potential murderer who had saved Detective Mike Cassel's life. I wanted that guy at a seminar at the New York Armory to instruct a room full of grizzled detectives. I was able to track him down at the jail on Rikers Island. He was there awaiting an early release, granted because Cassel had stood up for him at his trial. When I offered him the opportunity, he was understandably concerned about his reception, but I assured him it was the right thing to do.

Still, I had to go through a wringer of clearances with the DA, NYPD, and Department of Corrections. To secure the star of my show I put Detectives Tom Bowes and Charlie Paioli on escort duty, bringing him to the armory and gave our new consultant the code name: "Jesse the Robber."

Putting him in a mask like Jesse James, I stashed him off stage and gave him an introduction.

"It is always important when dealing with an adversary to gain as much information about their methods as possible," I said, pausing for effect. "In conducting an investigation, knowing the methodology of the criminal mind is critical. We have here today, someone who has had a long history of both successful and unsuccessful commission of armed robberies." A ripple of unrest washed though the room, and I stepped back. It was exactly what I knew would happen and what I wanted.

"We must all learn from our adversaries, and I'd like to add that this man—during the commission of an armed robbery—was also instrumental in preventing his accomplices from taking a police officer's life." That seemed to calm the room a bit.

It was short-lived.

"I'm now going to introduce you to him, a man who's going to tell you how he goes about his work, and I want you to listen and ask questions. Meet Jesse the Robber."

The room fell dead silent as Bowes and Paioli walked their charge to a seat at center stage. The air quickly went out of the room, replaced by stares and shifting chairs. The vast majority of detectives present were positively livid that I'd brought someone who was, in many of their minds, a perp to lecture them. Some of them might have even taken off the safety on their handguns.

"Who the fuck is this guy?"

I heard the murmurs.

"Why are we gonna listen to this asshole?"

Then, as Jesse slowly spoke and began to explain how he picked targets, assessed security, got in and got out, the room fell strangely silent. Pens suddenly began racing across paper, detectives' eyes opened wide, and many in the audience nodded as if Jesse was suddenly a fellow law enforcement agent.

That opened up Jesse, too, and soon questions were coming from throughout the room.

Two hours later, those same detectives gave Jesse a standing ovation. I was more than impressed. Jesse's talk was filled with observational detail and meticulous analysis on par with any detective's

134

investigative skills. He used professional, security-level risk assessment, and the information Jesse shared was transformative.

In some small way, I hoped Jesse would see his life in a new way, too.

Jesse had saved Mike Cassel's life. Now, he was doing more than that, and it taught me something critical that would only come to light later on when I became involved in counterterrorism. The vast majority of our adversaries were too often seen as one-dimensional and single-minded enemies. Instead, they were highly trained, extremely intelligent, resourceful, and strategic human beings with a multitude of motivations and goals. That meant their organizations, which pooled those talents, were even more capable.

As much as I enjoyed my new career as a department ambassador and lecturer, it wasn't something I had envisioned for myself early on. The post did, however, afford me the opportunity to bring many of my own mentors to the stage, where they could share some of the same amazing insights that they had shared with me. My brother Tom and Henry Mulhern from Delehanty came to the seminars, and the talks covered subjects as diverse as use of force, homicide and robbery investigations, and police and media. Tom signed up his friend and our DA's office colleague Linda Fairstein to help advise on rape investigations.

This helped propel Tom and me into speaking careers. Soon, our schedules had us traveling to cities around the country and getting paid for it. In some ways it made up for the low pay and lack of upward mobility inherent to the financial crunch. The money would prove important as by mid-1975, the city shook again under the weight of recession.

BRIGHT LIGHTS, BROKEN CITY

By the summer of 1975, one-fifth of all public workers had been laid off in New York City, and with substantially fewer firefighters and police officers, many crimes and fires went unaddressed.

The situation became so dire, in fact, that kids in the South Bronx were seen playing in burned-out buildings as if they were war refugees. Some such abandoned structures were turned into heroin "shooting galleries" or prostitution dens. The city seemed to be dying, and people were breaking laws just to survive.

This was the very summer when the New York subway system became jokingly referred to as "the muggers express" and where a couple of hundred felonies were committed every week. I have to admit, though, that in the midst of this dangerous citywide and national slide, this "paper tiger" wanted back into the jungle, but after four years in the Chief of Detectives Office, I may have lost sight of the fact that New York City was a far darker and more dangerous jungle than I'd ever encountered.

On an icy, windswept Monday, December 29, I was pulled deeper into the jungle when an emergency call came over the radio in my car. I was on the FDR Drive, maneuvering through sleet and ice alongside a partly frozen East River.

A bomb had just ripped through the baggage area at LaGuardia Airport, and there were dead and injured holiday travelers at the scene. I didn't even think twice as I quickly turned my car onto the Triborough Bridge and raced toward LaGuardia. It was to be my first direct experience with a bombing and, sadly, not my last.

I was acting on instinct, and there were others acting on the same impulse. One was a young FBI agent named Neil Herman, who was living in Manhattan. When he heard about the bombing, he jumped in a cab and took off for the same Triborough Bridge. Then as news of the bombing hit the airwaves, emergency vehicles choked the route, bringing traffic to a halt and locking Herman's cab in place. Undeterred, he jumped out into the icy downpour and ran the rest of the way to the airport on foot.

Neil Herman would carry that determination into a career as one of the more significant figures in the annals of counterterrorism. After the LaGuardia bombing, Neil was put into a new FBI unit known as M-9, designed to deal with acts of domestic terrorism. Until that time, cops and FBI agents frequently left whatever cases they were working on and rushed to bombings, where they often fought over collecting evidence and designating which labs would process it.

The NYPD had a unit called Arson & Explosion, but in those early years they didn't always mesh with their FBI counterparts. Regardless, neither the FBI nor the NYPD had the analysis capabilities needed for these events, so despite their evidence-based territoriality, they ironically had to rely on a third party—the military's Picatinny Arsenal research and manufacturing facility in New Jersey—for help.[38]

Neil Herman described the LaGuardia Airport bombing as grisly and shocking, and it was as major a terror event as New York had experienced to that date. The response, therefore, was a massive but makeshift task force of fifty FBI agents, thrown together in a single night. They learned as they went.

According to Herman, "The real modern age of terrorism began with the brutal murder of the Israeli athletes at the 1972 Munich Summer Olympics." The group responsible, the Black September Organization, was an offshoot of Yasir Arafat's Palestine Liberation Organization. A year after the Olympics, Black September member Khalid Al-Jawary planted three bombs targeting Israeli interests in

---

[38] Graff, Garrett M. *The Threat Matrix: The FBI at War.* Boston: Little, Brown and Company, 2011, pp. 156–157.

New York City. The bombs failed to detonate, but the explosives, fingerprints, and materials were traced to Al-Jawary and Black September.

For those who believe that the 9/11 attack on the World Trade Center marked the beginning of terrorist activities in the United States, the truth is that international terrorism was coming to our shores back in the early 1970s.[39]

Terrorism was already growing from within as well.

***

When I got to the LaGuardia scene it was blood, smoke, and mayhem, and I was greeted by Operation Fence's leader and chief of detectives for Queens, Edwin Dreher. He quickly assigned me to the temporary morgue to keep track of the bodies as they were brought in.

Twelve people were killed in the blast, and more than seventy-five were injured, including an off-duty FBI agent who had been collecting his bags. The powerful bomb was equivalent to fifteen sticks of dynamite and sent glass flying hundreds of feet, shredding structures and people. Limbs were blown off or hopelessly mangled, and victims were trapped in rubble and debris. Water pipes broke, and the freezing air coming in through broken windows produced white and blue icy waterfalls everywhere, filling parts of the terminal in strangely beautiful, crystal webs. It was a surreal war scene.

Then, we got the grim news that a caller had claimed that a second device was in place and counting down to detonation.

As the news coverage went live, networks speculated that a Palestinian group was involved, and then more copycats started calling, saying bombs were about to go off at airports as far away as Washington, DC, and Cleveland. Planes already loaded with passengers were ordered to take off and get clear of the area, while others full of extremely flammable jet fuel were pulled away from the terminals

---

[39] Temple-Raston, Dina. "Man Who Tried to Bomb Israeli Targets, Released." www.NPR.org, February 19, 2009.

to prevent the risk of being detonated by a second blast. All incoming flights were diverted. It was insanity.[40]

In the makeshift morgue, I had the grim task of recording casualties, which by my count were thirteen, not twelve. As it turned out, one was a heart attack victim who had died a full three minutes before the bombing.

***

In the early morning hours, as I drove home, I couldn't shake the images from that horrific night. Of the many bodies I saw at the morgue, one stood out, that of a young and handsome limousine driver. He was just twenty-one years old, and killed just trying to make a living. A completely innocent victim. That was why Neil Herman ran across that bridge, and that was why I had responded.

Of course, we were not alone. Among the many dedicated and talented people at the scene was another guy of note, Ken Maxwell, an already seasoned investigator who would later become a key counterterrorism expert with the Joint Terrorism Task Force in New York. While I was just the desk jockey doing my part to stay in the saddle, Ken Maxwell was miles ahead and would have a great career both in the public and private sectors. Next time you're on a flight, note the reinforced cockpit door, placed there to prevent a terrorist incursion, the kind of which created the 9/11 tragedy.

As head of security at JetBlue Airways, Ken made sure they were among the nation's first to install reinforced cockpit doors.[41]

The new trend of targeting planes and airports continued into 1976 when on September 10, TWA Flight 355 was hijacked en route from LaGuardia Airport to Chicago. The hijackers were from a militant Croatian separatist group that wanted that nation free from Yugoslavia. The hijackers claimed to have a bomb on board and

---

[40] Orenkes, Michael; Doyle, Patrick; and Stathos, Harry. "12 Die in LaGuardia Bombing." *New York Daily News*, December 30, 1975.

[41] Newman, Philip. "Ex-FBI Official Tapped to Run JetBlue Security." *Times-Ledger*, October 12, 2011. Web, July 12, 2018.

another planted at New York's Grand Central Station. While the plane was in the air, NYPD bomb squad personnel rushed to the city's main train hub, where they located and removed the pressure cooker device and brought it to a local range for detonation. Tragically, it went off prematurely, killing Officer Brian J. Murray, partly blinding Sergeant Terrence McTigue, and wounding Officer Hank Dworkin and Deputy Inspector Fritz O. Behr.[42]

After the hijackers were caught, it was discovered that the device on the plane was a fake. It was merely a pressure cooker mocked-up with wires and clay. Lead hijacker Zvonko Busic later claimed that all he wanted was the attention for his cause and that the bomb at Grand Central was never meant to go off. In line with Busic's claim, when the bomb's presence was phoned in during the Flight 355 hijacking, it was with explicit instructions on how to dismantle it.

Regardless of the actual plan, it was callous and reckless move—one that killed an innocent police officer.

The media already was prone to give top billing to stories of this sort. Ratings drove sensationalism, and sensationalism drove extremism. Serial killers from David "Son of Sam" Berkowitz to the Zodiac Killer who terrorized San Francisco followed the same pattern. Like the extremists groups of the time, both killers were motivated in part by their ability to garner press. Their letters were splashed across local and national headlines. Regrettably, none of those published messages did anything to help protect the public.

This seemed a long, long way from what Tony Hatch described as the public service and sacred trust of the press.

***

As law enforcement became an ever more complex puzzle, a necessary and natural evolution emerged—the increasing cooperation between the FBI and NYPD.

---

[42] Slotnick, Daniel E. "Zvonko Busic, 67, Croatian Hijacker, Dies." *New York Times*, September 5, 2013. Web, August 1, 2018.

Like my brother Tom's work with the Major Case Squad, the Bank Robbery Task Force was another of the department's first significant collaborations between the two agencies, as the money stolen in bank robberies was often stolen at the behest of mobsters, drug dealers, or extremist organizations. That landed these cases firmly on the radar of both the FBI and NYPD, so cooperation grew out of necessity and common cause.

Also, with money and manpower reduced due to deep budget cuts, the sharing of resources proved critical. Even so, there remained a bit of competitive enmity between agencies on the city, state, and federal levels. But the expanding web of crime was too big for any one organization to address alone. The fact was, we were falling behind, and something had to change.

The FBI's Bank Squad and NYPD's Major Case Squad provided critical proving grounds. Bank jobs were particularly focused with a single crime carried out in one location, so they provided a natural starting point for agency cooperation. Sharing intel not only helped cut down on repeat interviews and paperwork, it allowed each agency to play to its unique strengths. Federal investigative resources could be better directed and less bogged down by procedure, while NYPD boots on the ground were better deployed for gathering intelligence on the street.

Since the Major Case Squad addressed bombings, RICO crimes, hostage taking, and banks, my brother Tom got a lot of experience working with his FBI brethren like special agent Ed Petersen.

Thus, a lot of the groundwork was being laid for an FBI-NYPD Joint Terrorism Task Force. It began to coalesce in 1979, when FBI agent Ken Walton and former NYPD Commissioner Patrick V. Murphy hatched a plan for the first true joint operations, the Bank Robbery Task Force and then the Joint Terrorism Task Force, following the formula of the Major Case Squad.

Up to that point, while great work was being done by investigators like Tom and his FBI counterparts, these guys were bucking their respective departments and politics. Walton and Murphy seized upon what worked and hoped to expand it.

Ken Maxwell, the Major Case Squad investigator and former NY State Trooper who responded to the LaGuardia bombing, was also at the Grand Central scene. At one point he revealed to me that the LaGuardia bomb was the same pressure-cooker design as the Croatian bombs, thus connecting the two incidents.

Queens Chief of Detectives Dreher agreed. After he became the head of the task force that investigated the LaGuardia event, and before the investigation was turned over to the FBI, Dreher revealed that Busic had admitted the LaGuardia bomb was placed by the same Croatian group, again claiming it was meant to go off when the terminal was empty.[43]

***

In 1979, Ken Maxwell joined the FBI and, as one of the Bureau's top agents, preceded me into the Joint Terrorism Task Force. As so many of the people, places, technology, and eddies and undercurrents of the time converged, it seemed as if a great many things were headed on a collision course.

---

[43] Schindler, John R. "Why Hasn't Washington Explained the 1975 LaGuardia Airport Bombing?" *The Observer*, January 4, 2016.

THE RISE OF RAGE

In September 1976, a watershed moment arrived for law enforcement, one that revealed the brazen evolution of terrorism, along with the growing need to counter it.

It was a humid morning near Sheridan Square in Washington, DC, when the calm air was ripped by a massive explosion centered on a single car maneuvering in traffic. The force from the powerful remote-controlled bomb launched the car spiraling through the air before it rolled to a fiery halt by the Romanian Embassy.

Long before the shattered vehicle hit the ground, a former diplomat and driver of the vehicle, forty-four-year-old Orlando Letelier, was fatally wounded and a young female passenger, Ronnie Moffit, was sliced through the neck by shrapnel, left to choke to death on her own blood. Her husband, a passenger in the back seat, was miraculously thrown clear and survived, though left in shock and cradling his dying wife in his arms.

It was the first major act of state-sponsored terrorism on US soil and, as FBI Agent Carter Cornick observed at the time, counterterrorism was, "a specialty that did not exist in the mid-'70s…. It was the first time we were dealing with a foreign government as a suspect."[44] Like many others, I only learned of the assassination from the newspapers and evening news, but guys I would later be overseeing in the Joint Terrorism Task Force already were cutting their teeth.

---

[44] DeYoung, Karen; Montgomery, David; Ryan, Missy; Tharoor, Ishaan; and Lang, Jia Lynn. "This Was Not an Accident, This Was a Bomb." *Washington Post*, September 20, 2016.

This was when I arrived at 8th Homicide and had that hair-trigger dance with Teenager down the hallways of that dilapidated safe house on Bronx River Avenue.

***

Just as Jamie Villa, the human cobra, and I brought our deadly stare-down back down the forty-foot hallway to the apartment door, we heard the front door of the building explode off its hinges.

The distraction provided me the opportunity to quickly draw my revolver and grab for Teenager's. Incredibly, I ended up with both of our guns at the ready but our eyes still locked. I had no idea who was coming for us. Fortunately for me, it was the NYPD cavalry. Jack McCann ran over first, shotgun drawn and screaming at Teenager.

"*On your knees!*" Ron Marsenison instantly flanked us and did the same.

"*On your fucking knees now!*"

While Team C had no idea who this was—a martial artist and black belt who easily could have taken me down with a kick—they knew enough to act. It wasn't until later that we learned it was Teenager himself who had ordered Nector to execute Rafael Guzman after he had taken it upon himself to beat and rob a sixty-three-year-old rival drug dealer, a move that invited retribution.

The not-so-simple murder case was assigned to Detective Tom Davis, who tracked it through witnesses to a sports car that had been driven by another gang member, a dealer named Benny Escobar. When interviewed for this book, star reporter and writer Howard Blum, who wrote about the 138th Street War with fellow scribe Len Buder explained that after Teenager was arrested, Escobar was brought in for questioning and he gave up details on the whole war, becoming an informant.

With someone now tucked inside the Teenager-Ramins gang and Teenager himself in custody, Team C used their new source to begin a campaign of pulling high-ranking drug dealers and gang assassins off the streets. This, of course, didn't sit very well with the competing gangs on 138th Street, who placed a $20,000 price on the heads of each of the Team C detectives.

Very little of this was known to the public since the press at the time was far more occupied with the summer murder of Donna Lauria and the wounding of her friend Jody Valenti. They were the first two victims of the ".44 Caliber Killer" David Berkowitz, the serial murderer who would be later known as the infamous "Son of Sam."

After the airport bomb and my brush with death at the hands of Teenager, I felt as if I was back in the thick of it, but only about a week later the NYPD bureaucracy caught up with me and attempted to shift me to the Narcotics Division. I wasn't particularly enamored with that path and had to go before an NYPD Review Board to prevent the move.

Don't get me wrong, Narcotics Division made a real difference. It was a tough part of policing, extremely dangerous, and often undercover, though due to its autonomy and the proximity to drugs and money it could also become the downfall of a good cop, as seen in the famous Sidney Lumet film *Serpico* starring Al Pacino. Real-life NYPD whistleblower Frank Serpico got shot while working in the shadowy world of Narcotics.

I had direct experience with cops succumbing to their darker sides and knew from *The Kind of Guy I Am* what that dark side entailed. Back in 1969 and 1970, I'd experienced it first-hand. More was to come…

ONE WAR ENDS...

Knowing all too well what had happened to Rafael Guzman, police brought 138th Street War informant Benny Escobar in for questioning in September.

In his interview, Escobar sketched a picture that would embroil the 8th Homicide and Team C, the FBI, and the DEA in a deadly two-plus year battle that, in the words of *New York Times* reporter Howard Blum, ranged from "the bars and dance halls of the Bronx, into apartments where babies slept in cardboard boxes and into $350,000 ranches in Oklahoma, into shotgun battles and into helicopter chases, into pool halls in Los Angeles and into nightclubs in Puerto Rico as they pursued those who killed and those who ordered the killings."[45]

Benny also painted a detailed picture of the Teenager-Ramins gang, as well as the other belligerents involved in the conflict. Escobar recalled how news of Guzman's robbery made its way up the ranks of the gang until his murder was ordered by Teenager himself. Along with the DA's office, we knew we were onto something big but needed to move carefully as not to make the gangs of 138th Street suspect that we had an informant.

We needed to tread very lightly.

Then, on a Sunday afternoon that fall, with airport explosions and gang slayings on my radar, an upheaval of another sort ripped through my life. My father, Michael, only seventy-three going on seventy-four, went home from Sunday Mass and, as was his usual

---

[45] Blum, Howard, and Buder, Leonard. "The War on 138th Street." *New York Times*, December 17, 1978.

custom, sat down to watch the New York Giants football game. As he settled to watch his beloved team lose their second straight game of the new season, the TV started acting up and my dad got up to adjust the antenna to better the signal.

He barely made it off the chair before he collapsed to the floor.

While my father's passing was heartbreaking, I was particularly grateful that he had been alive to see my graduation from Fordham, though equally saddened that he hadn't seen brother Tom receive a bachelor's degree and masters, before becoming a candidate for a doctorate degree at the State University at Albany. Michael Hallinan wore our detective pins into the hereafter. The man had been a model father and had made sure that, despite my mom's early death, we would be raised correctly.

Joan helped me through Dad's death in so many ways and focused on the strong bond he had with his three kids. Looking back on his life, I realized that not only had he raised three children, but with me working so much and Joan juggling, he'd helped raise our kids, too. I decided to blame the Giants. To this day when we discuss Dad, it was "the Giants that killed him."

It was already well into October, and 1976 was far from over.

***

In the midst of family tragedy and Teenager Gang pressures, I was pulled into a very disturbing case. There had been multiple reports of rape in the 4-3 that fall, and on November 17 the body of a fifteen-year-old girl was discovered on an upper-floor landing of a Castle Hill apartment building.

The victim's name was Milagros "Millie" Otero, and she was a student at Adlai Stevenson Junior High School. By all accounts, Millie was a generous, brave, and caring young woman who earlier that night had volunteered to walk her mom's friend home, worried that the older woman was going to be walking alone. Horrifically, returning from her good deed, she was followed. Just outside Millie's apartment, nineteen-year-old John Battiste pounced and forced his way into the building behind her. Once inside, he dragged her to the eleventh-floor landing, savagely raped her, and, after Otero resisted, stomped on her neck and stabbed her multiple times.

It was after 10:00 p.m. and I was home, but when 8th Homicide Detective Tom Kelly called with the dreadful news, I jumped in my car and took off for the scene, where I met up with Kelly and Detective Larry Doherty. We all saw Millie's body and the ghastly purple bruise that Battiste's sneaker had left on her neck. The lab later matched the mark to the size and tread of a specific brand. We connected that with the testimony obtained from an area woman who was also a victim of Battiste. She helped us make a composite sketch, which hit the papers on Thanksgiving Eve.

That very night another woman recognized Battiste in the record section of an old Korvettes Department Store. After she called the precinct, officers nabbed Battiste and brought him in where Kelly, Detective Richie Gest, and I interviewed him for almost two hours. He clearly was a troubled kid, so we were gentle, feeding him and trying to get him to talk to us.

By around 4:00 a.m., he admitted to the rape but maintained he never meant to kill Millie and that it was some kind of terrible accident. Sadly, we figured it might just be the tip of the iceberg, so we checked with other potential victims and found one. We then went after the sneaker and found a dozen similar pairs in Battiste's apartment, one of which was confirmed by the lab as a match. Finally, after all the hard work and hours of investigation, we were able to go back to Millie Otero's mother and let her know that her daughter's killer had been caught and would be going away.

Mrs. Otero was grateful but utterly despondent. She cried through the entire meeting, and it was about as painful a time as ever in my career. Her daughter had done the right thing in walking a friend home, and this was her end. Later, as Detective Kelly and I left the Otero apartment and stepped into the street, the morning sun suddenly peeked up over the horizon, bathing us in a warm orange glow. It was cleansing, in a way, and after the exhaustion and trauma offered a moment of hope.

It did not last long…

***

Just a day after Mille Otero was raped and murdered, Benny Escobar came home from a meeting with Team C detectives and found a small group of gang assassins waiting for him in the front hall of his building. In the dim light of a dirty fluorescent bulb, seventeen bullets found their way through the haze and shadows and into Benny's body.

Miraculously, he survived, but Benny's life as an informant was over, and the 138th Street Drug War had begun.

As the volatile and deadly conflict continued into 1977, New York City was squeezed through the worst financial and social tourniquet yet, and nothing, it seemed, could stop the bleeding. Mayor Lindsay's years in office were just the start of it, as after the social democrat took power he brought with him a progressive agenda that, no matter your politics, promoted and supported '60s social activism above effectively running a municipality.

It didn't work.

When a handful of national movements turned to violence, grass roots and international agendas alike turned to bombs and assassinations. Things got so bad, in fact, that Mayor Abe Beam—who followed Lindsay—asked for federal assistance, prompting then President Gerald Ford to famously refuse. This resulted in the famous *Daily News* headline from October 30, 1975: "Ford to City; Drop Dead!"

"Nineteen seventy-seven was the break-point year," Democratic consultant Hank Sheinkopf, then a city police officer, said. "The romantic vision of what the city once was, died. Social democracy went into the toilet. People were less interested in free college than they were in safe streets."[46]

By April, my case load as one of three supervising sergeants of 8th Homicide was like living through a series of episodes of *NYPD Blue* or *Law and Order SVU*, only those later shows only aired once a

---

[46] Mahler, Jonathan. "Summer of '77." *New York Times*, June 30, 2002.

week. We had three or four episodes a night, and one particular crime was every bit as tragic and heartbreaking as the Millie Otero murder.

Seventy-seven-year-old Sydel Schwartz was raped and stabbed to death in her Co-op City apartment. What made the crime particularly sickening was the perpetrator, a married building tenant and grocery worker named Joe Delany. Imagine having to tell a wife and daughter that the husband and father they had known for years was a depraved sexual predator and killer.

It is cases like the murder of Sydel Schwartz that fill the ledgers and reports of policemen the world over, and sadly, you don't hear or read about them much, because they don't make for spectacular headlines. Those headlines belong to serial murderers like David Berkowitz, and while the "Son of Sam" case stole the press, the 138th Street War killed more than two dozen people. Such was the nature of the media. Drug gangs were old news, but a serial killer in New York City was a global phenomenon.

To me, the 138th Street War deserved the majority of the coverage, not just for the twenty-seven lives it took, but for the countless others who died via the heroin the war's combatants spread onto our streets.

***

By May, the depth and power of our adversaries, including the identity of Teenager-Ramins co-leader Armando Colon, was revealed. While we had always thought that Jaimie "Teenager" Villa was a bad player, even he was afraid of Colon, who not only hired and directed assassins for drug-related hits, he also sometimes participated in the gruesome murders.

As the gang roundup continued through early 1977, Team C got a lot closer to Colon, who was identified via a mystery that had befuddled the members of Team C for months. A 1974 gray Pontiac had been seen at the kidnapping of several young men, most of whom later turned up dead. One night, for example, three strippers working the stage at the South Bronx Myrurgia Lounge watched through smoke and flashing lights as two rival gang members were brutally executed by shotgun fire in the crowded club. The strippers, too, then went missing, last seen in that same 1974 Pontiac.

After the killing, Detectives Jack McCann, John Meda, Ron Marsenison, Mike McTigue, and John Taldone—who had been assigned to Team C for a related murder case—got wind of something astonishing. There was a seemingly unconnected robbery in Congers, New York, not far from my own house. A connection came to light when Rockland County resident Detective John Meda picked up the morning paper on May 22 and read about the local crime. Sifting through the article, Meda noticed an interesting detail: witnesses had seen a gray 1974 Pontiac flee the scene.

Meda quickly called local police and asked for the plate number, which he then traced to the city and to another astonishing find—a guy named Reinaldo Olivera, who was a member of Teenager's gang. When we brought him in, Olivera gave up more details of the story. Apparently, members of the Teenager gang, under the direction of Armando Colon, had been impersonating police officers to steal from rivals and to maneuver them into position to be kidnapped and murdered. Through that same 1974 Pontiac, a brutal picture emerged.

The car was also seen when the two local men who had been tortured and killed with an electric chainsaw were abducted. Then, after the robbery in Congers, a body was discovered nearby. It was a drug dealer named Anibal Rivera. He, too, had been kidnapped, stabbed, and shot, his lifeless body rolled in a rug and dumped in the back parking lot of the Bully Boy Restaurant in Congers. Before Rivera's execution, the gang took two and a half kilos of heroin and $5,000 in gold jewelry from him.

Detective Meda then tracked the Pontiac to Olivero, the man hand-picked by Colon to play the role of "cop" for the kidnap-murders. Olivero then led Team C to Colon, who according to multiple sources, quickly fled to Mexico.

For Team C, it was a tantalizing near-miss, and the Teenager gang was ready to seize upon it. They did so on a Friday night in June, while the seven Team C detectives were dining at a back table at Marlain Steakhouse in the South Bronx. The guys were barely cutting into their steaks when bullets tore through the front windows and walls, sending Team C diving for cover. It was meant as a warning, but more was coming.

According to Len Buder and Howard Blum's great *New York Times* piece on the 138th Street War, not long after, "squads of uniformed officers, acting on a tip from an informant, raided a roof near 138th Street and St. Ann's Avenue. On that roof, police officers found four men with two high-powered rifles and two shotguns." They had a clear shot into the bar. Had they walked out a few minutes earlier, they might all have been dead.[47]

In a bizarre twist, religious gang members had also enlisted voodoo against Team C by having their guns, bullets, and drugs blessed. Through street informants, Team C knew all about it, and Ron Marsenison hatched a plan to counter. After the shoot-up at Marlain, the whole team went back to the establishment and gathered around a table in the still-damaged dining room. There, Marsenison rather publicly bathed the bullets of his Walther PPK in garlic. He knew word would get back on the street about it and, that to a practitioner of voodoo, getting shot with a garlic bullet was a damnation worse than hell itself.

Marsenison was a real piece of work, tough, determined, and as focused as they came. He looked the part, too, with a scowl so sharp it looked like it could cut through glass. Howard Blum recalled how *People* magazine ran a picture of Marsenison and the other Team C detectives in an article featuring the "Son of Sam" case. Frantic readers quickly sent letters to 8th Homicide, convinced from the photos that Ron Marsenison was the serial killer we were looking for.

***

As the holidays approached, Jack McCann and I talked about needing extra cash for friends and family. He said a lot of the Team C guys had

---

[47] Blum, Howard, and Buder, Leonard. "The War on 138th Street." *New York Times*, December 21, 1978.

a security gig hookup with a retired US Secret Service agent who had a company with some pretty big clients. They included the shah of Iran's twin sister, Princess Ashraf; the Rockefeller family; Chairman of the Federal Reserve Paul Volker; and Ski Industries America, one of the world's most influential winter trade shows. Jack was a godsend, and I jumped at the opportunity he offered.

The first job, with the Rockefeller family security team required being present in David and Margaret Rockefeller's estate in Westchester and also at their townhouse in Manhattan. I eventually got my brother Tom involved in the off-duty job, and one of our main assignments was the midnight-to-eight tour at the Rockefeller estate.

Our job entailed staying up while the family slept and keeping tabs on the vast estate, a compound of buildings that overlooked a large farm. We were to remain in the main house all through the night, so I often brought study materials with me and spent most of the night reading in the kitchen and preparing for an eventual lieutenant's test. On breaks, I would walk through the downstairs area at different intervals to check on things, stretch my legs, and stay awake.

Rather amusingly, it was widely known to security that Mrs. Rockefeller would often come downstairs in the middle of the night and touch the couches to see if they were warm from an unauthorized and forbidden nap. Peggy Rockefeller didn't need security. She *was* security.

Gigs like these led to more high-security adventures, including transporting the priceless King Tut exhibit to Washington, DC. On details like those, I honed my abilities to build teams and coordinate with local and federal law enforcement.

***

Long before the summer of 1977, a depleted and stretched police force also was dealing with a huge uptick in bank robberies. Bank jobs were most often tied to the usual suspects of desperate individuals and mobsters, but as mentioned earlier, there was an ominous new wrinkle by 1977—antiestablishment anger and funding for radicalism.

By late in the decade, in fact, there were as many as four bank holdups a day, totaling more than a hundred a month in the city alone. With the growing mix of suspects came an appropriate mix of law enforcement responses. Some cases were local; some tied to international players; still others tied to organized crime.

Necessity brought the FBI and NYPD together, but on which cases? Some led to mobsters, some to domestic militants, and still more to just desperados. Regardless, the NYPD had to do something better on its own, yet with so many cuts in services, manpower, and equipment, a bit of a bluff had to be employed.

During that year, police cars and crews not on assignment—even stopping for coffee—were directed to park in front of banks as a deterrent.

We were undermanned and unprepared for what was coming. In many ways, both the city and department were up against a wall.

PART FOUR

THE RISE OF TERROR

◢ TROUBLED WATERS

August 3, 1977, may have been yet another milestone moment in the shape and scope of global and domestic terrorism. It was the day two bombs went off in Manhattan—one at the city offices of the Department of Defense and the other at the city headquarters for Mobil Oil.

After the smoke cleared, one person was dead and seven injured. Dozens of bomb threats quickly followed, targeting multiple banks and the World Trade Center. The resulting mayhem caused one hundred thousand New Yorkers to flee their offices and the city, snarling traffic and choking public transport. In the chaotic aftermath, the two crude devices ended up costing the city millions of dollars in revenue.

The FALN took credit. It was the same group that had bombed Fraunces Tavern and dozens of other financial and government targets around the country.

What caught eyes from the NYPD to the FBI were the methods used, the careful planning and infiltration of targets. The Fraunces Tavern bomb had barely gotten through the front door, and the Grand Central and LaGuardia bombs were placed in public lockers. The Department of Defense device, however, was smuggled deep inside a building using a woman's purse. The bomb at Mobil Oil, too, had apparently been placed in a closet using a coat or some other garment.

Both devices, therefore, revealed a worrisome level of long-term surveillance and a study of routines, and pointed to possible inside help. After the August 3 bombings, a note was found in New York's Central Park outlining demands for the release of political prisoners. It cautioned that the two explosions were "just a warning" to "multinational corporations that explore and exploit our national resource" and "are part of Yankee Imperialism."[48]

Looking back from the present day, this was eerily similar to the kind of playbook used by Islamic jihadists—the same mix of oil and accusations of imperialism, aimed at the same targets. This trend would lead to the 1993 attack on the World Trade Center, culminating, of course, in the tragic September 11 event.

In 1977, though, these were merely a few deadly pieces of an emerging puzzle. Life went on, though as previously noted, the press had its own mind as to what the people needed to focus on.

For example, on August 10, "Son of Sam" serial killer David Berkowitz was finally caught. Over the course of a year, he'd claimed just six victims, yet he'd created more fear—and headlines—than the JDL attacks, and the Croatian and FALN bombings combined. After the FALN bombings, Police Commissioner Codd and NY Mayor Abe Beam actually had to go on TV to assure the public that police would not be removed from the "Son of Sam" serial case to investigate the explosions. I still scratch my head about that, about the actual danger and the response, greatly fueled by the amount and editorial slant of press coverage.

Then, as winter approached, the mercury bottomed out, and some of the bombing cases went equally cold. Other matters though—ones in my immediate view—spread toward an incendiary finale.

In November, the guys on Team C learned through an informant that Teenager-Ramins gang leader Armando Colon had snuck back from Mexico to attend the birth of his first child. We knew Colon would be holed up with people he trusted, and one the best leads pointed to Armando's half-brother, Leonard Beauchamp Jr.

Detectives Ronnie Marsenison, Jack McCann, and the rest of Team C took immediate action, and on a cold, early December night McCann scaled a barbed wire fence off 136th Street to place a tracking device on Beauchamp's late-model, brown Camaro. By then the FBI and DEA were involved, and the departments coordinated on

[48] Breasted, Mary. "100,000 Leave New York Offices as Bomb Threats Disrupt City; Blasts Kill One and Hurt Seven." *New York Times*, August 4, 1977.

tracking the car and getting Colon. For the next seven days Team C and our law enforcement partners followed Beauchamp's every move.

We learned of an arranged meeting of the brothers, set to take place on December 14. A helicopter and van filled with Team C, DEA, and FBI personnel closed in. The operation dragged on for hours and when no Colon materialized, it was almost called off. Later that night, though, Beauchamp led law enforcement on a twisting ride from the Bronx to Manhattan and then through the Lincoln Tunnel into New Jersey. Seven vehicles in all closed in on a four-story house on 48th Street in Union City, and as Beauchamp stepped from his car, he was immediately arrested for harboring a fugitive.

Taking Beauchamp was the easy part, as Armando Colon was still waiting inside, likely armed and *very* likely unwilling to go down without a fight. As Beauchamp was tucked into a waiting police car, he snuck a gesture toward a third-floor apartment window.

The response was immediate.

Wearing bulletproof vests and carrying shotguns, Detectives Ronnie Marsenison and Charlie Summers raced into the building as the rest of the officers surrounded the adjacent lot. Fortunately, Colon recognized he had no possible escape and gave up without firing a shot.

***

The apprehension of Armando Colon and the close of the 138th Street War not only marked the end of my 1977, they also turned a critical page on my career. At that time I was serving as detective sergeant of the 8th Homicide Zone; the year 1978 would bring a time of significant changes, some stemming from my past and others that pointed me toward a more tumultuous and unknown future.

Future and past collided just after the new year when 8th Homicide detectives and I responded to an evening killing on Tremont Avenue in the Bronx. The body of Louis DeAngelis was found near a payphone just outside a bar that was known as an organized crime hangout. According to people we interviewed at the scene, the deceased had been told of a phone call, and after he exited to take it, DeAngelis was sprayed with gunfire from a passing car. Riddled with bullets, DeAngelis fell back into the dirty snow and died on the spot.

Organized crime cases were always some of the hardest to solve, since witnesses were understandably tough to come by. We did an immediate background check on DeAngelis and found a long criminal record. That led to many hours at the scene and video camera walk-throughs that we studied at the station. This was the first of our crime scenes in which this new video examination was utilized.

The day after the killing, I received a call from the Chief of Detectives Office and was directed to contact a Lieutenant David Durk, who claimed to have information that could be helpful. This was the famous David Durk who'd stepped up with Police Officer Frank Serpico and exposed the department corruption that culminated in the Knapp Commission Hearings. A fellow detective and I met Duke at a dilapidated apartment just off 117th Street and First Avenue, where he opened the door cautiously and only after we showed our gold shields.

Strangely, Durk seemed extremely nervous and was very general with his information. It was kind of a dry hole, leading me to wonder if Durk was gun-shy and afraid that my partner and I might not be legit. What really hit me, though, happened after leaving the building.

As we walked back to our car at First Avenue, we had to pass between 117th and 118th Streets. I stopped at the corner of 117th Street and looked back up at the building where Durk was. Something held me in place, and it took me several moments to realize that I was standing over the very sewer grating where five years prior, Desiderio Caban had lain dying after being gunned down by Arnie Squitieri.

Stranger still, it wasn't just a memory.

It was a preview of things to come.

The next day the funeral for Louis DeAngelis was held at St. Raymond's Church. Since it had all the earmarks of a mob killing, I elected to attend, along with part of my team, while others in the unit hovered outside and copied licensed plate numbers of attendees. St. Raymond's was about half full for the service, and my partner and I took seats halfway up the center. I sat on the aisle.

The organist began to play, and the priest and the altar boys silently walked down the aisle to the front of the church. I turned to watch as the polished dark coffin was carried in and blessed, after which the family of DeAngelis escorted the casket up the center aisle and to the front of St. Raymond's.

As the casket approached, my eyes went past the priest to the solemn faces of the pallbearers, and there, to my complete shock, the pallbearer closest to me was none other than former Police Officer Patrick McCooey from the Arnold Squitieri case. He was coming right at me and about to pass within inches.

I was transfixed.

Seeing one of my ex NYPD blue escorting a mob soldier into the hereafter was, to say the least, extremely disappointing. It was sad to see how far these men had fallen and the life they had embraced. As McCooey passed, he realized that I was locked in on him and looked directly at me. My pulse pounded. As the blood ran to my face, it drained completely from McCooey's. He quickly looked away.

Two days in a row this case had jumped right back into my life, and I began to think I was in the *Twilight Zone*. It took me the entire service just to calm down. Then, after the final prayer, the casket made its trip back down the aisle, but something was missing.

Patrick McCooey.

Another man had taken his place.

It was like being shown a movie of where my life had gone so far—almost like a challenge to continue and step up. In the space of forty-eight hours a mob murder, the Knapp Commission, and Pleasant Avenue had served to remind me that the only sane way to look at this job was straight ahead.

Straight ahead, though, lay an entirely new type of trouble.

***

In mid-April, an informant named Frank Sisto decided to pull a handgun and rob his ATF contact of his weapon, shield, and cash. Sisto was a known wannabe wise guy and had a serious drug problem to boot. To fill out his dance card, he was also rumored to be connected to East Harlem's infamous Purple Gang.

Reporter Howard Blum described the Purple Gang as a Pleasant Avenue group of teens and young men who often handled drugs and money for the Five Families of Mafia. The gang began their activities working alongside the Lucchese family in their heroin business. This was during the time that I was occupied with Squitieri, Sisca, and "Fats" Inglese, who was known to run heroin for the very same bosses.

When the famous French Connection bust took down parts of this secretive network, the Purple Gang receded into the shadows and became more independent, though the mob still relied on them to help transport drugs to the Harlem streets and, when needed, for gangland executions.

Seemingly distanced from the Five Families, the Purple Gang became emboldened by the fear their growing reputation engendered and formed what many called a "sixth Mafia family," a development that threatened to launch a bloody new turf war centered on Pleasant Avenue.

Still, at the time, nobody in the ATF had any idea that Sisto, one of their trusted informants—a kid who had provided so much good intelligence—would pull a gun on his federal agent handler. Worse still was the notion of having a genuine ATF shield floating out there, along with a registered government firearm. The Teenager-Ramins gang had used shields of their own, along with falsified police credentials, to lure victims for kidnappings and murders, revealing the deadly scope of the problem.

Sometime after Sisto robbed Dunham—around 10:00 p.m. on April 13, as I recall—the ATF arrived at 8th Homicide to ask for assistance in tracking him down. We gathered our forces, got a few leads on Sisto, and spent the next three or four hours combing the area looking for our man.

The next afternoon, ATF Special Agent Alex D'Atri arrived at 8th Homicide with information that Sisto, along with his girlfriend, had been spotted at a methadone clinic in Pelham Bay; so, with two matching descriptions we had a pretty good lead. We also had a lot to worry about. Frank Sisto was armed, dangerous, and considered highly volatile, but the guys from the ATF were a ready bunch. Like Team C, they were young guys who, despite their ages, were already battle-tested and street-hardened.

They were also highly independent—so much so, in fact, that some in Washington wanted to rein them in and even disband them. It reminded me of the cautions I'd received regarding the lure of being so close to the criminal element and mindset. This was seen as a necessary risk for the big reward, though. Drug running involved the street and a volatile sense of immediacy, making it a young man's game—for younger, generally single cops with less to lose.

It wasn't the time for overanalysis, however.

That very evening, April 14, a combined unit from 8th Homicide—including Detective Tom Kelly, me, and several others—went to assist a team of ATF agents in apprehending Sisto. I brought along Team C's Jack McCann, who knew the area best and had some experience with the Purple Gang. When Jack and I caught up with the group, some of the ATF team were already tracking our suspects as they came from the clinic. Shortly thereafter, 8th Homicide and ATF teams pulled over the target car as it pulled onto Westchester's Hutchinson River Parkway.

The unknown girl climbed out of the car first, and Jack McCann took her aside. Another man named Frank Chismar exited the car next, but the driver—the one matching Sisto's description—refused to exit. As ATF agents became insistent, he started screaming and cursing at them, and when agents attempted to remove him, the man hooked his arm over the steering wheel and dropped his other hand out of sight.

The ATF agents pried the suspect from the wheel and pulled him straight through the driver's-side window, forcing him to the ground. The man wasn't Frank Sisto.[49]

---

[49] Castellucci, John. "US Grand Jury Probes Incident on Hutchinson." *Reporter Dispatch*, October 12, 1978.

***

The shit hit the fan, and then the US attorney got involved. All three in the car that night brought a suit against the ATF and police department, claiming a civil rights violation.

Mind you, I was there as leader of my team, so the growing mess was destined to drop in my lap. Sure enough, the very next day the FBI, with whom we had a great working relationship, called to inform us of the coming storm. Certain factions in the US Attorney's Office were looking to clip the ATF's wings, and the mistaken takedown gave them political leverage to do so. Captain Jim Trainor saw the whole picture and was extraordinarily helpful in helping us navigate the swirling fallout.

From his work in the Bronx Homicide Zone, Trainor was keenly aware and very supportive of highly specialized and proficient investigative teams, and knew all too well that embedded and undercover teams could gather amazing amounts of timely information. Yes, sometimes this fast-acting structure could lead to mistakes, such as with Frank Sisto, but nobody at the scene had ended up with more than a few minor scrapes.

Had it been Sisto that night, a far more disastrous outcome might have resulted, or a very dangerous man and his accomplices would be off the street.

Regardless, the ATF and the Sisto case quickly exploded into the political football of the year, exemplified by a 1980 congressional hearing regarding regulatory agency oversight, during which, the "Hutch Incident" was prominently referenced.[50]

While this was brewing, I was blindsided by something that hit far closer to home.

---

[50] "Gun Control and Constitutional Rights." Committee on the Judiciary. Serial No 96-83. September 15, 1980. Web, September 3, 2018.

BOUNCING OFF THE WALLS

I was on the FDR Drive and headed into work when Joan called to let me know she was in an ambulance on the way to Nyack Hospital. After a quick U-turn, I raced back upstate, and when I got to Nyack, grim-faced doctors met me with news of a shadow they'd found on X-rays.

It was near my wife's adrenal gland, not a good sign. Joan had been with me since high school, through four children and a police and consulting career that had taken me away for long hours. She was my rock and truly my better half. Joan raised our kids, and where I merely entered a room, Joan lit it. I would never have gotten as far without her.

What on Earth would I do if she were gone?

We acted quickly and set up an appointment in the city for the next day at Mt. Sinai Hospital in New York, and the diagnosis was downright scary. It looked like cancer and carried the terrible prognosis of six months. The glimmer of hope was that the doctors still needed a biopsy to be certain.

The morning Joan went under the knife, everything became a blur. I wandered out of Mount Sinai and onto the street before finding my way to nearby St. Francis de Sales Church at 96th Street. There, I prayed to and pleaded with God, promising to be a better and more available father and spouse. I sat there for hours until my brother Tom took me to lunch and worked to occupy my mind with the job, his and mine.

Joan's operation lasted nearly seven hours in all, and when I got back to the hospital, the news was worse than before. The doctors were certain that the growth they had removed represented terminal cancer. It took another agonizing week for the tests to come back, and I truly don't know how, but forces intervened on our behalf.

The doctor, too, seemed amazed, though happily relieved when he called.

"It's benign," he told me.

For years, Joan had been a pillar of strength and an inspiration, running every aspect of our home and finances, keeping me together through the Squitieri case, my brushes with IAD, and my father's death.

The whole scare got me thinking again about my career—past, present, and future—and with the advice of John Culley still echoing in my brain, I put in my application for the FBI Academy. I'd spent my whole life just following along with whatever adventure came my way. The time had come to choose what was best for both me and my family.

***

May brought a return cha-cha dance with my friend Jamie "Teenager" Villa, only this time in front of a grand jury. I testified in both federal and state courts, recalling the circumstances of Villa's capture and my part in it. The entire time, the chiseled defendant glared at anybody who dared meet his eye.

Villa offered me a strangely different reaction.

Each time I began telling of our hallway confrontation, Teenager broke out in a grin and just shook his head. It was then that I realized how fortunate I had been in walking away from this event without being seriously hurt or killed. Villa seemed amused somehow, stunned even, perhaps by his own misread of me.

The grand jury wrapped. Teenager and his confederates were charged with more than thirty murders, along with dealing drugs. In some way, the whole experience seemed to cement my belief that applying to the FBI was a solid career move. Yet at the same time, I also wanted to make lieutenant or maybe even leave the department to become the next Chris Borgen. Even though my intended direction was the FBI National Academy in Quantico, my compass was still pointed toward remaining in law enforcement.

But that needle was wavering...

Such indecision wasn't exactly healthy for an active police officer, but so much was happening that I was off balance. And to top it off, I arrived at *another* backup plan—to follow Tony Hatch's advice from years prior and go for a master's degree in communications. And as with every other choice I had made, the classes at the New York Institute of Technology opened new doors and pulled me toward new adventures. To my surprise and delight, during those classes I found famed *New York Times* reporter Len Buder as one of my adjunct professors.

Buder had made his name covering hot-bed education issues, including teacher's strikes, desegregation, and budget crises, then had transitioned into crime reporting, covering among other cases the capture and arrest of "Son of Sam," David Berkowitz.

Buder and a photographer came to one of my presentations at the Police Academy, during which I showed homicide detectives how video surveillance could be used for better crime-scene analysis. During my talk, Len's photographer caught a picture of me standing in the middle of the class, arms outstretched making a point—only with my eyes closed.

The paper printed it. Upon seeing it, my brother Tom ribbed that the picture was a perfect representation of how I did my job.

If justice is blind, I certainly looked the part.

After that, Len started poking around for more stories and began looking deeper into my career. Predictably, the first item he gravitated toward was my time at the 2-5 Precinct working the Squitieri case. He suggested that I produce a series of newspaper articles or a book. I recall thanking him for his interest but making it very clear that the *last* thing I wanted was an exposé revealing my experiences with bad cops and failures in the system.

"There's too much scar tissue," I told Len. Instead, I offered the story of the 138th Street War, in hopes of passing the glow to the guys in Team C.

"It's the Bronx, Kevin. Who cares?" Buder replied.

One evening, though, he invited me to toss back a couple of beers with the previously mentioned Howard Blum, one of today's most influential writers and journalists. At the time, Blum was a *Village Voice* and *New York Times* reporter and fresh from a bestselling book. Maybe twenty-five or twenty-six, Howard was successful, ambitious, and adventurous, though—as he later admitted—maybe without a real direction other than the next big thing. We had that in common.

Over drinks Blum told me that he was fascinated by police stories and admitted that as much as his generation mistrusted the system, in the role of a *Village Voice* reporter he'd gone out with cops and had seen the other side. Blum admitted that he was captivated by the blue-collar mentality of most of the men in blue, their ethics and desire to help others. He also found many of them a far cry from the monochrome antiestablishment view of the time.

Later, in that smoke-filled bar and with the conversation moving again toward Squitieri, I made my move and, in spite of Len Buder's indifference, proceeded to tell Blum about Team C. His reaction was quite different, and he thought the adventures of Team C made for a great story. With a smirk, Buder grudgingly let me weave the tale.

I was about three-quarters of the way through when Blum turned to his colleague.

"Len, I think we oughta do something about this."

That fall, on radio and television, the *Times* began promoting the stories about 138th Street War. The articles that followed were real and gritty and captured how these guys were in the crosshairs every day, relying on informants and contacts who might turn at any moment. For a full week that very December, the story splashed across the headlines, and I was grateful that the guys from Team C were going to get their due. Jim Trainor had always talked about the value of horse trading. Team C was the horse I preferred to back.

***

As some of the craziness that was the summer of 1978 ebbed like a wave out to sea, a fierce undertow returned as outside forces began circling the April Hutch Incident.

Those of us who had been involved had by then chalked it up to an honest though regrettable mistake, but many—in both DC and New York—wanted blood. A grand jury was called, and civil rights charges were leveled at the ATF and the police department. The situation took an even more ominous turn when two fresh-faced FBI agents appeared at 8th Homicide to question me.

While it seemed a bit strange on the surface, I happily invited them in, and the interview started benignly enough, with the two asserting that they had some simple questions about the "incident" and just wanted my take. Before the questions began, however, they stopped to advise me of my rights!

A sickening feeling appeared in the pit of my stomach, and I began to connect the dots.

My application to the FBI Academy had been mysteriously held up. Class was scheduled to begin in January, and it was usual to hear by midsummer if you had been selected. Such a delay likely meant I was still being investigated. Well, here were two investigators, sitting right in front of me advising me of my rights.

"Gentlemen, with all due respect," I said as I gestured toward the door, "this interview is over." Thanking them for their time and interest, I slid out of my chair. "I don't know of too many witnesses that have to be advised of their rights."

Before showing my federal colleagues out, I reiterated that I was one of the supervisors at the scene but only there as an observer. I further advised I wasn't going to talk to the grand jury and added that if I or any of my men were under suspicion of impropriety, none in 8th Homicide would testify without proper immunity.

As the FBI men exited the precinct, it struck me that the FBI had sent two rookies so as not to poison the waters with agents with whom we might have worked. It felt like a bureaucratic setup and an assumption that my team and the ATF had become more than fodder for a civil case, suspects in an over-the-top ATF arrest and alleged beating.

There was a move in Washington to break up the ATF, so the serious level of maneuvering made sense. Worse, the "Hutch Incident"—as the papers were calling it—had grabbed headlines and become the centerpiece of that witch hunt.

A week or so later, the detectives who had been involved were served with subpoenas, as was I. We were ordered to appear before a federal grand jury and directed by the grand jury to appear in an FBI lineup, only separately and on separate days. Furthermore, we were directed to wear the same clothes we wore at the scene and told to leave our guns at home.

That was the clincher.

Lineups were commonplace for patrolmen and detectives, but generally we'd only be asked to forego firearms if we were going to be charged with a crime. With that glaring red flag raised, I instantly picked up the phone and called a lawyer at the Sergeant's Benevolent Association (SBA) to ask him what I was up against. Thankfully, the attorney wasn't as worried as I was and didn't see the big deal with the lineup.

I felt differently. It was an embarrassment to be put in this position after an entire career of service. Nevertheless, I had to just shake it off, go home, and relax as best I could.

It was far from over.

If I'd suspected a witch hunt, it certainly seemed to arrive after I got to the FBI office on East 69th Street in New York. Nobody in that lineup looked remotely like me. Then, in the brightly lit, scuffed and soiled lineup room, I was asked to pick a number and grabbed spot number five near the middle of the pack. My mind raced with scenarios, and just before the window opened, a guy next to me spoke up.

"What are you in here for?"

It was the kind of thing a perp would ask another.

"I'm in for helping a federal agent."

He blinked at me and then looked away. As the screen slowly opened, he started acting very nervous on purpose and seemed to pull all of the attention away from me. Turned out he was an FBI agent who I suppose knew of the case and, I guess, was trying to help me out of it.

That night, I chose not to mention any of this to Joan. She had been through enough already, and the last thing I wanted was to burden her with the possibility of a reprimand or, worse, the career blow of a rather politically charged suspension.

As events continued to unfold, the motorists involved claimed the arrest had been over the top, and the more I thought about the way the incident was being handled, I developed the urge to talk about it.

Surely I'd get my chance in the grand jury.

Or would I?

◢ CLEARING THE AIR

After the grand jury was announced for October, word spread that no immunity was forthcoming, and my SBA attorney promptly demanded that I not testify. Honestly, it didn't matter to me.

Immunity or not, I was upset and wanted to set the record straight. With my attorney in full protest mode, I bristled. "I'm one of the people responsible, and I have a duty to clear the record. I'm going in, and that's it. I'm going in with no immunity, and I'll take the heat. It's gotta be brought back to reality here."

I also knew that if we didn't testify, we'd likely be arrested for obstructing a government investigation, yet that wasn't the point. It felt like forces were trying to pressure us—and specifically me—to hang the ATF out to dry and was eerily similar to being raked over the coals during the Squitieri investigation.

The whole mess quickly escalated after news of the grand jury hit the papers. There was no keeping it from friends and family, and I had relatives in Rockland and Westchester calling the house and office.

Regrettably, it all took quite a toll on the other guys in 8th Homicide. The night before the grand jury, Jack McCann revealed that Tom Kelly had gone home and prepared his family for a likely suspension and possibly even an arrest. According to both the Civilian Review Board and Jim Trainor at the Bronx Homicide Zone, we hadn't done anything wrong, yet there we were, about to be paraded as suspects. The ATF, too, had simply made a mistake—one that could have saved lives and, in reality, injured no one.

It didn't matter.

If the lineup had been surreal, the grand jury was something else entirely, a real dog-and-pony show that was presided over by civil rights heavyweight Michael Johnson. As a federal prosecutor for the Department of Justice, he had led the tense and politically charged investigation into the terrible Greensboro Massacre of 1979, during which neo-Nazis and Ku Klux Klan members opened fire on civil rights protestors.

The presence of Johnson sent shockwaves through the ATF, the 4-3 Precinct, and the department. The government spared no expense, either, and carefully constructed an intricately detailed 3-D model of the entire Hutchinson Parkway scene, complete with opposite lanes, witness car positions, and our positioning at the traffic stop.

In the grand jury room, Johnson asked me to approach the model and explain each and every detail, as well as the sequence of events as I recalled them. The entire time I spoke and paced, a short second chair US prosecutor, Dan Rinzel, furiously scribbled notes on a yellow legal pad, stopping only to glare at me. After the initial tense minutes, I began to feel a little more at ease, especially as my re-creation of the events, along with a little editorializing, got past the grand jury and attorneys without much interruption.

Then Rinzel caught my eye again.

He was filling that legal pad with notes, and, at times, all eyes were on him, almost as if he was sending a signal to the room that my entire testimony was setting off a sea of red flags. The mood in the room slowly deteriorated, and I knew I had to do something about it. As Johnson finished his questions and paced back to the prosecutor's table, Rinzel began to violently tug his boss's jacket.

"I have a few more questions," he announced as he rose, faced me, and rather dramatically tossed his yellow legal pad behind him. He approached. "Sergeant Hallinan," he said, hovering. "Do you know what I think? I think you have done an excellent job of covering up for the ATF and what transpired that day!"

I just looked at him and waited, giving him a few moments to stew and also to make sure the jury knew I felt there was nothing to hide. Rinzel returned to his position alongside his boss. Finally, I exhaled and eased back into my seat. My heart, of course, was racing, but I had a job to do.

"Counselor," I began, as the unease inside of me shifted into a slowly brewing Irish anger. "I've been a police officer for seventeen years." I then leaned toward the jury and began to list my career highlights, including being under the microscope of the Knapp Commission and facing down the Pleasant Avenue crews.

"I have a *spotless record*," I thundered. "I've been committed to this job, and so was everybody present that day. I saw the job they did," I continued. "I saw the resistance that was put up by a man matching the description of one known to carry guns and not being afraid to use them. Everything was done correctly."

Then, I relaxed a bit as I felt the weight of it ease. It was good to get it out in the open.

"It was all done by the book," I directed the next comment to the judge. "I had a responsibility to both my men and the suspects, by my oath to protect both sides." I waited another beat and then did my best to put a punctuation mark on it all. "My *integrity* is *not* on the line here today. Yes, I was in charge that night—I was responsible then, and I'm still responsible here and now." I then looked past Dan Rinzel and to his boss, Michael Johnson. "If I saw anything illegal, I'd be duty bound to stop it. It was unfortunate, but it was professional and the best job that could be done."

At that point Rinzel rose to come at me again, but this time, it was his jacket that was the one being tugged on and by Johnson, his boss.

"Sit down," the DOJ prosecutor commanded his second as if he was pulling back a trained attack dog. Johnson then stood and approached me. "Sergeant Hallinan." His demeanor eased, and a slight smile glinted across his face. "I want to thank you for coming in here today. Please let your detectives know that if they are willing to testify, they may do so with full immunity." He then walked back to the table, and I was excused.

What a relief to know that the guys in my command, those brave souls who had risked so much to do so much good, were going to be treated accordingly and with all due respect and trust. Having expected the worst, I suddenly felt buoyed by the whole experience. Still, as tough as he was on me, I understood Dan Rinzel's approach. I can only just imagine the pressure that the whole system was under, with the politics swirling.

After the grand jury broke for the day, I approached Michael Johnson to thank him. Instead, he thanked me again for coming in without that same immunity and asked if there was anything else he could do for me. There was, and I mentioned to Johnson my worry that the whole incident had held up my application to the FBI National Academy. I politely asked him if he had any friends there and was told that he did.

"I'd appreciate a good word on my behalf," I added. Johnson smiled and said he'd do what he could. Whether Johnson made a call, I'll never know, but the very next day Bill Kelly—who handled applications for the FBI in NY—called to inform that I was going into the January class. In a very real way, it was a culmination of lessons given from inspirations and mentors as far back as my own father, brother Tom, through the police academy and my first gigs on the beat.

The lesson was simple. It might take months and it might take years, but you will be found for being up to a certain set of standards. No matter how hard or how long the road, doing the right thing is always better than taking the short route or doing nothing at all. After that grand jury and my FBI invitation, I felt renewed.

◢ THAT ONE CASE

Every cop has that case—the one never solved, the one that stays with them for life.

It was my turn to take that journey, and, in a strange way, it came right back around to Pleasant Avenue in East Harlem. It all unfolded on a brisk fall night a couple days before Thanksgiving, a somewhat routine call for a shooting at Crosby Avenue and Westchester Square.

Two young teens, barely eighteen, had been crossing the street when a speeding car turned the corner and almost struck them. Angered, both pedestrians yelled at the driver, who screeched his car to a stop, jumped out, and opened fire with a handgun. Seconds later, both teens lay wounded, and later at the hospital, the assault turned to homicide as both died from their wounds.

After some solid detective work by elements of the 8th Homicide detectives unit, uniformed police officers brought in a suspect, a mob wannabe named Maurice "Moe" Anzisi.

My cubicle was at the far end of the homicide office, and once Anzisi was brought in, four of us in all packed into the cramped space. Almost in a sitting huddle, I watched Anzisi closely as two homicide detectives questioned him. Knowing I was in command, Anzisi eyed me angrily as I stared down at his name on the arrest report.

Suddenly, something deep inside pulled at me, a shadow of a memory, a haunting from Pleasant Avenue. I knew the name Anzisi from the 2-5 Precinct—it was the same last name as that bartender on Pleasant Avenue, proprietor of one of the very same bars where Tom Bowes and I shook the tree during the Arnie Squitieri investigation.

That bartender was Moe Anzisi's older brother.

Here was Squitieri again, in a way—at least everything he stood for, the indifference and callousness, and only inches away from me, his legacy, a kid following in his footsteps. Moe Anzisi was only nineteen at the time and stood a diminutive five-foot-five. At most he tipped the scales at maybe one hundred twenty pounds, a kid in body.

What struck me about him was his eyes. They were cold and as empty as those of a man who had seen a lifetime of violence and depravity. Honestly, it was the first time I looked into a man's eyes and thought I could not find a soul. As the detectives continued to question Moe, he growled just enough to make it abundantly clear that he had zero remorse. It didn't matter that he'd killed two people that evening, Anzisi's only admission was his disgust and anger at being in custody.

The next morning, Anzisi was arraigned and charged with the double homicide. Anzisi entered a not-guilty plea, then walked out of court after easily posting bail. To nobody's surprise, more than a few Pleasant Avenue connections came to light, pieced together by detectives Tom Kelly, Jack McCann, and me via area informants.

A close relative of Anzisi had put several buildings up for collateral, and that relative was, in fact, Moe's father, a rumored mob associate. Stranger still, Moe's dad had worked with the department, too, as a paddy wagon driver.

Investigators quickly gathered enough evidence to charge Anzisi with several other murders. Only problem was, he was out on bail. Soon after leaving our company, Anzisi contacted his seventeen-year-old girlfriend, Theresa Panarese, and informed her he was going to run. Panarese, we later learned, tried hard to convince him to stay and face the music. A high school senior and studying to be a beautician, she didn't want to live on the run and told Moe she wouldn't leave.

Hoping to convince her otherwise, Anzisi asked her to meet him the day after Thanksgiving at Jack's Diner in Westchester Square. Theresa Panarese had a plan of her own though, a tragic plan. Hoping to prevent her boyfriend from further complicating his life, Panarese called Anzisi's father and informed him of Moe's plans and her hope to prevent them. Moe's dad allegedly told Theresa to go to the diner and stall his son while some "friends" moved in to compel Moe not to go through with his flight.

On November 24, at Jack's Diner, Panarese and Anzisi were joined by three young men who likely were members of the infamous Purple Gang, guys the mob sometimes used for coercion or executions. According to witnesses, the small group left and drove about fifteen minutes away to nearby Orchard Beach, where the three men tried to "convince" Anzisi to take the heat. With Anzisi undeterred, the group next drove a mile away, stopping on Shore Road.

A passing witness, a young woman driving home from work, observed a car, a brand-new blue Cadillac Seville. It was up off the road and parked on the grass with a young couple fitting the description of Moe and Theresa Panarese. They were being pulled from the back seat and made to kneel down in the high grass. Before the witness drove past, she noted the look on Theresa Panarese's face, and the way she described that look of sheer terror has stayed with me to this day.

Panarese was just a kid with dreams and an entire life ahead of her. There she was, trying to help keep her high-school love from running and, instead, got a bullet in the head and a muddy and shallow Pelham Bay Park grave as her reward.

After the bodies were found, detectives received a lead from another motorist who had witnessed the same blue Cadillac as it sped from the scene. That person got a plate number. There was no other information provided, other than the vehicle was occupied only by three white males possibly in their twenties. To punctuate the deadly crime, the vehicle registration pointed back to Moe's own father.

Apparently, had Anzisi succeeded in disappearing, Moe's dad would no longer have title to the several buildings he used as collateral to post his son's bail. The revelation was especially disgusting.

Anzisi's dad then, as the saying goes, "lawyered up" and vanished. Only his attorney contacted us after that, and he, of course, was known to be closely affiliated with organized crime. The lawyer advised that his client would not come in for questioning unless we provided a list of questions first. We refused and instead looked for other avenues of leverage, but with few tangible leads to the actual killers, it was frustratingly slow going.

Honestly, I didn't really care as much about what had happened to Moe. It was disturbing enough that his own father would kill him over a piece of real estate, but Theresa Panarese was truly innocent, and her murder got to all of us. Me perhaps most of all.

As the trail went agonizingly cold, John Taldone of Team C offered a last desperate suggestion. He said he would be able to get us a sit-down with Paul Castellano, who at the time was the head of one of the five organized crime families in New York, the Gambinos. From his undercover work with Team C, Taldone had some good connections who sometimes cooperated with crimes that they too found unbearably disturbing. This might be one of those, so we all agreed it couldn't hurt.

The meet with Castellano took place in the back of a pet store on Second Avenue in East Harlem. I went along in the hope that the mob boss would find the murder of the innocent young Italian girl as repugnant as the rest of us.

Let me tell you, "Big Paul" Castellano was as intimidating a sight as his nickname. Nearly six-foot-three-inches and easily two hundred seventy pounds, he was built like an old gladiator and had a reputation that was equally dangerous. He was extremely polite, though, and listened closely as I explained the situation in some detail. Unfortunately, I couldn't detect any interest in providing assistance, likely because it would not only mean turning in an associate, but perhaps also a potential run-in with the already out-of-control and hyper-violent Purple Gang.

We left empty-handed but eventually found a possible suspect. Given the tight-lipped nature of organized crime, we pushed for a grand jury, whose subpoenas sometimes helped compel witnesses to provide information that they previously may have been reluctant to share. That was a dry hole, however; so I decided to bring some pressure to the Bronx District Attorney's Office.

A meeting was called by the district attorney's chief assistant and attended by representatives from the three homicide zones in the Bronx. We were pushing for a grand jury, but at the last moment—and for reasons unknown—Bronx District Attorney Mario Merola refused to approve the arrest of our suspect. We were left out in the cold.

The homicides of Moe Anzisi and his girlfriend, Theresa Panarese, were never solved, and Detective Kelly and I had the grim task of informing the girl's mother that her daughter's killers most likely would escape justice. It was truly heartbreaking and stands as the one case I will take with me into the next life.

**

The ugly business with Moe Anzisi was yet another grim reminder of Pleasant Avenue and reinforced for me just how correct I was in pushing the 138th Street War story over my own.

Then a couple weeks before Christmas, Pleasant Avenue rose again—only this time to offer a gift in the guise of New Orleans mentor and fellow cop Dick Olpe, who, along with Terry McKeon, was such a big part of my growth as a law enforcement professional.

Olpe never forgot the Squitieri case, and since he moved through some pretty influential circles, he again offered to set up a meeting for me with Michael Korda, the wunderkind editor in chief of literary giant Simon & Schuster. I was grateful, of course, but reminded Dick that I didn't want to pursue it.

"Just take the meeting and see what he has to say," Olpe pressed, so just before the holiday, I walked into Korda's office on 6th Avenue. The piercing and ever-curious editor was on me instantly.

If there was ever a man of many hats, it was Michael Korda. The protégé son of artists and influencers, he presented an immediate and formidable combination of pleasant and grim, relaxed, and razor sharp. Like his tapestry of interests, Korda's office was a clutter of shelves and sections, all filled with items and knickknacks including books, awards, and this collection of miniature helmets from the world's military and police.

Maybe, he wanted to add me to the collection as for the first half-hour Korda grilled me about police life and my experience with NYPD history. At times I felt like I was back in the grand jury room. Don't get me wrong; Korda was quite charming, but there was an intensity, an uncompromising vibe behind his wire-rimmed glasses, like it was only a matter of time before he broke me like an exposé.

Soon enough he pressed me on the Squitieri story, telling me how big a part of history it was. I just wasn't ready, and the harder he pressed, the more I fell back on tactics I'd honed under pressure from prosecutors. I tried hard to steer him back to other items, most notably the 138th Street War, which, I reminded Korda, was set to hit the front pages of the *New York Times* as an explosive and action-packed exposé of its own.

That shifted his attention, and I weaved the tale from my first contact with Teenager and Team C through the thrilling conclusion of the gang war takedown. After absorbing my blow-by-blow, Korda's eyes went inward and even before I was done, he mused that having the *Times* piece in hand was a marketing homerun, almost like a free press kit in the hands of millions.

He was sold, and I walked out of his office excited to share the news with Team C. I felt as if I'd just delivered a whole bag of holiday gifts to some of the most deserving people I knew.

A few weeks later, the publishing giant came back with the revelation that none other than famed columnist and crime writer Jimmy Breslin was going to be hired for the book. Korda also wanted to set up a meeting with the huge William Morris Talent Agency. Needless to say, when I shared this news with Jack McCann and Team C, the guys were excited. They had long and distinguished careers, sure, but their professional lives were lived mostly undercover and, as I knew all too well, lived vastly underpaid, too.

This was a career-making moment for them, and I was very happy and proud to be the conduit. Unfortunately, Breslin was hit with the untimely death of his wife, the book was delayed and, sadly, didn't quite turn out as intended.

It was time to turn the page.

"FEDERALIZED"

▰ BACK TO SCHOOL

In all the excitement of reaching the FBI National Academy, I'm not entirely certain I realized just how rapidly the world around me was descending into ever more danger and complexity.

Up to then I had done a reasonable job of taking each life and career adventure as it came. Even through some pretty serious trials and tribulations, I was generally comfortable in the reality that each task and hurdle was well defined by established procedure. There was comfort there, a usual outcome. The FBI National Academy, however, would soon reveal itself as just the beginning of an incredible new life chapter, one that would severely test every ounce of knowledge, experience, and bandwidth I had.

For NYPD guys like me, just getting into the program was like getting voted onto an all-star team. It was both an honor and a privilege, and I certainly recognized that it was going to be hard and serious work, accompanied by profound expectations.

Indeed, many of the men and women of the FBI set high bars for cops from New York, considering all the city had to offer in experience. NYPD invitees to the FBI Academy included Deputy Inspector Bill Conroy, known as a tough-talking, red-headed New Yorker with a wise guy sense of humor. Bill and I hit it off as city Irishmen, took the drive down to Quantico together, and while I thought the academy was a big accomplishment, Bill Conroy quickly set me straight.

For Conroy, acceptance into the FBI program meant little when compared to the differences he felt he could make well beyond it, so unless this new training was well implemented and built upon, the experience and accomplishment would amount to little.

I certainly had some things to learn, and there would be plenty of telling lessons ahead. The first lesson came in the form of the Quantico welcome.

It was more akin to being inducted into the armed forces. We were just two of the two hundred fifty guys in the 116th annual class, and as soon as we walked in, Bill and I were weighed and measured and assigned our dorm rooms. As seriously as the training was meant to be taken, honestly, I was just so happy to be there that I decided to hold an impromptu class party that first night. The nice twenty-five-year-old bottle of Scotch I'd snuck in with me was a good start, too.

Before any party could begin, though, I had to get settled.

Finding my way to my simple dorm room, I found that I had no roommate. Thinking I'd caught a break, I called home to let Joan know I'd arrived and then set off on a tour of the facilities to look for potential party guests. I hadn't gotten far when a guy named Tom Elfmont grabbed me in the hall. His room was across the way and said he had overheard my "New York Irish" from outside and wanted to say hello.

Elfmont was a lieutenant in the Los Angeles Police Department but originally hailed from Long Island. I guess I provided a familiar face and voice, and from that moment on we hung out so much that he became an extra roommate and a lifelong friend. Tom was raised in a small town in West Hampton, New York, and saw policing as a community affair, like I had with the familiar neighborhood beat cops of my youth. We bonded over the shared experience and agreed the more personal approach had, by 1979, become lost in a more by-the-book approach.

To Tom Elfmont, policing was becoming more about risk aversion than community security. During the writing of this book, Tom reminded me that present-day cops can get quickly reprimanded and even suspended for doing anything off the book, even if it's the right thing to do in a given situation.

Elfmont had experienced quite the career before the FBI Academy, too, from a stint in the Army ROTC program to a dangerous Vietnam post as an advisor in intelligence and counterintelligence. After the war, he spotted a job for police officers in Berkeley, California, and jumped at the chance for what was then envisioned as a "progressive" new kind of department.

The Berkeley into which Elfmont walked, though, wasn't what he expected. By the early '70s, the whole area was losing parts of its progressive agenda in the face of simple survival during the rise of the Black Panther movement. On one of Tom's early patrols, in fact, he was on the side of the road talking to a couple of young women who had been involved in a minor traffic accident when a carload of Panthers ran him down just for being a cop.

Tom recovered from the blow, but the town was hit even harder as the radical movement of '70s took firmer hold and Berkeley became an epicenter for protests and riots.

By 1971, the orchestrated unrest spread to politics and several area activists were elected to the city council, which only made matters more volatile as the council was faced with the realities of leading an entire community. Even the most radical leaders had to make sure certain services were provided and order was kept. They had to compromise, which to some on the front lines felt like a sellout.

In turn, the grappling with fiscal and social reality seemed to some like a betrayal, fueling even more militancy. By the time we became classmates, Tom Elfmont had already lived a law enforcement life far beyond my own horizons. His Berkeley adventures included regular bombings and homes routinely flying communist North Vietnamese flags.

From there, he had taken a notoriously tough assignment with the 77th Division of the LAPD, Southern California's epicenter of radical and gang-related violence. He then joined Los Angeles's 7th Homicide Division, which boasted more than ninety murders a year.

Tom Elfmont was the real deal.

***

As the party in my room got rolling and as my bottle of Scotch circulated, Tom and I wondered if there was a way to switch him across the hall, as I had no roommate.

That's when the seas parted and in strolled this hulking bear of a man in a snow-dusted fur coat and a ten-gallon cowboy hat. When he saw me staring up at him, he just tipped his hat like he was the new sheriff in town. Then he pulled out a photo of a wife and kids and carefully placed it on a dresser. My new roommate's name was David J. Hungness, the district sergeant for the Bismarck Police Department in North Dakota.

Prior to the Academy, Hungness had been in charge of keeping the peace on the local Native American reservation. It was a dangerous job as the mostly self-governed reservation had constant problems with alcohol abuse and the resulting disputes. During our time in the Academy, he would regale me with stories of his job and of nearly always being outnumbered and outgunned when responding alone to calls.

"When you come up on a group of angry guys," he'd advise, "you knock out the biggest guy right away...or get beat up or killed." He said it so matter of fact, it had a certain romantic charm. David stood out, both literally and figuratively. Sadly, David Hugeness died in 1993 at the very young age of fifty-five.

***

With the party behind us, the 116th Class of the FBI Academy was tossed into the thick of it, and I quickly got a good look at just how comprehensive and detailed the Bureau could be.

One of the first courses that really stood out for me involved professional sports gambling. Having brushed so closely with organized crime, and being such an avid sports fan, I had seen the perils of teams and athletes alike as targets of mobsters. Our instructor was an FBI agent named Charlie Parsons, the FBI Academy's expert in gambling technologies.

Parsons talked at length about having an openness to learn from anybody and their experiences, and he meant *everybody*—from friend to foe and professional competitor. True to the sentiment, Parsons knew every step of the gamblers trade and outlined how each sport was bet, how odds were figured out, and how organized crime made their money—what is known as their "vig." Short for "vigorish," the vig, or to some "the juice," was the percentage amount charged for taking a bet.

He also detailed the mob's strong-arm tactics and the extortive and coercive tools they deployed to compromise athletes, their friends, and their employers. As it turned out, athletes could be pretty easily influenced or assessed when establishing the odds. It was as simple as finding out from insiders if guys like quarterbacks or starting pitchers were fighting with their wives or likely to be hung over. Anything—no matter how trivial—could sway game results and move thousands if not millions of dollars around.

Athletes could be bribed and coerced too, set up by hookers, for example, or extorted by planting drugs. Point shaving, insiders' reports, you name it—all were viable methods of separating a gambler from his money. This class would play a major part in my future—in ways I could never have imagined.

As Academy training progressed our group—the 116th FBI National Academy class—was tasked with choosing a representative for the session and, wouldn't you know it, it came down to Tom Elfmont and me. I ended up getting the nod, and my new position allowed me to compete for class spokesman at the March graduation. Tom was gracious, so much so that he volunteered to do some digging on my behalf and returned with the information that a very impressive Royal Canadian Mountie, assigned to the FBI in Washington, also coveted the precious speaking role.

I had to further distinguish myself.

The 116th class was engaged in a fast and furious volleyball competition and once the field was pared down to two teams, things got heated. One team was ours, and both were from the class I represented. After a split of the first two games, the last, tense winner-take-all contest devolved into a brutal affair.

The players were hyper-competitive, bruised and hitting balls as much at each other as for points. After a few angry and violent exchanges, one of the guys actually broke an elbow. Push came to shove and guys got in each other's faces, so I walked over to the leader of the other team.

"Are we trying to prove who's a better team, or are we gonna prove we're a *larger* team?" I asked. "Why don't we call it a draw and both get a trophy?" I don't know if it was my words or just the breath they provided, but the situation was defused and all the guys shook hands.

Having proved my diplomacy skills, I had a real shot at becoming class representative speaking at graduation. To win that honor, though, I would have to best four other class leaders, including the Canadian Mountie, in what amounted to a winner-take-all "speech off."

For that competition my remarks captured how I felt in the Academy, the honor and responsibility of it. I stressed how each of us not only represented a city and a police department, but also the embodiment of the career and what it stood for to the public trust. In my closing remarks, I saluted the remarkable and diverse audience as a great law enforcement team that consisted of all-star individuals.

It got me a thundering ovation.

Then, I proceeded to lose—by one vote!

A few years later, Bill Conroy and I had lunch during which he confessed that it may have been his vote that took me down. As a ranking deputy inspector, Conroy had felt it would have been awkward for him back in New York if I, a sergeant, had been selected for such a prestigious honor.

All was good. In the end, our colleague from Canada gave an amazing graduation speech, one that made us all proud.

WALLS CLOSING IN

Following my graduation, and as things often went in the age-old "Brothers in Law" competition, my brother Tom followed to the same FBI Academy program and, of course, got elected class spokesman for graduation by an overwhelming margin.

In the meantime, upon my return to New York I was informed that I was being promoted. So as the summer came and passed, I got ready for a new assignment, this time at Midtown's historic 19th Precinct on 67th Street, a post known for its mix of international embassies and affluent residents.

The Soviet Mission to the United Nations was directly across the street from the station, and the rich and famous lived in great numbers all around us. While the 19th was known as a pretty safe but complex patrol, a deep recession had changed it drastically. In fact, on my very first day fellow cops were quick to point to the bullet holes in the walls behind the reception desk where I'd be spending a lot of my time. The holes had come courtesy of crazed gunmen who had burst in one night, hoping to kill some cops.

It became clear almost immediately that the job of lieutenant did not suit me. It was far more desk jockey than active cop. To remedy the situation, I began angling for a path back to the detective bureau. Thankfully, my new precinct commander, Deputy Inspector Jack Clifford, was very supportive and advised me to write to the police commissioner. This surprised me, as I figured that would be a breach of protocol. Jack pressed on and assured me that the commissioner's office would be happy to hear from somebody with my record and desire to do more.

Buoyed by Jack's support, I followed his suggestion…and waited.

Meanwhile, I think he got busy trying to figure out just what to do with me. I give a lot of credit and thanks to Jack Clifford as a mentor and leader. He was a no-nonsense guy and, even under pressure, always seemed to find a silver lining, something hopeful to smile about.

Clifford also had this wonderful first-floor office that looked out on the posh neighborhood and the Soviet Mission. When I joked to Jack that the Russians were likely watching back, he not so jokingly replied that he knew they were. Atop the mission building was an array of video devices, all trained on the front gate, the neighboring firehouse, and us at the 19th.

***

After only a month of desk duty at the 19th, I was going absolutely stir-crazy. Fortunately, life offered me a way out.

The department, ever short on manpower, sent down a new order allowing lieutenants to serve as operations officers. This meant guys like me would be given the choice to stay on desk duty or assign a sergeant to the desk and elect to go on patrol. I could get back into the action, though it also meant double duty of a sort as the operations officer was also expected to supervise both the station house and street activities.

Working several jobs at once was my forte, so I jumped at the chance to be the 19th's very first operations officer. All I had to do was sell Deputy Inspector Clifford on the idea so, order in hand, I went straight to his office.

"Jack, when you're not here, I'm the highest paid member of the force."

"Yeah, so?" He smirked from behind his desk, knowing I was angling for something.

"Well," I responded, "I think your money could be better spent allowing me to be the operations officer, instead of just a desk lieutenant."

"You want to go out again?" He shrugged. "Sure, go ahead," he announced it as he passed the window, almost as if he wanted the Russians to know. "But you're going to have to cover both jobs."

That was fine with me.

***

My new situation had its advantages, and among them was my very own driver. Gerry Gorman was a former US Marine who had served in Vietnam. An outstanding police officer, he was also—via marriage to Joan's sister—my brother-in-law, though we kind of kept that aspect of our relationship under wraps. I wanted no special treatment for him, and Jerry wanted none for himself. Yet he had to drive a lieutenant, anyway, so we figured it may as well be me.

Gorman was a big, strapping sort, which most people mistook as his calling card. In reality, he was an extremely thoughtful and intelligent law enforcement professional. Before our time together, we had both attended Fordham University, where Jerry quickly outdid me in school. His career was more active, too—more akin to my brother Tom.

My adventures with Jerry were many and some quite poignant, including a time when we prevented a woman from committing suicide on the Manhattan Bridge. Outside of work Jerry may have done even more for my career when he volunteered to help me coach the local Catholic Youth Organization basketball team in Congers. On that team we found a kid named Willie Kennelly, a class act who became team captain and eventually a fine police officer who later figured quite prominently in my story.

Jerry and I were on duty together when the 19th Precinct got decidedly more international in flavor. This occurred when the shah of Iran, Mohammad Reza Shah Pahlavi, came to New York City. A controversial figure, Pahlavi had been living abroad for almost a year after forces loyal to the Ayatollah Ruhollah Khomeini remade the country into the Islamic state it is today. After his exile, the shah traveled from country to country until a diagnosis of lymphatic cancer brought him to the prestigious Cornell Medical Center.[51]

As operations officer, I was tasked with the shah's security and the hospital's, as well. Once word got out that the shah was in a New York medical facility, demonstrations quickly materialized. Jack Clifford gave me full control of the crowds and thankfully assigned Gerry Gorman as my personal aide. We certainly needed the shorthand knowledge of working with each other as more than a hundred police officers and eight to ten sergeants were assigned each day outside of the hospital. Ambulances still had to get through, and people needing treatment, support staff, and doctors needed safe access.

It created an immense challenge just to allow for the right to protest without endangering other lives.

Word of my role in the NYPD part of security spread to my colleagues in the department, including the guys from Team C with whom I was still friendly. Not long after the shah left the city, Jack McCann called and offered me a security job moonlighting with the shah's twin sister, Princess Ashraf. I quickly enlisted brother Tom and thus the "Brothers in Law" entered the world of personal VIP security.

It was a critical education for us. The Ashraf job taught us both the grim reality of life as a foreign dignitary, a life in which no moment was safe and no post or job in such a detail was trivial or part-time. It was like going to Secret Service school, and getting paid to do so.

Then as I dipped my toes further into international waters, a wave began heading toward the 19th and my future.

***

The first swells arrived in the form of an improvised explosive device that, on the night of December 11, was tossed from a passing car and into the driveway of the Soviet Mission.

The explosion shattered hundreds of windows on surrounding blocks and injured several people, including four police officers,

---

[51] "Mohammad Reza Shah Pahlavi." *Encyclopedia Britannica*, October 22, 2018.

nearly blinding the officer manning the mission gate. By the time I got to the office the next morning, the anti-Castro Omega 7 Group had taken credit. They had, just two weeks prior, attempted a bombing of the Cuban Mission to the UN, as well. Newspapers described the scope of the explosive:

> The shock of the blast, which occurred shortly before 10 P.M. and was heard 20 blocks away, smashed a gaping hole in the driveway to the mission's underground garage, sent bricks flying, blew out windows as much 17 stories above the street and knocked residents of neighboring buildings to the floor.[52]

One interesting and little-known note from the bombing was the care taken by the Soviets in terms of our injured men in blue. Our "enemy" the Soviets offered to bring the blinded officer to Russia, free of charge, where they said surgeons had developed a new procedure for just such an injury. I don't know what became of that, but it did reveal a moment of humanity that went beyond ideology.

That being said, the thought went through the ranks that after they fixed the officer's eye, they'd likely fix his allegiance, too. That joking bit of foreshadowing proved to be more correct for me as the year ahead would bring me up to and just *across* the line between diplomacy and espionage.

What I didn't know yet was that the bombing at the Soviet Mission was a combination of last straw and inciting incident. As the various activists and militant groups of the decade became more and more aggressive, various units of the police and FBI were busy uncovering a degree of organization and linkage that was both daunting and terrifying in its scope—and they were only seeing the tip of an immense iceberg.

---

[52] Thomas, Robert Jr. "Bomb Damages Russian Mission on E 67th Street." *New York Times*, December 12, 1979.

Along with the Omega 7 Group, the May 19th Communist Organization, another affiliate of the Weather Underground and Black Panthers, was very active. Their agenda included freeing domestic radicals and attacking commercial enterprises in order to staff and fund a coming Marxist revolution. Recall here that while I was in New Orleans, members of the Black Liberation Army targeted, killed, and wounded NYPD cops and was at least partly responsible for the murder of Louis T. Sirgo.

Joanne Chesimard, alleged mastermind of the cop-targeting for the BLA, had since changed her name to Assata Shakur and had been tied to crimes as far back as 1971, including bank robberies and police assassinations, including the 1973 murder of New Jersey State Trooper Werner Foerster.[53]

The year I got to the 19th, in fact, operatives of the BLA led by Mutulu Shakur, along with members of the May 19th Organization, stormed the visitor's center at the Clinton Correctional Facility for Women in upstate New York. They took two guards hostage and freed Chesimard/Shakur in a brazen move that landed her on the FBI's Most Wanted List. What was particularly notable about that incident was more than just the ties to the BLA and Black Panther legacy and mission. The operation showed military-style planning and precision execution, as well as a level of inside infiltration that would give pause to the most seasoned espionage professional.

Also in 1979, members of the BLA arranged and assisted in the escape of FALN member William Morales from Bellevue Hospital in New York City. The same FALN, or the Fuerzas Armadas de Liberación Nacional separatist, nationalist group, was behind the Fraunces Tavern bombing and was also responsible for the 1977 bombing of the Mobil Oil offices in Manhattan. When he escaped from Bellevue, Morales was recovering from an injury from a bomb.

---

[53] Johnston, Richard J. H. "Trooper Recalls Shooting on Pike." *New York Times*, February 14, 1974. Web, October 31, 2018.

Only problem was it was his own bomb that had gone off prematurely. William Morales was the bomb maker for the FALN.[54]

The FBI'S Ed Petersen, who'd worked with brother Tom at Major Case and with me as a liaison to 8th Homicide, was there when police burst into the bomb factory and found Morales hiding behind a curtain. According to Ed's recollections, cops asked Morales who he was.

"I'm a prisoner of war," he replied.

The arresting officer's reply was, "We have your fingers if you want them, and we can find out who you are when we print them. Or you could just tell us your name."

After Morales was taken from Bellevue, the FBI tracked him to Mexico, where he escaped again via a shootout between FALN-supporting Sandinistas and the Mexican national police, the Federales. In that shootout, one of the badly wounded cops eventually got Morales into the trunk of his car, but died on the way to bringing him in. Leaving the dead Federale's body behind, Morales ended up in Cuba.

Still closer to my own work life, nationalist Jewish groups like Meir Kahane's Jewish Defense League became very active in the city, mostly targeting Russian concerns over the communist state's support of Israel's enemies and treatment of Jewish dissidents at home. That also meant a potential attack on the Soviet Mission, right smack in the middle of the 19th Precinct, and under my watch.

Meanwhile, yet more of the iceberg was coming into view.

The Croatian group that was the prime suspect in hijackings and the bombing at LaGuardia Airport in December 1975 revealed itself to be a multistate organization.

"According to the Federal authorities, Croatian nationalists were responsible for at least 21 acts of terror…. Eight were in the New York metropolitan area and included the death of a New York City policeman when he tried to defuse a bomb; the hijacking of a Trans World Airlines jetliner; the mailing of a book bomb to a New York

---

[54] Yuhas, Alan. "Cuba-US Thaw Brings Fate of Cold-War Era Fugitives on the Island into Focus." *The Guardian*, April 21, 2015. Web, September 22, 2018.

City publishing company; the bombing of Rudenjak Overseas Travel Agency in Astoria, an agency that arranges trips to Yugoslavia; and the bombing of the museum section of the Statue of Liberty." They also seemed centered in Chicago, where extortion and bomb plots unfolded, aimed at gaining funding for their operations.[55]

The FALN had expansive operations in Chicago and the Midwest, fell under notice from the FBI, as did the east-west and southern tendrils of the Black Panthers movement and the affiliated BLA.

***

I want to return to the LaGuardia bombing for a moment here, as it brings Ken Maxwell back into the timeline and further explores the forces circling the city and nation.

The former state policeman turned FBI special agent represented part of a sea change in law enforcement that was intricately tied into the militant agendas affecting the city. Back as far as 1975, a kind of task force mania took hold across law enforcement, and one was designated to tackle the twisted and often hidden web of a new and far more dangerous enemy, that of coordinated international terrorism. These dangerous organizations weren't like organized crime with their families and menu of businesses and money schemes. These separatist, nationalist, and revolutionary groups weren't about making money; they were about *appropriating* money as fuel for terror attacks against existing power bases and governments.

Many of the groups had no aversion to killing opponents and attacking high-profile targets where civilians might end up in the crosshairs. Also, while organized crime—with the exception of young, violent, and careless groups like the Purple Gang—acted like roaches when the lights went on, scurrying into every dark corner and hidden nook, these new groups preferred the spotlight and used the press as part of their strategic advantage.

---

[55] Sheppard, Nathaniel, Jr. "Arrest of Nine Brings Uneasy Calm to Croatian-Americans." *New York Times*, July 23, 1981.

They also shared information, training, and resources, making them far more like a dark web.

The FBI saw it early on and reacted by exploring the concept of a special task force to bring together various departments and resources from around the country, developing a central resource for comparing notes and information. Unfortunately, as the dangers intensified, so did competition within law enforcement, and rifts often formed between the FBI and the NYPD—the latter of which considered New York City to be *their* turf and responsibility.

While brother Tom and his FBI counterparts had interfaced wonderfully on a Bank Robbery Task Force, combining assets on a larger scale and on more international crimes proved to be much more difficult. While the leaders of the two organizations knew they had to do more than coexist, it was extremely hard to overcome individual personalities and territorial biases. Thus, guys like Ken Maxwell—who had been both cop and FBI agent—would have to be part of the plan. From the beginning and from his unique vantage point, Ken saw first-hand the next evolution in anti-terror law enforcement.

In a sense, it came together while I was at home on the very night the Soviet Mission was rocked by that Omega 7 bomb. No-nonsense FBI Senior Agent Ken Walton and NYPD Chief of Operations Pat Murphy responded to the scene of the attack. While watching their organizational counterparts scurrying about the site, they discussed bringing the NYPD and FBI together on counterterrorism.[56]

Both the FBI and NYPD, it turned out, were already on the case with Special Agent in Charge Joseph McFarland and Commissioner Robert McGuire already beginning to plan just such a new task force.

Ken Walton and Pat Murphy were given the ball to roll, a meshing of police and agents that would take what the Bank Robbery Task Force had so successfully accomplished and bring it to a next level. It certainly helped that Ken Walton was bit of a detective at heart and a man who loved a good reconstruction and investigation.

---

[56] Hahn, Richard S. *American Terrorists—The True Story of the F.A.L.N.* Seal Beach, California: R. Hahn & Company, Inc., 2011, p. 70.

Detective Elmer Toro, my future compatriot in the Joint Terrorism Task Force, recalled that Walton would walk onto a crime scene and quickly stash his FBI ID in favor of a hastily borrowed NYPD shield. Ken wanted to walk a scene without creating one.

THE ROTTING APPLE

As was the case with much of my professional life, when the calendar flipped to 1980, the New Year became an omen of things to come by ushering in what was statistically about the worst crime spree in New York City history.

For years the NYPD had been crunched by shrinking budgets, shortages, and the sheer volume of recession-fueled crime. The city put up a brave face during the early months of the year as outside of the department nobody really knew just how bleak things had become.

Even with all of the positives in my life—my ever-evolving and engrossing police career, the FBI Academy, a wonderful family, and Joan's miraculous diagnosis—I still found myself again at a crossroads. I'd made lieutenant sure, but in the 19th Precinct, with a part-time desk job as operations officer and bombs going off in the city. I thought, *Where exactly am I going?*

Another security job came to me courtesy of Jack McCann, this time for Snowsports Industries America, and their trade show at the Las Vegas Convention Center. SIA was founded in 1954 and was considered the standard-bearer for winter sports, holding the preeminent trade show for snow sports suppliers worldwide. Working that show and others in subsequent years offered me a critical education, watching over alcohol management and acting as liaison for show security, management, local police, and the FBI.

The seemingly innocuous escape to Las Vegas was a godsend, allowing me to combine several facets of my career and experience while providing an engrossing nexus between my love of sports and a life dedicated to law enforcement.

Theft was a huge concern at the Snowsports show, as was industrial espionage. The show featured prototypes and new products that were at least a year out from public release. Buyers came from all over the United States and from countries throughout the world, yet in the midst of all of this excitement, intrigue, and potential espionage, SIA head David Ingeme gave me full authority to do my job. He also helped me understand how to maneuver the complexities and politics of handling corporate events in other law enforcement jurisdictions.

Still, I approached the job with all the experience I could bring. My goal was to blend in, vanish into the crowd, hobnob and talk and feel the lay of the land. The show spanned about a million square feet of space, with booths and millions of pounds of freight and product. It was a four-day setup, with thousands of people involved.

As one of the largest trade shows in the country, it was important grooming for what lay ahead of me, even if I had no idea at the time what was to materialize.

Then back in the harsh winter of New York City, I hit the wall or more accurately, the wall came for me...

***

It was just after 3:00 on a frigid January morning in 1980, when the tinny radio of an aging patrol car crackled to life with an urgent dispatch. A 10-31R, burglary in progress at a five-story residential walkup in the Upper East Side of Manhattan, just a block or so off the icy and windswept East River. As was my prerogative, I went out on patrol that morning with John Yandrasits, or as he was known "Johnny Y."

Yandrasits was kind of the prototypical patrol cop you'd see on 1960s police dramas. He had a medium complexion and sported a thick mustache and bushy black hair. Set against me, all totally clean shaven and pale Irish, we kind of looked like Starsky and Hutch in uniform. I liked working with him.

As we stepped from our patrol car and into the screaming wind tunnel outside that Upper East Side apartment, the whole scene suddenly pulled at me. It was a strange feeling. Quickly, though, police training and duty had me shaking it off and racing inside and up the hard marble stairs toward whatever awaited.

The woman who called in the initial complaint met us on the second-floor landing. Still shaken, she said she'd awoken to a burglar trying to break through her bedroom window. The bedroom window part was especially troubling as at meant the burglar had come down via the fire escape and might still be at large. On that thought, I quickly left my partner behind and raced alone toward the roof where I reflexively pulled out my service revolver, opened the heavy access door, and plunged into the dark and icy whirlwind beyond.

Outside on the roof, a jagged and forbidding patchwork of ice, shadows and city light spread out before me. It looked like immense shards of broken glass reflecting an equally shattered city and somewhere in that visual jumble, I caught sight of my adversary as he darted away. All I could make out was the shape of a midsized man—black, white, purple, or orange, it didn't matter in the slightest. My next move could be a life-or-death decision.

Across the way, loomed a high wall that separated the roof from an adjacent building, and the burglar was headed straight for it. It was maybe eight or so feet high but that shadowy shape hit it and went over like Batman. It was Delehanty all over again.

I never slowed a step and hit that wall fast and high, hooked a leg, and went over in pursuit. As I landed on the far side, I saw my suspect zoom across the next roof and through the access door there. By the time I caught up, I found the door had been locked from the inside.

Then as my adrenaline gave way to a growing awareness of fatigue, I took a moment to assess, catch my breath and slow my fight-ready heartbeat.

Then I cautiously walked to the edge of the roof and looked down toward the street, perhaps in hopes of catching a glimpse of our thief under the dim street lights. There was nothing down there but dirty slush, briny water, and ice. I stood there, mind blank until the bitter chill of the wind crept back into my awareness.

As I looked back up, a gigantic billboard caught my eye. What it advertised is long lost in the shadows of memory, but that billboard became a strange and telling symbol for me that night, a symbol of things I had been chasing after.

What exactly was I running after anyway? A burglar who had been frightened off by an older woman in her apartment?

Where was I going at forty-one years old?

Yet there I was, standing atop a city at 4:00 a.m. and suddenly wondering what difference I had made, with an eight-foot wall behind me and a locked door in front and all around the sides a five-story precipice.

Maybe for the first time in my career, my mind raced. What if this burglar had been waiting for me just over that wall and killed me there? I would have been just another cop, bleeding to death on a rooftop, another chalk outline, and another funeral with a flag and a gun salute. My wife, Joan, another widow left to raise fatherless kids.

My world went eerily silent, the wind vanished, and the cold and I became one. My police life had begun with a training wall. Had it just ended the same way? I didn't see it coming. Even after I shook it all off, it wasn't over.

Something was coming for me.

***

Not long after that rooftop and soul-searching, officials from the FBI's New York field office and New York City Police Department met for lunch to detail how to combine their expertise to track down the many terrorist organizations responsible for the wave of violent attacks in the city. Even before the bomb went off at the Soviet Mission in December 1979, an official MOU, or memorandum of understanding, sketched out the initial plan, though the final version would not be signed until May 19, 1980.

A galvanizing moment came in April of that same year when "the arrest of 10 FALN leaders, including Carlos Alberto Torres...by local police in Evanston, Illinois, [led] to the discovery of a network of FALN safe houses in New York, New Jersey, Wisconsin, and Illinois." The realization of a multicity organization, similar to the Black Panthers and BLA, mandated the need for far-closer interaction with federal, state, and local law enforcement across the country; so, that October MOU evolved into a meeting of the minds and organizations that took place on the twenty-eighth floor of 26 Federal Plaza.[57]

Present were Deputy Assistant Director in Charge Ken Walton and Police Commissioner Robert McGuire, along with FBI Supervisory Special Agent Barry Mawn and NYPD Lieutenant George Howard, who would both be tasked with heading up the newly designed unit starting with ten agents from the FBI's New York Field Office and ten New York Police Department detectives.[58]

Instantly it was rocky, and when the formal MOU came down the resistance was palpable, with some guys in the FBI doubting it could ever work. Cops for their part were instantly angered by background checks and good men on both sides quit or requested not to be included. There were also concerns over expertise, with many citing the division of tasks as the main sticking point.

According to guys like Detective Charlie Minch, a task force standout, while FBI agents saw bank robberies as more evidence-based and therefore fertile investigative ground for detectives, terrorism involved far more preemptive and predictive analysis, based mostly on surveillance. That wasn't usually found in the shorter-term mentality and structure of the NYPD.

Though I had no inkling of it at the time, the new Joint Terrorism Task Forces (JTTF) was certainly my kind of organization.

Ken Walton, who possessed a rare combination of showmanship, style, and grim determination, played a major part in any success the

---

[57] Valiquette, Joe, and Donald, Peter J. "The History of the First Joint Terrorism Task Force That Began in New York." ticklethewire.com.

[58] Ibid.

task force showed in the beginning. Walton had movie star looks and hair that earned him another of his nicknames, "the Fonz." Fun names aside, Walton had a steely demeanor, a biting sense of humor, and an uncanny ability to rapidly size up people and situations.

A lesser-known secret to Walton's success was his background as a Midwest reporter, which helped him develop top-notch people skills and big-picture thinking. Everybody knew the stakes—perhaps most of all Ken Walton. Police were short-handed, the recession was squeezing everything in sight, and these new domestic and international terror groups were becoming bigger, stronger, more organized, and interconnected.

Ken Maxwell recalled the day it got done, and Ken Walton pulled him and his squad into his 26 Federal Plaza office: "You guys might have heard the rumor. Well, it's not a rumor." Walton continued in what I'd later learn myself was his trademark mix of suggestion and directive. "I want your input, but only to a point." Then he laid down the gauntlet. "But let me be clear, anybody that doesn't want to work this way, you can leave and get transferred. Nothing punitive. But if you stay, I don't wanna hear another fucking word. You will make this work from day one."

When his turn came at the pulpit, the NYPD's Robert McGuire delivered an identical message.

"Make it work, or work someplace else."

Somehow, I knew the feeling.

PART SIX

THE GUY I HOPED TO BE

INTERNATIONAL WATERS

Drastic budget changes always led to department reshuffling and reallocating, but in 1980, with things in such flux, I actually caught a break.

The administrative lieutenant of the 19th learned that he was about to be promoted to captain. He approached to inform me that he'd taken note of my work with the shah and hustle from Operations to street and back again, and wanted to recommend to Jack Clifford that I become the 19th's next "him." While I was honored by the consideration, the job of the administrative lieutenant was far more expansive than that of the operations officer and, in many ways, more than I'd ever tackled before.

On top of that, I wanted back in the Detective Bureau, and this position would only pull me deeper into the bureaucracy.

Regardless, duty called, so I accepted the opportunity with the appropriate enthusiasm and, alongside partner Lieutenant Larry Haggerty, set out to move department resources around to better serve the public need. Hearkening back to my stint in the 4-6, task one was to move guys who needed motivation or needed out. So effective—or perhaps feared—became Hallinan the administrator and Haggerty the integrity officer that we were given the moniker "Heaven and Hell." Thankfully, as the guy who usually found use for bored or shopworn cops, I was the Heaven part of the deal.

My new office chair was barely warm when Jack Clifford directed Ivan Mirishkin, the ranking official at the Russian Mission, to contact me. As administrator it was my responsibility to deal with any and all police matters where diplomats and embassies were concerned and, boy, did Mirishkin take full advantage.

From my very first week on the job, Ivan was in my office a minimum of twice a week, and I have to admit that my first impression of him was that of a foil in a James Bond film. Standing easily six-foot-four and weighing a hefty two hundred fifty pounds, the round-faced and pale man was every bit the proverbial Russian bear. It certainly didn't help that my first meeting with Ivan came not long after the February 22 "Miracle on Ice" in Lake Placid, when the US Men's Olympic Hockey Team defeated the previously invincible Russians en route to an improbable gold medal. Despite my best efforts to get Ivan to talk about the game, however, he always changed the subject.

Instead, he was quick to remind me that the Soviets had a lookout post at the Mission and cameras on the roof.

Mirishkin could be both gregarious and funny but just as quickly irascible and confrontational. There was a lot behind his bravado, too, as he was reportedly the ranking New York City agent in the KGB, at the time Russia's expansive national security service. His first visit also came only a few months removed from the December '79 Omega 7 bombing, which according to Mirishkin was an ominous portent of things to come.

The Miami and New York–based Omega 7 group was only part of the Soviets' security concerns in the city, as their attention also included ongoing threats from Rabbi Meir Kahane's Jewish Defense League, or JDL. Since the group's 1968 founding, Kahane maintained its purpose to "protect Jews from antisemitism by any means necessary." Over the years, those means grew from protests to attacks throughout the city, specifically against Russian and Arab interests.

By the early 1970s, the JDL was implicated in a series of violent, attacks against Soviet interests. These included a bombing of the Soviet Cultural Center in Washington, DC, and planned kidnappings of Russian diplomats to protest Soviet treatment of Jews in Russia. Kahane and the JDL took to protesting the Soviet Mission on a regular basis and, regardless of your politics here, with pipe bombs in the JDL repertoire, the Soviets were appropriately concerned.

I was, as well, since officers from the 19th and simple support staff at the mission were all at risk, along with innocent passersby.

I'd soon get to know Rabbi Kahane myself when he brought his protests directly to my desk. We had more than a few disagreements about harassment of the Mission staff and the unrest JDL protests caused in the precinct, but Kahane always excused his actions by saying the Soviets were taking pictures of his protesters and threatening to harm or harass any relatives they had back in the Soviet Union. While I understood Kahane's concerns, I was a law enforcement official, and any violent tactics were going to affect the people in my precinct.

Whenever Ivan Mirishkin visited, nearly ten minutes after he left two FBI agents would suddenly appear in my office with a list of questions about my Soviet guest. During one of these meetings, I was informed that not only had the Russians placed cameras atop the Mission to spy on neighboring buildings, but the FBI had responded with cameras on the roof of the nearby firehouse to spy on the Russians. We had a full-on camera Cold War going on, and it was right next door to the 19th.

On a more personal note, Mirishkin and I knew all too well which sides of the fence we were on, but under the circumstances we had to coexist. For that reason, we got along very well—so much so, that come May of 1980, the bearish Mirishkin invited Deputy Inspector Clifford and me to a Soviet May Day celebration at the Mission. Of course, the FBI was in my office soon after the invite and directed me to attend but made sure to provide me a couple of very pointed intelligence-gathering questions to ask.

I was intrigued. It was time to put my FBI training to work.

The afternoon of the party, Jack Clifford and I rang the bell at the Mission and waited. After we were no doubt studied by a hidden camera, the door suddenly opened to reveal a fully dressed and fully armed, stone-faced Russian solder. Silently he escorted us inside and to a reception line where Mirishkin was waiting to introduce us to a long line of Soviet officials. As Clifford and I went from person to person, Ivan started in with the vodka, and I could swear that soon we were being induced to sample each and every brand made in the Soviet Union.

We were there about two hours in all, and I don't recall eating any food. We may have, but after all that vodka I was lucky to find my own two feet, much less my way back to the front door. For added measure, my new Soviet "friend" presented me with two more bottles as a parting gift.

Stumbling across the street to the station house, I gave one bottle to the desk officer and swayed toward the station dormitory to sleep it off. The FBI was disappointed that I hadn't remembered to ask the questions—not that I would have remembered the answers, anyway. Though I had passed the FBI Academy with flying colors, I scored far less impressively on my first assignment as a field agent.

***

As summer arrived, the steep rise in city crime was accompanied by the violent return of terror when the same Croatian group suspected of bombing LaGuardia Airport claimed credit for a June 3 bomb that destroyed the Story Room Exhibit at the base of New York's Statue of Liberty monument. For this crime, again enter Ken Maxwell, now working in the new Joint Terrorism Task Force and extremely familiar with the Croatians, the JDL, and the aforementioned Omega 7.

At the Statue of Liberty scene, Maxwell and his NYPD partner Charlie Wells found bomb fragments that matched the Croatian group that claimed responsibility. FBI Special Agent Lenny Cross had recruited an informant in the Croatian community, but the highly skilled Croat group soon discovered the leak. In response, they marked Lenny for assassination.

Lenny was told that there was a package waiting for him at the post office. The sudden arrival of the unexpected parcel was immediately suspicious, so Maxwell and Wells checked it out. Sure enough, it was a bomb.

Later, when Maxwell and other agents went to check on Lenny's home, they were then followed by a white van that had one of the back windows removed and replaced with a simple cardboard cover. This maneuver turned a van window into a possible gun port.

Tracking the Croat suspects and their van eventually led law enforcement to a Dobbs Ferry, New York, warehouse where the nationalist group holed up and met. There FBI technicians led by Jim Kallstrom—a household name today—wired a microphone to a beam over a pinball machine. Unfortunately, group members discovered it and tore it down, and then openly gloated that they were too smart for their FBI adversaries. How did the FBI know they gloated? After placing the first device, the brass-balls agent wasn't to be denied, and Kallstrom went in again to put the bug back in the exact same spot, correctly thinking nobody would have the sense to check twice.

By December 1980, FBI agents learned that the Croat group was planning to blow up a holiday party being held by the Yugoslavian ambassador at a dance studio in Union Square, Manhattan. Ken Maxwell and his team—including future JTTF personnel FBI agent Lenny Cross and NYPD detective Jimmy Cassidy—watched as two men left the warehouse with shopping bags and drove to Union Square, circling in a van. After a cat-and-mouse trip through Manhattan involving both FBI and the NYPD, the Croat group returned to the warehouse with the suspicious bags, all under the watchful eyes of the FBI and Dobbs Ferry Police.

The FBI obtained a search warrant via US District Attorney John Martin, who was former NYC Mayor Rudy Giuliani's predecessor in the post. One December night at the Dobbs Ferry warehouse, FBI agents took down the two drivers, Ivitch and Stanbuck, along with the four main members of the New York–based Croatian group. Inside the hideout, agents found a cache of weapons and a large supply of dynamite meant for the assassination of the Yugoslavian ambassador.

The story is noteworthy first for the sterling combined efforts of FBI and NYPD assets and second for the remarkable work of the new Joint Terrorism Task Force as a whole, which proved itself the most effective weapon yet against terror groups operating on US soil. The case also provided a critical example for the effective use of surveillance in counterterrorism investigations and led to the discovery of a money trail that allowed federal prosecutors—most notably the well-known Stuart Baskin, assistant US attorney in the Southern District of New York—to use the organized crime RICO statute for the first time ever for a domestic terror event.

The successful apprehension of Ivitch and Stanbuck led to the bigger fish behind them and later broke the back of the Croatian group. Meanwhile, a parallel future was unfolding for me as the increasingly effective FBI/NYPD Joint Terrorism Task Force was making great progress, specifically with the militant Puerto Rican separatist group, the FALN.

Earlier in 1980, FALN operatives had taken control of the George H. W. Bush and Jimmy Carter campaign offices in New York City and Chicago respectively. They looted both sets of delegate lists in order to send threatening communications about violence to come if Puerto Rican independence wasn't pursued politically. By midyear, the scope and abilities of the FALN were still relatively unknown, as both local and state law enforcement efforts were uncoordinated and sometimes at odds with FBI investigators.

In Chicago, however, the FBI and Illinois police forces had already set aside many differences and, by sheer chance and circumstance, identified a known FALN member named Edwin Cortes. Nicknamed "the Rabbit," Cortes was nothing so benign, having been tied to more than a hundred bombings and attempted bombings going back to 1974. The Chicago FBI, in concert with surveillance teams from local police, followed Cortes for sixteen hours a day during the week and twenty-four hours a day on weekends.

By March, agents observed Cortes carefully dry-cleaning his every move—employing professional spy-level countersurveillance measures—but after tireless surveillance, they spotted him entering a safe house. After obtaining a court order, agents then entered and found a cache of weapons, bomb materials, disguises, training manuals, and information on targets including plans for attacks and prison breaks.

Still they didn't act. Instead, they chose to render the explosives and weapons inoperable, return them, and continue the surveillance. This decision to keep the operation clandestine eventually led to the capture of those eleven members of the group in Evanston, Illinois. As the Homeland Security Report from 2012 described it, "Locating the address of an active terrorism safe house was the first successful outcome of the new intelligence-led strategy."[59]

A subsequent robbery bust in Illinois that May revealed more of the true scope and danger posed by the FALN, an organization with a careful and insular cell structure that would make a present-day international terrorist network proud. The bust in Illinois brought with it an informant named Freddie Mendez, a new FALN recruit who had no intention of spending a long term in jail for crimes in which he was only now becoming complicit.

His information caught the attention of a young FBI agent named Rick Hahn, who "had gained experience working on FALN bombings both in New York and Puerto Rico. Thinking of the FALN's multi-city presence, Hahn proposed a plan during a monthly meeting between the Secret Service and the intelligence units of the Chicago and State Police. Since the FBI did not have sufficient manpower to carry out the kind of intensive surveillance activities Hahn had in mind, he asked the police and state investigators to participate as partners by committing their own manpower."

Hahn's requested expansion of interdepartment cooperation was a high-functioning version of the JTTF in Illinois and, as the scope of the Puerto Rican's organization's tentacles in New York were revealed, pulled the FBI/NYPD JTTF into the mix in a big way.[60]

***

January 1981 brought me a fresh chance to get out of the city and stretch my longer law enforcement legs again. I was offered a return

---

[59] Belli, Roberta. *Effects and Effectiveness of Law Enforcement Intelligence Measures to Counter Homegrown Terrorism: A Case Study on the* Fuerzas Armadas de Liberación Nacional *(FALN), Final Report to Human Factors/Behavioral Sciences Division, Science and Technology Directorate, U.S. Department of Homeland Security.* College Park, Maryland: START, 2012, pp. 24–25.

[60] Ibid.

to the Snowsports International show in Las Vegas and again set aside my vacation time to do it.

Upon my return, my boss Jack Clifford seemed to really sense just how stir-crazy I was going and offered a high-profile post helping organize security for the March wedding of New York Giant's football legend Frank Gifford's daughter Vicki to the late Senator Robert F. Kennedy's son, Michael. Coordinated with the NFL league office, the event went off without a hitch, and afterward Clifford rather clairvoyantly mused that head of security for a major sports league like the NFL would be a great career move.

If he only knew where I'd eventually end up.

Honestly, at the time, whether back to the Bureau or into one of the new robbery squads, all I wanted was to get back to the detective bureau, but in the department that was a hard row to hoe. I even went so far as to formalize a request to the commissioner, a move that Clifford supported. Even so, I received a gentle rebuff from the commissioner's office, noting a shortage of lieutenants on patrol, so I sent my horse-blanket overcoat to the cleaners in preparation for a long, cold winter.

Then my friend Jim Trainor, now commander of the newly formed Central Robbery Division, saw an opening. New robbery squads were being organized under a central umbrella, and while there was no opening for me anywhere, Trainor slipped me in as his administrative lieutenant.

The new post was a whole new ballgame.

As Jim Trainor's right-hand, it was my task to help identify and allocate the right people for the right jobs as we rebuilt five all-encompassing robbery squads throughout New York. Working alongside Trainor was a remarkable and educational experience, especially with his constant guidance to stay patient, seek quality, and never settle. Within a month, all five boroughs were up and running, and all commanders were in place.

Part of the reason I accepted the Central Robbery assignment was the hope of receiving a post that could get me back to the street. It would take ten more months, but Trainor was able to reward my work and dedication and give me the nod as commander of the newly re-created Manhattan Robbery Squad.

It was my first command, a big accomplishment, and a post that quickly afforded me everything I could have hoped for and more. While I usually downplayed all my promotions and new posts, Joan and the kids certainly knew I was a happy camper.

Part of the new Central Robbery Division, the Manhattan squad was tasked with investigating and prosecuting the most serious robbery cases, major crimes involving businesses and high-value targets. It was a full plate from the start and too, as one of the more forward-thinking and analytical units in the ever-evolving NYPD Central Robbery, had a full set of tools available. I had three or four detective sergeants in my command at any one time, coming from various highly experienced backgrounds including precinct units, street crime units, and narcotics.

One of the people who made a huge difference was Detective Sergeant John Loughran, a streetwise and seasoned leader who had excelled in a very tough narcotics unit. Like me, Loughran started as a beat cop before moving through various jobs and departments. More like my brother Tom, however, he took a far tougher career path. A graduate of the Marine Corps' Parris Island recruit depot, Loughran was out of the academy in '62, narrowly missed a call to Vietnam, and then went straight into some of the NYPD's toughest assignments.

After making detective sergeant, he did yeoman's work undercover, one time dressing as a decoy nurse to break up a rash of muggings near Central Park. Later, he went to the 6th Precinct in Greenwich Village and worked alongside my former 2-5 commander Al LaPerch and the incredibly accomplished Harry O'Reilly. He spent time with the Organized Crime Control Bureau, which took him onto Pleasant Avenue and into the teeth of the Mafia beast I'd barely escaped. John also worked Mafia details in Brooklyn, investigating the same Bonanno Mafia family that FBI Special Agent Joseph D. Pistone—also known as Donnie Brasco—was working undercover.

Loughran's flexibility and integrity eventually got him noticed by Al McGuire, a ranking NYPD man who had worked with brother Tom in the expansive Safe and Loft Squad. McGuire cherry-picked John for a job with the Narcotics Division before I got him for Manhattan Robbery.

My time as commander of the Manhattan Robbery Squad put me back in touch with some notable crimefighters—namely the FBI's Ed Petersen, who was called in for many major cases of domestic terrorism or organized crime, including when FALN bomb maker William Morales was apprehended after nearly blowing himself up at a lower Manhattan bomb factory.

That March, the May 19th group participated in a brazen daylight theft in nearby Danbury, Connecticut, and in April, BLA members opened fire on two NYPD officers during a traffic stop, while the JDL fire-bombed a Holocaust denial exhibit in Los Angeles. Then in May, the aptly named May 19th organization appeared again, assisting in the robbery of a Brink's Company truck in Mount Vernon, New York, and then a subsequent armored car heist at a Chemical Bank branch in Nanuet, New York.

Fast on the heels of both robberies, associates of the FALN booby-trapped a bathroom at JFK Airport, killing a twenty-year-old man who had gone to wash his hands. It was May 17 and only a portent of far more to come.

◢ DIPLOMATIC IMPUNITY

In early September, several bombs were discovered at the Soviet Mission, including one that went off under a parked car. Nobody claimed responsibility, but somewhere in my mind I knew my life was ratcheting up to something more clearly defined.

On October 20, 1981, I was safely manning my desk at Manhattan Robbery when, unbeknownst to me, my future path was lurking nearby at a renovated Harlem brownstone at 245 West 139th Street. The red-and-tan-checkered brownstone was the headquarters of the Black Acupuncture Advisory Association of North America, or BAAANA, though little therapeutic acupuncture actually occurred there.

What did occur, specifically on the morning of October 20, was preparations for a violent armored truck robbery in Nanuet, New York. By that afternoon, two police officers and one security guard would be dead and 1.6 million dollars stolen to fund the activities of various radical groups, including the Black Liberation Army, the Republic of New Afrika (RNA), the May 19 communist organization, the Black Panther Party, the Weather Underground organization, and the Prairie Fire Organizing Committee.[61]

According to the 1985 *Report of the Policy Study Group on Terrorism*, the men who met at the acupuncture clinic included

---

[61] Blumenthal, Ralph. "F.B.I. Wiretaps: An Ear on the Brinks Case." *New York Times*, August 9, 1982.

"Mutulu Shakur, Donald Weems, Edward Joseph, Cecil Fergusen and Samuel Brown."[62]

Six men in all would participate in the crime.

It was just the opening act.

The group then moved to a Mount Vernon safe house that had been rented under an alias by BLA sympathizer Marilyn Jean Buck, who had been convicted of buying ammunition for the group in 1973. This before she escaped from prison on a furlough and became intimately involved in the daring 1979 prison escape of BLA leader Joanne Chesimard/Assata Shakur.

After picking up Buck, members of the growing robbery and assault team manned multiple vehicles including a small Honda, a light-colored Oldsmobile, a red van, and a U-Haul truck, and later—with the Honda and U-Haul stashed nearby as getaway cars—drove the red van to the National Bank at the Nanuet Mall.

Moments later, after a Brink's armored truck arrived containing driver David Kelly and two guards, Joseph Trombino and Peter Paige, several masked attackers moved in, and a firefight ensued. Peter Paige was killed at the scene, and both Trombino and Kelly were wounded. The assailants then fled and jumped into the stashed Honda and U-Haul, where they transferred their haul and escaped.

Fortunately, the transfer was spied by a witness, and the chase was on. Two of the fleeing killers sped their U-Haul down State Route 59 toward Nanuet and the ramp to I-95 East and an attempted escape across the Tappan Zee Bridge. Fortunately, police had just set up a roadblock there, and the U-Haul became ensnared on the narrow chokepoint of Mountainview Avenue.

That's when all hell broke loose.

To the surprise of police, the U-Haul contained only a driver and a woman in the passenger seat. This did not match the initial report of more assailants, so they had no idea that the passenger was Weather Underground member Kathy Boudin. With law enforcement trying

---

[62] New York Criminal Justice Institute. *Report of the Policy Study Group on Terrorism*, November 1985, p. 29.

to figure out if it was the same U-Haul from the mall, Boudin got out, raised her hands, and pleaded her innocence, frantically screaming about all the guns. This, just as Nyack detective Arthur Keenan was trying to figure out how to open the U-Haul's rear door.

Suddenly, it burst open on him and six members of the robbery team leapt out and opened fire with automatic weapons and pistols. In the hail of lead Sergeant Edward O'Grady and Patrolman Waverly Brown were left dying on the asphalt while Keenan was severely wounded.

In an especially sinister turn, O'Grady and Brown both survived the initial fusillade but were coldly executed while bleeding on the ground. Boudin and the driver then took off on foot, whereupon off-duty New York City corrections officer Michael Koch, who happened to be passing the scene, gave chase and caught Boudin.

Another assailant, Samuel Brown, was picked up by a yellow Honda containing Weather Underground members David Gilbert and Judith Clark. The Honda, driven by Gilbert, then sped away on Nyack's Mountainview Avenue, where it was chased down by South Nyack Police Chief Alan Colsey, causing the Honda to crash and resulting in the capture of three of the suspects within.[63]

Inside the wrecked vehicle, police recovered nearly $800,000 and a 9mm handgun belonging to Clark.

As police continued to fan out across Route 59 and into neighboring Nyack, I was driving home from work, and the level of congestion I faced increased substantially, leading me to wonder what was happening. It was well past rush hour, so I switched my radio from a sports show to the news outlets and heard the reports of the attempted robbery and the tragic aftermath.

Then as I came off the Palisades Parkway at exit 5 and turned north on Route 303, a long line of police vehicles from every jurisdiction spread out before me. It was unnerving. My home nearby was supposed to be a safe haven and refuge. Instead, the evening and

---

[63] Ibid., pp 29–31.

location suddenly became a grim reminder that bad things can happen at any time and any place.

***

After the robbery and manhunt, my next day at Manhattan Robbery felt somehow *off*. The Brink's case was the major topic of conversation in the squad, especially as it presented every deadly and dangerous facet of theft imaginable—high stakes, organized planning, and murder—but this case was well beyond the purview of the Central Robbery Division.

Then as the calendar flipped to November, the Brink's case only deepened and the law enforcement community began to discover the immense and tangled web of militant activism that had led all the way from the radical '60s, to that brownstone acupuncture clinic in Harlem. The unfolding drama landed in the lap of the still somewhat embryonic Joint Terrorism Task Force, and, to put a context to this, what went on behind the scenes in the aftermath of the crime was unprecedented.

The day of and just after the deadly robbery, several local law enforcement arms had to quickly coordinate with all the fine dexterity of a cohesive entity. The FBI, too, responded to the scene after two special agents overhead the radio chatter and came to assist, bringing in a significant and needed piece of the developing puzzle. As the elements of a larger and more ominous picture came to light, the NYPD became involved and helped surveil the BAAANA offices alongside their FBI counterparts.

The license plate on one of the getaway cars led investigators to an apartment in New Jersey that had been rented by BLA's Marilyn Jean Buck. Inside was a cache of weapons, bomb materials, and chillingly detailed blueprints of six Manhattan police precincts. There was more—the address of another apartment in Mount Vernon, New York—and what was found there broke the initial phase of the case open. Aside from receipts for rental cars and disguises were names and out-of-state addresses and a witness, "an eagle-eyed building super [who] had identified several of the Brink's network, loading a tan van with items. The van was later traced to New Orleans."[64] Perhaps most incriminating from the Mount Vernon apartment, the bloody clothing worn by Marilyn Jean Buck during the robbery.

Three days after the Brink's robbery, NYPD detectives including friend and colleague Detective Lieutenant Dan Kelly, tracked a set of license plates seen at the Mount Vernon safe house to an unknown new vehicle driving through Queens and, after attempting a traffic stop, got a high-speed twenty-minute chase and a gunfight instead. In the subsequent shootout, suspect Samuel Smith was killed, and Nathanial Burns, a.k.a. Sekou Odinga, was taken into custody. It was the Brink's crew, and both men were clad in the very bulletproof vests they'd worn during the violent robbery, a fact later backed up by cooperating witness Tyrone Rison, who told investigators that Smith once showed him the Nyack Police–issue bullet that his vest had stopped in the Brink's shootout.

Indeed, when Smith's body was later autopsied, an impact bruise precisely matched witnesses' accounts of the shootout.

What unfolded next took years and involved several militant and political groups, loosely unified by ideology but chillingly aligned by expertise, propensity for violence, and the targeting of police officers. I've already referenced the bloody trail from the militant groups of the '60s to nationalist groups like the FALN and the Republic of New Afrika group and their affiliations with the Black Panthers, BLA, and others, but Brink's was where it all seemed to come together as never before, and right at the time when the JTTF was coming online.

Looking back, it may have been one of the most formative moments in the history of anti-terrorism in this country and the world.

Certainly, the Croatian group I knew about. They had assaulted diplomats, hijacked planes, and exploded bombs throughout New York, Los Angeles, Chicago, and more, and were a big contributing factor to the formation of the JTTF, but the Brink's crime involved unprecedented cooperation.

---

[64] "Heading for the Last Roundup." *Time*, November 9, 1981.

The JTTF was brought together exactly at the time when terrorist organizations were evolving and organizing in chilling new ways. Just a look at the people, prior history, and organizations involved; the BLA attacks on police; the FALN bombings; and daring prison infiltrations and escapes—it all painted a bloody line straight to the Brink's robbery, with connections to suspected BLA operative Joanne Chesimard, the Harlem BAAANA clinic operator Mutulu Shakur, and several other dangerous fugitives including Tyrone Rison and Marilyn Jean Buck, whose relative anonymity made her perfect for renting apartments and securing transportation.

Even the partial picture was chilling.

It meant that members of the Weather Underground, Black Panthers, May 19th Group, and others might all be working together and across state lines. In fact, much later—during a 1987 trial of the remaining Brink's defendants—Tyrone Rison took that bloody trail from the '60s and painted a fuller and more terrifying picture when he asserted that Mutulu Shakur, who had presented himself as a simple acupuncturist and therapist, had been present during the 1979 Clinton Correctional Facility breakout of Joanne Chesimard/Assata Shakur. This operation was carried out by a group known as "the family," or an offshoot of the BLA.

Marilyn Jean Buck was the getaway driver that day, too—according to Rison—and later rented a villa in the Bahamas as a hideout for Chesimard. According to the *New York Times*, Rison also stated during his trial that a full three months before the deadly robbery, "Mr. Shakur, Ms. Buck and others [participated] in the robbery of a Brink's armored car in the Bronx on June 2, 1981," during which Rison brutally executed a handcuffed guard and wounded another.[65]

Rison stressed that Matulu Shakur was the key to it all and had roots going back to his involvement with the Republic of New Afrika. In 1969 Detroit, Shakur was involved in a shootout with police during which one officer was killed and several RNA members were arrested.

---

[65] Lubasch, Arnold H. "Killer Says He Helped in Chesimard's Escape." *New York Times*, December 2, 1987.

Shakur somehow walked and turned up in Los Angeles, where he became by most accounts a noted acupuncturist who used his skill to help people get off of heroin without the dangerous risk of methadone.

In Los Angeles, however, Shakur—still a member of the RNA—also became involved with the Weather Underground and eventually folks like Kathy Boudin and Marilyn Jean Buck. He then moved to Harlem and opened his clinic. He continued his work, though soon significant evidence emerged that the facility was also being used as a front for the RNA, Weather Underground, and May 19th operations.[66]

---

[66] New York Criminal Justice Institute. *Report of the Policy Study Group on Terrorism*, November 1985, p. 34.

THE SECOND GUY THEY WANTED

It was a Thursday, as I recall, when Chief Jim Sullivan reached out to me from the Chief of Detectives Office. Usually such calls regarded personnel or some new initiatives, but that day Sullivan got straight to the point.

"Did you put in for the Joint Terrorism Task Force?"

Practically nobody even knew of its existence, let alone me.

"I didn't even know there was one."

Without so much as an inkling of explanation, Jim said, "Okay," and hung up. It was an instant mystery, one which only saw explanation recently when former COD insider John Culley shined a light for me during the writing of this book.

Even before the Brink's robbery, winds of change were whipping up all around the city, and in many ways the center of the gale was the new JTTF. The plan had always called for a ranking NYPD commander.

I wish I could say I was excited by the idea of participating in something so new and ground-breaking, but, quite frankly, I had no idea there was even a plan for such an organization. Regardless, the difficult post of NYPD leadership initially fell to George Howard, a standout from the Arson and Explosion Squad, since A&E was the unit that most often interfaced with counterparts on the FBI.

Unfortunately for Howard, a terrible personal tragedy took his father, forcing him to bow out. In the rush to replace him, the FBI pushed back at guys who had no previous experience working with them. Case and point; when George Howard was installed as the NYPD commander, it caused a dustup that required FBI Deputy

Assistant Director in Charge Ken Walton to step in and put people in line.

As mentioned before, while an affable and colorful sort, Walton did not suffer fools lightly and suffered grumbling even less so. In November 1981 he and Police Commissioner Patrick V. Murphy coauthored an article for the FBI's *Law Enforcement Bulletin*, and the opinion piece read more like a directive and warning. It opened with a paragraph on competition, stating that it might be good for the free market but when "competition erupts between individual law enforcement officers and agencies, the ultimate goal of law enforcement is lost in the labyrinth of real or imagined slights. The fact that an investigation is being conducted to lead to a successful prosecution all too often becomes secondary."[67]

When Howard stepped down, my old friend US Assistant District Attorney Ken Conboy—the man who'd grilled me during the Squitieri case—sent what was described to me as a "flaming arrow" straight into the desk of Jim Sullivan, basically demanding that I be given the post. It was alleged at the time that my ability under fire in the crucible of the 2-5 Precinct had made the difference.

I'm also certain that my having graduated the FBI National Academy made me far more palatable to the FBI contingent of the task force. Brother Tom likely had a lot to do with it, too. Tom's yeoman's work alongside the FBI showed that if one Hallinan was okay, maybe the other wasn't so bad.

After the call from Sullivan, I just sat at my desk with my head swimming. Then, the phone rang again. It happened that quickly. In organizations like the NYPD, big changes often take an excruciatingly long time to begin, but once set in motion things can't happen fast enough. On the other end of the incoming call was Police Commissioner Bob McGuire, and he was only marginally more upbeat than Sullivan.

---

[67] Walton, Kenneth P., and Murphy, Patrick J. "Joint FBI/NYPD Task Forces: A Study in Cooperation." *FBI Law Enforcement Bulletin*, vol. 50, no. 11, November 1981, pp. 20–23.

"You've been transferred and assigned as commander of the FBI/ NYPD Joint Terrorism Task Force, effective immediately," he said. "Report to 26 Federal Plaza at 8:00 a.m. Monday morning."

No interview, no congratulations, and no warning.

In the span of maybe ten minutes, the Brink's case was mine, too— manhunt, traffic jam, and all. I didn't know whether to be excited or terrified. I settled on stunned and focused on the task ahead. That was my reflexive coping method, I guess.

The phone rang again, and this time it was a far friendlier voice, that of NYPD Detective Sergeant Dan Lenahan. Dan had gone to the JTTF along with several others from the Arson and Explosion Squad so the no-nonsense, "get things done" Lenahan was already an insider. But while Dan Lenahan had found a niche, at the moment I was an extra apple in the cart.

"I hear you're taking over as the new commander," he opened. "I'm calling to welcome you to the agency and give you your first briefing." I truly appreciated his reaching out and asked if he'd like to stop by for lunch the following day. "How about a beer instead?" he asked. Dan knew how far out from left field the post had come. He knew I needed the drink.

***

The next day, Friday, the official Personnel Order came down. I met Lenahan at a restaurant not far from the 13th Precinct and we had that beer. Dan Lenahan had an easy manner about him, but also a focused intensity and directness that I knew served him well in his chosen career.

Lenahan had one immediate quirk though—he was, and is to this day, the only person I ever saw put ice in his beer. Maybe he ran hotter than was apparent. About six feet and built like stone, Lenahan was an interesting contrast in appearance, with brown, curly hair and a mustache that stuck out from his light complexion, suggesting it was part of a disguise. I recall opening our conversation by assuring him that I liked an open book in my command. Sergeant Lenahan took that as marching orders and began to brief me on a dizzying caseload of operations and intelligence.

I didn't even have my "Top Secret" clearance yet.

Nor did I know all that much about domestic terrorism, and as Lenahan spoke, I realized that this assignment was going to take me into a lot deeper water than I was perhaps prepared for.

What else is new? I thought. I slowed things down and suggested that first I needed to properly maneuver my exit from Manhattan Robbery, and make sure it was in good hands before I dove in. Instead of continuing the breakneck briefing, I suggested to Lenahan that we reschedule a full one for the following Monday at the JTTF offices.

When Monday rolled around, I went from draft pick to spotlight pretty quickly. The job of commander was obviously a highly sought-after and prestigious position, but that certainly wasn't apparent on my first day. From the very moment I walked into the looming gray slab of 26 Federal Plaza and grabbed the elevator for the twenty-eighth floor, I had to be on my toes.

Just as the doors closed, I noticed a very attractive young woman in the elevator with me, about thirty to thirty-five years of age, and spied that she was watching me somewhat closely. She had already pressed the button for the twenty-eighth floor, so I simply settled in for the ride. I'm sure I gave her a quick smile as we made our ascent, and when we arrived at our destination I motioned for her to step out first.

Across the way stood a large steel door with a combination keypad beside it. The woman lingered a moment, as if to keep track of my position behind her, and then punched in her code. A buzzer sounded, and the door opened. As I moved in behind her, she stopped and turned.

"Where do you think you're going?" It was only then that I noticed the FBI photo ID hanging from her lapel. My detective skills hadn't made the trip from the lobby, so I quickly fumbled for my shield and NYPD ID.

"I've just been transferred to the JTTF."

"Follow me," she said offhand and, appearing unimpressed, then crossed the threshold into the JTTF office. It felt more as if she was taking me into custody than welcoming me as the agent promptly deposited me in an office and left me there.

A few moments later she returned with Agent Barry Mawn in tow, my official counterpart. Mawn was tall and silver-haired, with thin-rimmed glasses and a firm, thoughtful gaze. Despite his professorial appearance, Mawn was a significant figure in the intelligence community who had cut his teeth and as a field agent in the FBI's Bank Task Force, where he worked closely with brother Tom.

With the confused female agent watching, Mawn stuck out his hand, welcomed me to the team, turned to her, and smirked.

"He is your new boss."

The air escaped audibly from her lungs, and, tossing a sheepish look in my direction, she smiled warmly.

"I guess I'll see you around then—welcome aboard."

Mawn then ushered me down the hall and to the assistant director's office, where I finally had the pleasure of meeting Ken Walton in person. At first blush Walton struck me as a showman with his perfectly coiffed auburn pompadour.

To further the image, Ken's personal space looked like a miniature version of the White House Oval Office, with two large flags behind his desk and a large FBI logo perfectly framed between them. The surrounding walls were covered with photos, mostly of Walton at various moments in his anti-crime career, and while I might have drawn the impression that Walton was self-promoting, the opposite was true.

According to the agents and police who worked with him, Ken used his high-profile post strategically, to better the public perception of the agency. Many saw this as flamboyant, but Ken Walton was all about his command and his people.

He was a supremely dedicated workaholic, too. I often found Ken in the office early and almost always leaving late. He obsessed over cases and resources and was always ready and willing to go against his own bureaucracy to get results. In the time I worked with him, Ken Walton never shied from strong positions or heat, and I appreciated his distaste for politics when it got in the way of safety and effectiveness.

Terry Booth, a recently retired FBI man who worked with Walton called him "Old School" and "a Legend," and said that Walton always had his agents' backs.[68] Former NY Police Commissioner Bob McGuire agreed, saying, "Ken Walton was the operational reason [the JTTF] succeeded...he had the complete trust and confidence of the cops because he was more of a street detective than a button-down bureau agent."[69]

After Mawn introduced me to Walton, the three of us sat down for a very open conversation on teamwork. Thanks to brother Tom I knew all too well the potential bumps in the road between FBI and cops, but Walton was adamant that he wanted none of that in the JTTF. Since I was a graduate of the FBI Academy, and had worked with FBI liaisons at 8th Homicide—most notably, Ed Petersen—I had some experience putting the FBI in the lead where necessary.

This was a whole new level.

After the meeting I felt much better about my new job...well, until Walton asked another agent to escort me to my cubicle and get me situated. The walk took a couple of minutes, and along the way, through the maze of the twenty-eighth floor, I began to feel as if my workstation was in another borough. After I found myself seated among FBI agents who weren't even part of the task force, I noticed an immense stack of open investigations and briefings waiting on my desk.

I slumped down into my chair and wondered what I had got myself into.

After about ten minutes, I called Barry Mawn and asked for another quick sit-down with Ken Walton. Mawn seemed somewhat confused.

"What's up?"

___

[68] Lengel, Allan. "Ken Walton, the Most Flamboyant Agent Ever to Head Detroit FBI, Dies at 76." Deadline Detroit, June 2, 2016. Web, December 15, 2018.

[69] Roberts, Sam. "Kenneth Walton, FBI's Bold New York Face in the 80's, Dies at 76." *New York Times*, June 16, 2016. Web, August 1, 2018.

I told him I would explain in Walton's office, then took the long hike back.

Ken Walton was surprised to see me again so soon, until I told him and Barry that while I wasn't there to lead the parade, I certainly wanted to be part of it—at least in the same zip code. Walton's eyes sparkled. He grabbed his phone and directed that my cubicle be back-to-back with Mawn's and in the center of the task force.

Just like that.

With a hint of a smile, he invited Mawn and me to join him for a cup of coffee while our "office space" was being reconfigured.

Mawn later explained that the initial reason for my seating arrangement was due to the still-uneasy working relationship between the FBI and NYPD, even after a year of operation. During coffee, the three of us talked about the tension, and it put me at ease to have Walton and Mawn assure me that breaking down walls and building close partnerships was their priority.

Indeed, Ken, Barry and I would be friends from that moment on. I can't say it enough: Ken Walton was something special and made sure from that day on that I would never suffer from a lack of access. He was never hesitant to have me join him for conferences with domestic and international chiefs of police and law enforcement leaders, and made me one of the chosen few he would invite to occasional break-fast meetings with then-FBI Director William H. Webster.

Walton maintained an obvious appreciation for—and even desire to be—a detective, a respect and admiration he reinforced by hanging a green lantern outside his office, as if it was a mini-police precinct. Obviously, the guys in blue loved it.

Ken Walton also saw and appreciated the pressures related to my new position, especially with the anti-Bureau feeling among some ranking NYPD personnel. After I established myself as JTTF commander, my visits back to police headquarters were sometimes met by demeaning snipes like, "When did you get federalized?" I never mentioned the sometimes-hostile environment to Walton or Mawn, but my sense was that both men understood and appreciated that I was dealing with the issue as best I could on my own.

Chief Pat Murphy understood and worked hard with Walton, both publicly and privately, to change the climate.

As for me, I simply wanted to find my footing as expeditiously as possible. But who were the players, and what were the key roles? With Walton and Mawn, my relationship with brother Tom had already provided me a lot of currency, but I didn't yet *really* know that much about them. In his excellent book, *American Terrorists*, Chicago FBI Agent Richard Hahn—who was a key player in the Midwest portion of FALN investigations, provided an interesting inside look at Ken Walton.

Hahn described him as a guy who brought a true people-based investigative view to the task force. While Walton's reputation preceded him, Hahn revealed that Ken hit the ground running and that once in the Bureau, "quickly established himself as an irreverent, 'I want to see for myself' manager, [who after arriving] in New York in November 1979 had taken to going to the bombing scenes to see what was happening and how they were handled.

"Having no prejudice against any investigative agency, Walton befriended Commissioner of Police Robert J. McGuire who also would show up at some of the high-profile scenes." Walton's propensity for roaming crime scenes brought him and Murphy together to help create the JTTF.

I didn't yet know any of this, of course, but apparently it worked in my favor at some point. Initially, I was simply assessing who the assets were in the unit, how they worked together, and where the rough spots were. Thanks to the leadership of Walton and Murphy, the guys on the ground were already coming together.

Yet the picture of what we would face was only just emerging, and the initial files and top-secret briefings that Barry Mawn dumped on my desk backed it up.

They were overwhelming to say the least.

THE MAN ON THE MOON

I had been in the detective bureau, Sex Crimes Unit, and Anti-Crime Squad. I'd investigated drug cases, robberies, and homicides, tangled with Teenager and the Pleasant Avenue mob families, but what I saw in my first couple of weeks at the JTTF was above and beyond anything I'd seen before. Honestly, it had me wondering what I brought to the table.

Where did I fit?

Could I help?

Could I be a resource at all?

So much of anti-terrorism involved utter mystery. Tracks were so often and so well covered, evidence blown to fragments, informants hard or impossible to come by.

Following what I'd already seen from Ken Walton, I decided that if the JTTF needed resources, we'd get them. If those resources didn't exist, we'd invent them. Fortunately we had plenty of great resources of our own: the FBI agents and NYPD detectives who had already come together as a team.

FBI Agent Larry Wack was an early standout, and while he was not a particularly big man, Larry's work and dedication left an extremely large footprint. Coming from the New York FBI's bomb investigations squad, a.k.a. Arson and Explosion, Larry was a top analyst and field agent, often following the trail of the Omega 7 anti-Castro group. The Florida and New York–based Omega 7, led by bomb maker Eduardo Arocena, was composed of about twenty or so Cuban exiles whose stated goal was to overthrow the Cuban dictator by any means necessary.

Those means included multiple bombings and funding of these deadly operations via drug trafficking.[70] According to the Global Terrorism Database, the Omega 7 group was responsible for more than fifty known attacks and four known killings, including the bombing of the Soviet Mission in the 19th Precinct and the assassination of a Cuban delegate to the United Nations named Garcia Rodriguez.[71]

To track down the terrorist group, Larry Wack worked alongside NYPD Detective Bobby Brandt and the two men meshed into a machine of investigative efficiency. Wack had his intel and coordination with the Miami FBI down pat, which gave him eyes and ears in the anti-Castro community of South Florida. Bobby Brandt was great support in New York, filling in the local gaps and tracking Miami connections to Cuban communities in the city.

Larry Wack, who recently lost a tragic battle with cancer, was one of the most dedicated guys we had and a key FBI agent on the 1976 Sheridan Square assassination of former diplomat Orlando Letelier. Not one to rest on laurels, even before leaving the FBI Larry dedicated countless extra hours to helping track down World War II Nazi war criminals, including the nefarious Auschwitz concentration camp doctor, Josef Mengele.

Another great pairing was Special Agent Lenny Cross with Detective Jimmy Cassidy. Cross was a natural analyst and likely one of the smartest guys we had. His big-picture view meshed perfectly with Cassidy's hardscrabble New York street smarts. Coming out of the US Navy, Cassidy took a hard path through the NYPD, from street cop to Tactical Patrol and finally the Narcotics Division. The Narcotics guys were a driven bunch, often staying on jobs with no overtime and using their own family cars to follow or stake out suspects.

Jimmy was the real deal and had taken the opportunity to work with the Major Case team, including brother Tom. After the FALN's bombing

[70] Associated Press. "Reputed Omega 7 Leader Found Guilty of Murder, 20 Bombings." *Fort Walton Beach Playground Daily News* Archives, September 23, 1984, p. 18. Web, December 21, 2018.

[71] Global Terrorism Database. Omega 7. www.start.umd.edu. Web, December 20, 2018.

of Fraunces Tavern, Cassidy was pulled—along with a few dozen other white shields—into a newly expanded Arson and Explosion Squad, where he credited the A&E guys for much of his success, guys like former Marine Joe Mulligan and Billy Burns, who taught him what to look for in a bombing investigation, what parts, wires, and residue.

If Pat Murphy and Ken Walton had been watching the FBI and NYPD after the Russian Mission bombing, sketching out the JTTF, Jimmy Cassidy and Lenny Cross were a big part of the finished picture. Cassidy and Cross worked together as far back as the Croatian Separatist bombing of LaGuardia Airport and broke the barriers between Bureau and department, dealing with the competition between agencies.

They also caught a glimpse of the competition in legal circles, too, where state and federal prosecutors competed for evidence and the lead in emerging high-profile cases.

In the new agency, Cassidy and Cross worked alongside teams like Special Agent Ken Maxwell and Detective Tommy Dale, seriously compromising the Croats. In many ways, the successful investigation transformed the early JTTF. It was proof of concept that our young organization needed and as FBI agent and writer Richard Hahn pointed out:

> The arrests [of Croatian Separatist leaders] resulted in a shutdown of Croatian terrorism world-wide. When that happened, cops and agents who had worked together on the cases saw one another in a new light. There was a genuine mutual respect and recognition that together they could make a difference. From bitter seeds of resentment had come a sweet success. Coupled with the resources of cars, radios and money, suddenly the JTTF members, both Federal and NYPD, were an elite group.[72]

---

[72] Hahn, Richard S. *American Terrorists—The True Story of the FALN*. Seal Beach, California: R. Hahn & Company, Inc., 2011, p. 71.

***

Agent Ken Maxwell was lead on the Croatian investigations. The former New York state trooper knew the city well and, along with NYPD Detective Tommy Dale, located the informants and connections needed to break up the Croatian network.

Both men also worked closely with Dan Lenahan, who also came to the JTTF via the Arson and Explosion Unit. Yet it could still be a political minefield. After a cop from Bay Ridge came to Lenahan and Dale with information of a Croatian waiter who'd been talking openly about freeing his native land—by force, if needed—Lenahan asked the cop to wear a wire. The cop agreed, but it caused quite a bit of consternation that the NYPD and not the FBI would wire one of their own.

I found it both strange and troubling that a known terrorist organization could sometimes work closer and more openly than cops and the FBI. Fortunately, through the tireless and constant leadership of Ken Walton and Pat Murphy, along with the very willing partners in the early JTTF, we worked hard to create an atmosphere of transparency and communication.

***

For the first year, members of the Joint Terrorism Task Force didn't just need to learn a new level of anti-crime skills, they needed to teach one another.

For example, detectives generally did a better job of hiding in plain sight while working the street and sources, conditions under which some FBI guys didn't blend quite as well. That said, while NYPD detectives were great at assembling elements of individual crimes and smaller cases, the analysis skills of the FBI guys—combined with their vast network—provided incredibly powerful tool for tracking and assessing broader and more spread-out criminal enterprise.

I watched it all come together.

Soon the FBI guys were helping their NYPD counterparts analyze and plan, all while the NYPD gave the bureau some amazing lessons in covering the street and digging out sources.

There were other issues, however, involving money. Detectives got overtime, so when teams had to go on long ops, the FBI guys got upset because the NYPD guys made more money. NYPD personnel were also worried about grades and shields, promotion opportunities that were alien to the FBI field agent.

On a lighter note, written reports could be a riot as FBI 302s read like dime-store novels, with police DD5 reports seeming by comparison like stereo instructions.

Regardless, it had come together through the Croatian Separatist investigation, which, by mid-1981, was well on its way to completion. Following a lead team of FBI and police from Chicago, the JTTF helped take apart a group that had bombed targets and killed people since the mid-1970s.

The Croatian case also provided something even more significant in the annals of law enforcement and anti-terror activity—it gave us a chilling look at just how organized and embedded a criminal group could be. Unlike organized crime with its major families and brazenly open appearance, even defiance, domestic terror was a secretive component of international terror.

The Croatian group would reveal just how stitched into the fabric of the community these militant groups were. The kicker was the home base for their violent operations, a seemingly legitimate Croatian-based political organization in Chicago that had been infiltrated and found its younger members turned militant by zealous separatist leaders with ties overseas.[73]

The Jewish Defense League, which had been very active in their attacks against Russian interests, became increasingly so during my stint with the JTTF. By 1981, the JDL was ramping up operations into a near-monthly attack or protest.

---

[73] Sheppard, Nathaniel Jr. "Arrest of 9 in Terrorist Group Brings Uneasy Calm to Croatian-Americans." *New York Times*, July 23, 1981.

At this point in 1981, both the FALN and the Brink's case—with its ties to the May 19th Organization, Weather Underground, and BLA—held center stage. Alongside the Brink's group huddled a more shadowy entity called "the Family," with Harvard doctoral-student-turned-militant Randolph Simms, a.k.a. Coltrane Chimurenga. He directed the group to commit more deadly robberies in the Brink's mold. Another affiliate group, the New Afrikan Freedom Fighters, began planning to blow up NYPD cars and then open fire on police personnel as they fled the station houses.

What was especially troubling was that these groups had for years been gathering detailed intel on us. They knew exactly who they were up against, our routines, and, more ominously, where many of us lived.[74] Meanwhile, the full picture of exactly who *they* were remained murky. The Croatian groups may have provided a key to the door, but these others presented the deadly house of horrors that lay beyond.

Neil Herman, the FBI man who had literally run across the Triboro Bridge to the LaGuardia bombing, explained that the Brink's case created a watershed moment in the history of counterterrorism. When we began to realize what they had been responsible for accomplishing up until that point—a seemingly random pattern of prison breakouts, assassinations and bank robberies—the game changed.

Up to that point we had no idea they were related or connected to groups like the Panthers, May 19th, Black Liberation Army, New Afrikan Freedom Fighters, and Weather Underground. The elders of these groups had been '60s activists who'd seemingly assimilated into society, with some teaching at prominent universities. The linkage was chilling.

Ken Walton addressed it just after the Brink's robbery, telling the press that we were indeed aware of the linkage between several groups, "and possibly some foreign organizations."[75] Bringing our own forces together would enable us to connect the dots.

---

[74] Republic of New Africa. GlobalSecurity.org.
[75] Hudson, Edward. "7 Are Indicted in Rockland for Robbery of Brinks Car." *New York Times*, November 30, 1981.

***

By 1981, FALN had gone eerily silent. As any in intelligence or law enforcement could tell you, when militant groups dropped off the radar, it almost certainly meant they were busy planning something. That something would be a challenge that was almost beyond the capabilities of the JTTF.

At the time I read the top-secret briefing on them, and something seemed especially troublesome, even after the spring 1980 arrests of nearly a dozen network members in Illinois seemed to indicate a level of closure. We still didn't know all that much about them. We only had pieces.

This isn't to say that we were without actionable intelligence. In fact, several months before I joined the task force, the FALN recruit named Freddie Mendez "flipped" and brought to light some new information about the group's size and organization.[76]

Jeremy Margolis was and still is a significant figure in the legal side of law enforcement worldwide. When I knew him best, Margolis was in the middle of an eleven-year stint as assistant United States attorney in Chicago, working some of the nation's most prominent prosecutions. As his private practice biography stated, "[Jeremy's] cases included both domestic and international terrorism involving bombings, air piracy, hostage taking and seditious conspiracy... [and Margolis] was one of the co-founders and coordinators of the multia-gency Chicago Joint Terrorist Task Force...."[77]

Margolis stayed on the trail of the FALN, even after the successful arrests and convictions of what seemed like the leaders of the group. He was certain these defendants presented just the tip of the iceberg,

---

[76] Belli, Roberta. *Effects and Effectiveness of Law Enforcement Intelligence Measures to Counter Homegrown Terrorism: A Case Study on the* Fuerzas Armadas de Liberación *Nacional (FALN), Final Report to Human Factors/Behavioral Sciences Division, Science and Technology Directorate, U.S. Department of Homeland Security.* College Park, Maryland: START, 2012, pp. 21–22.

[77] Loeb and Loeb, LLC, website. "White Collar Criminal Defense and Investigations." People: Jeremy D. Margolis, co-chair.

and to try and leverage their cooperation he employed a heavy-handed seditious conspiracy charge, a legal hammer most often used for organizations bent on overthrowing the government.

According to Margolis, this charge was a perfect fit for the FALN case, given that the evidence couldn't tie individuals to specific incidents but rather warlike ideological ones.[78] While the initial Illinois defendants stayed silent, the sedition charge proved highly effective in the case of Freddie Mendez, who called Margolis from prison to spill what he knew.[79]

What's important to note about the turning of Freddie Mendez was that his information was critical in bringing the information needed to begin evolving the task force into the kind of organization needed to properly meet the coming threats.

The Homeland Security Report put it this way:

> For the first time since the beginning of the investigation, the FBI had finally found an insider who could shed some light on the structure and functioning of this secretive organization [the FALN]. Mendez's contribution…allowed the Chicago team to experiment with an innovative strategy which combined traditional criminal investigation tactics (i.e., physical surveillance) with state-of-the-art intelligence-gathering measures.
>
> Crucial to the realization of this strategy was the newly formed Chicago squad, which began as an informal cooperative effort between the FBI, the

---

[78] Belli, Roberta. *Effects and Effectiveness of Law Enforcement Intelligence Measures to Counter Homegrown Terrorism: A Case Study on the* Fuerzas Armadas de Liberación Nacional *(FALN), Final Report to Human Factors/Behavioral Sciences Division, Science and Technology Directorate, U.S. Department of Homeland Security.* College Park, Maryland: START, 2012, p. 20.

[79] Hahn, Richard S. *American Terrorists—The True Story of the FALN.* Seal Beach, California: R. Hahn & Company, Inc., 2011, p. 6.

Secret Service, local and state police, and became progressively more established.

To give more credit where credit is due, it was FBI Agent Richard Hahn who proposed an operational plan on how to blend cops and agents, and it was his working model that provided the proof of concept of what we had employed in New York.[80]

In the top-secret briefing I read, the most chilling part of the Mendez information was the revelation that the FALN employed the same kind of secretly coordinated cell-structure as present-day terrorists. Mendez outlined how insulated some of the arms of the FALN were, so that even if we took down one part, it was going to be extremely hard to use that part to help uncover another.

He also explained in frightening detail, the spy-level counter-surveillance training being used against us.

Indeed, some of the FALN's network operated like sleeper agents, living normal, unassuming lives until activated. Then, after passing on weapons or information, they would just blend back into the scenery until called upon again. Mendez also revealed how he was coached in the use of disguises and how to avoid being followed by jumping on and off public transportation, constantly checking for surveillance and tails. FALN safe houses stretched well beyond Illinois and into other states.[81]

More than ever before, we had to be better.

---

[80] Belli, Roberta. *Effects and Effectiveness of Law Enforcement Intelligence Measures to Counter Homegrown Terrorism: A Case Study on the* Fuerzas Armadas de Liberación Nacional *(FALN), Final Report to Human Factors/ Behavioral Sciences Division, Science and Technology Directorate, U.S. Department of Homeland Security.* College Park, Maryland: START, 2012. pp. 22–23.

[81] Hahn, Richard S. *American Terrorists—The True Story of the FALN.* Seal Beach, California: R. Hahn & Company, Inc., 2011, pp. 22–31.

◢ PUZZLE PIECES

Agent Tom Terjeson, a multifaceted professional who had inherited the long-running Fraunces Tavern bombing investigation, was a key man on the FALN case.

He was partnered with Arson and Explosion Detective Elmer Toro, an outstanding investigator in his own right who had worked at my old 2-5 haunt. As a fluent Spanish speaker, Toro often maneuvered the same dangerous drug areas patrolled by Team C. More than most he knew well the ties that existed between Spanish Harlem and Latin America, ties that included drug kingpins working with the Colombo crime family and FALN.

Toro also knew domestic terrorists, having personally interviewed bomb maker William Morales before he blew himself up in lower Manhattan. Knowing of the FALN long before most of us, Toro tried unsuccessfully to turn Morales into an informant. Later in Mexico, and after Morales had been detained by Federales, their familiarity turned into vital intel as Morales revealed to Toro—then with the JTTF—the details of his escape from New York.

Morales's flight included a woman named Diane Campbell, who turned out to be the Weather Underground's Marilyn Jean Buck, a driver in the Brink's heist and accomplice to Joanne Chesimard/ Assata Shakur. Thus Toro, more than most, saw the linkage between domestic groups—possibly even before the rest of us fully did.[82]

---

[82]   Hahn, Richard S. *American Terrorists—The True Story of the FALN.* Seal Beach, California: R. Hahn & Company, Inc., 2011, p 116.

When the Arson and Explosion Squad was formed, Toro was certainly on their radar but, like me, needed help from on high to get in. Once there, he excelled in his new post and, after working closely with FBI counterparts like Tom Terjeson, was noticed by the JTTF.

Toro and Terjeson were a fast fit, though, as Toro recalled, a lot of cops and FBI personnel bowed out over early territory problems. In Toro's eyes it was Ken Walton who not only held the early unit together but, when hearing about problems that Elmer had with late promotions, went straight to the NYPD to get action on his behalf.

Their friendship gave Toro a unique insight into the man. He recalled how Walton "would roll into scenes and tell guys, 'I'm not here to take charge or do anything. I just want to know what happened and how I can help.'" Walton cemented their friendship in 1982 by calling ahead to the FBI Academy to make sure Toro got a good welcome for his training session.

What stood out most for Toro, though, was Walton's insistence on personally visiting or honoring any NYPD officer shot in the line of duty.

Ken Walton knew a key piece when he saw one. Elmer Toro was skilled and obsessive in his work and quickly became a high-profile problem for the FALN—so much so that during one of their congresses, the terror organization put a large contract out on his head.

"When water got hot, as they say," Elmer recalled, "the JTTF gave me a 1975 Monte Carlo that was reinforced with steel, making it so heavy that in the snow, I couldn't stop it!" Still, one night during the height of the FALN case, Elmer walked out to his car and on the windshield found a photo of a woman holding a baby.

His wife had just had a child.

It was terrifying.

Steadfast and undeterred, Toro was our guy on Brink's and often shuttled between New York and Chicago and even traveled to Puerto Rico and Mexico for the expansive investigation. When FALN insider Freddie Mendez was turned and brought to New York, both Terjeson and Toro interviewed him and used the information gleaned to help convince New York Assistant US Attorney Charlie Rose to reinvigorate the grand jury process that had stalled after the Evansville FALN cell was broken.[83]

For all intents and purposes, in the legal and "official" circles the FALN was a done deal, though at the time we knew better. Yet we had little concrete information to go on.

***

Our case against the Brink's defendants was vastly strengthened by the October 1981 arrival of FBI agent David Mitchell to the JTTF. He was about as expert as anyone on Earth in the playbook and roster of the Brink's crew and brought with him a series of connections that filled in vital missing bits of the puzzle.

Prior to his arrival at the JTTF, the Tennessee-born Mitchell was already a seasoned FBI investigator, having done an extremely serious tour in New Orleans where he tackled violent crimes, kidnappings, bank robberies, fugitives, and acts of domestic terror. As tough as Dave could be as an investigative force, he was smooth as glass with his NYPD counterparts. Soft-spoken, friendly, and always ready for a joke or light moment, Mitchell bore the distinction of being the only member of the task force with a Southern drawl, which prompted Ken Walton, always fond of nicknaming or poking fun, to wonder if our new JTTF "hillbilly" wore shoes when not in the office.

He wore marching boots.

It was Mitchell's very Southern ties that yielded much of our amazing early intel on the scope of the challenges we faced, with probably the *best* understanding of the tangled and multistate structure of the Brink's group. For example, when electronic surveillance picked up a phone call that tied BLA member Anthony LaBorde to the brutal May 1981 traffic stop murder of NYPD officer John Scarangella and the wounding of his partner Richard Rainey, Mitchell was already on the job from down south.

---

[83] Hahn, Richard S. *American Terrorists—The True Story of the FALN*. Seal Beach, California: R. Hahn & Company, Inc., 2011, pp. 72–73.

On May 1, Scarangella and Rainey had stopped a van in St. Albans, Queens, that matched the description of a vehicle used in several burglaries. "[S]uspects emerged from the van and pumped 30 shots into the police patrol car, hitting Scarangella two times in the head. The 42-year-old died two weeks later from his wounds."[84]

Investigators at the time also believed that none other than BLA ringleader Joanne Chesimard was in the ambush van that night, as she was still at large and hadn't yet fled to Cuba.[85]

A lot was riding on our investigation. Mitchell had tracked Nathaniel Burns (Odinga), William Johnson (Bilal Sunni-Ali) and Cynthia Bolton (Fulani Sunni Ali) as they moved down south. Mitchell was also tracking Anthony LaBorde and other elements of the Brink's group that were involved in the Scarangella and Rainey, a full three months before the fateful Brink's robbery in Nyack.

Mitchell and a surveillance unit traced phone calls to the location of a gray van with Louisiana tags that was being operated by Nathaniel Burns, a.k.a. Sekou Odinga of the Brink's robbery crew. Burns and van were traced to a remote Georgia farmhouse, which prompted the FBI there to contact the JTTF in New York. In New York, supervisor Barry Mawn connected Mitchell and his team to Ed Petersen, who at the time was working in Newark. It was how the puzzle pieces fit, and Mitchell had found a key one. It didn't matter who picked them up, spun them sideways, as long as they got put into place.

Ed filled in more of the picture with known accomplices of Burns, LaBorde, Ward, and Chesimard, and more than a few more pieces fit—especially the van. It fit the description of the same one seen by the Mount Vernon building super after the Brink's theft, being loaded by known Brink's heist members.

Sadly, the news was so new and the picture still so unclear and, as Mitchell later described, "We didn't know what we had going on

---

[84] Murphy, Mary. "Targeted by Their Uniform: The Disturbing 43-Year History of Assassinations of NYPD Cops." WPIX pix.com, December 20, 2014.

[85] Stepansky, Joseph. "Retired NYPD Officer Richard Rainey, Hit with 14 Rounds in 1981 Shooting That Killed His Partner, Dies." *New York Daily News*, March 5, 2015.

exactly, but we knew they were up to no good." Three months after the Brink's robbery occurred, the fuller picture of the vast and generational network behind the crime slowly came to light, prompting Ken Walton to have David Mitchell quickly transferred to New York as a case agent alongside NYPD Detective Jimmy Haefner.

Walton knew an asset when he saw it.

***

Keeping our lives "interesting," to say the least, the Jewish Defense League became increasingly violent in 1981, bombing an Iranian bank in San Francisco before carrying out similar attacks against an alleged Nazi war criminal on Long Island later in the summer, then two more New York bombings in the fall. What was notable about the JDL's activities of the time was the careful split the group maintained between its attacks and official statements.

In earlier years, the JDL proudly took credit for attacks directly, but upon falling under scrutiny during the 1970s, they seemed to learn a lot from other militant groups of the time, shielding the core by using satellite organizations and groups.

For example, after a dozen bullets were fired through the sitting room window of a Soviet ambassador, JDL founder Meir Kahane released a statement.

"We have no exact knowledge of who fired into the home, but we have no doubt it is the work of Jewish activists." And despite describing the shooting as an "unlawful act," Kahane added, "We heartily applaud it."[86]

Regardless of the sleight of hand, it was our job to bring the JDL organization to justice, and it would require a deep dive into the underground organization. This required evidence gathering and human intelligence, but as the JDL often switched between bombings and simple acts of vandalism, it was especially difficult to tie it all together outside of a common ideology.

---

[86] The Jewish Defense League. "Extremism, Terrorism and Bigotry." adl.org.

TICKING CLOCKS

Toward the end of 1981, with the FALN case just simmering, we began making progress on Brink's. All of the various law enforcement players—local and state departments—were involved, and more pieces of the puzzle began to turn up from all corners of the New York-New Jersey-Connecticut tristate area.

A cohesive and cooperative new form of law enforcement was emerging, bringing a powerful and broad spectrum of skills and bandwidth to bear against the complex web of networks we were finding. The 1979 brainchild of former Police Commissioner Patrick V. Murphy and the FBI's Ken Walton was truly coming of age.

The new leverage helped convince the captured participants in the crime to begin to reveal where some of those pieces fit. A significant break came when the JTTF gleaned critical information from captured Brink's participant Samuel Brown (a.k.a. Solomon Bouines), who was apprehended along with Judith Clark and David Gilbert.

Whereas Clark and Gilbert refused to talk, Brown provided names, places, and sequences of events. He had been a career criminal before joining the BLA and was suspected of firing the fatal shots in the execution-style murders of officers Edward O'Grady and Waverly Brown. His detailed information, gleaned under federal guidelines, got us the court permission needed to begin electronic surveillance at the May 19th and BLA safe houses and related businesses.

One of those businesses was, of course, the BAAANA office in Harlem, which Brink's ringleader Mutulu Shakur managed. A small problem was that in the task force we were mostly white and fairly easy to spot on the street. We had to construct a special surveillance unit, and fast, so we began recruiting Black and Hispanic detectives into the FBI and provided them a crash course in surveillance.

Through their herculean efforts, we learned that the groups involved in Brink's also had a safe house in the Lower East Side, at 85 Barrow Street. We needed more surveillance teams and had to get our intel faster, often having to rely on outside resources.

After forming up, the JTTF had secured an agreement with Jim Kallstrom's FBI Special Ops Unit, which was part of the Foreign Counterintelligence (FCI) division. When Special Ops had available manpower, we could tap them. Kallstrom was the FBI's first real wiretap expert, and according to a *New York Times* article on his 1997 retirement, he all but built the Bureau's engineering research facilities at Quantico.

"He took the bureau sort of light years ahead of where we were at the time," former FBI director Louis J. Freeh was quoted as saying, "and has put us in a wonderful position today."[87]

Jim Kallstrom was a creature of higher duty from day one and, after high school, joined the Marines and did a stint in Vietnam. When the Safe Streets Act was passed, Jim jumped at the chance for a meaningful career that to him was all about taking responsibility and helping others.

After graduating from the FBI Academy, he did a stint with the Baltimore Bank Task Force. Then, after the RICO laws went into effect and brought with them new tools and procedures for mob surveillance, the FBI suddenly needed a domestic unit to go alongside the Foreign Counterintelligence group.

Kallstrom stepped up there too.

On the domestic front, the FBI had little structured or organized surveillance capabilities, and Kallstrom credited his own mentor and leader, Neil Welch, as the key. Like Kallstrom, Welch always looked for the next hill to climb, and after graduating law school he came to the FBI, where he promptly "vexed his bosses in Washington, by focusing

---

[87] Weiser, Benjamin. "F.B.I.'s Kallstrom, Head of Flight 800 Inquest, to Retire." *New York Times*, December 10, 1997.

his investigations not on bank robbers and draft dodgers but on organized crime and corruption."[88] FCI had a tall order with organized crime, but it turned into a fertile though incredibly dangerous training ground. The Mafia maintained hardened targets of street-fortress strongholds like Sullivan and Mulberry Streets in Manhattan, protected with systems of lookouts and informants.

According to Kallstrom, when Neil Welch initially called on him to create five surveillance teams from his pick of 1,500 agents in the NY Office, "There was immediate blowback from within the Bureau as guys didn't want to lose their best to the new units no matter how important it may become."

What eventually won out was success.

As the local surveillance units came up to speed and grew, the intelligence they gathered and provided to the rest of the FBI and law enforcement became a precious resource. As Kallstrom put it, "We got provable cases against leadership of all five families, their effect on legitimate businesses and their stranglehold of produce and construction and sanitation and such." As it's been said time and time again, however, success has many fathers, but failure is an orphan.

"We had to create our own driving school," Kallstrom explained. "Show our new agents how to follow guys, when to break off, parallel them and so on." Another huge challenge was the limitation inherent in the available technology of the time. "During our early years," Kallstrom observed, "we had no protected channels on our radios and there was no encryption, so we had to create a system of codes and when to flip channels. We even had to make fake broadcasts as bad guys monitoring the system could get spooked by something as seemingly harmless as an accidental mic key."

It worked, slowly but spectacularly so, and as the new Special Ops units grew more effective and opportunities increased, Kallstrom needed cars and surveillance aircraft, which were expensive and came at premium in any arena of law enforcement. "Wires and Fliers" was

---

[88] Robert, Sam. "Neil Welch, F.B.I. Mastermind in Abscam Sting Operation, Dies at 90." *New York Times*, July 11, 2017.

how he described the unit's ground-based and aerial surveillance capabilities, ones that would later prove crucial to the JTTF.

Thanks to Jim Kallstrom, Neil Welch, and the determined work of so many FBI agents and police, the Special Ops Units dealt the American Mafia a blow from which it never recovered. Neil Welch, along with Long Island FBI Agent John F. Good, oversaw the famous ABSCAM political corruption operation that in the late '70s and early '80s took down a corrupt US senator and six congressmen.

JUGGLING BOMBS AND RESOURCES

In early 1982, as we focused on Brink's, the FALN announced their return with three bombings in New York's financial district, hitting the Merrill Lynch Building, the New York Stock Exchange, and Chase Manhattan Bank's corporate headquarters. In a subsequent communiqué, the organization implied a connection to Brink's, albeit only in the ideological sense as far as we could discern.

A month before the blasts, Assistant US Attorney Charlie Rose in New York began grand jury proceedings against Brink's defendants David Gilbert, Judith Clark, and Samuel Brown, and the communiqué specifically mentioned "the three North-Americans captured in the Brink's expropriation." It declared, "By linking up with your Black comrades and making their struggle your own, you have put into practice the Leninist principle which states that the duty of the working class…is to actively assist and fight for the liberation of the colonies."[89]

It was just an inference of broader cooperation between our opponents, but what unfolded over the next two years went from threat to a chillingly clear warning.

To be sure, we would need that surveillance capability, and need it yesterday. To get it, we had to break through any internal walls that might stand in our way.

---

[89] Hahn, Richard S. *American Terrorists—The True Story of the FALN*. Seal Beach, California: R. Hahn & Company, Inc., 2011, pp. 100–101.

Jim Kallstrom again led the charge. It was mission-critical to him that communication, leadership, and the willingness to set aside internal politics rule the day.

"Not that we had a lot of resources," Kallstrom explained, "but we did an awful lot of work on major cases. We rallied, and guys really set aside everything for a higher need and cause. For at least a decade if not longer, we did most of the surveillance work in the country, and other agencies called on us when they needed our expertise."

Kallstrom himself did whatever it took, and it was his unit, with Jim himself present, that twice placed the wire taps that all but smashed the Croatian group. On another such case, involving the New Afrikan Freedom Fighters, Kallstrom did what nobody else could do. When his own Special Ops guys tried and failed more than once to get a bug into the group's heavily guarded Brooklyn stronghold, Kallstrom went in alone at night and got the job done.

But even with Kallstrom's willing and eager support, there was only so much manpower available the JTTF could count on in the New York area. The Special Ops guys had a lot of sticks in the fire, including support for larger FCI initiatives and foreign intelligence gathering. As a result, in those early days we could mostly go after tidbits, unless something major happened to bring our investigations more of an international flavor.

Though always short on something, we received a tremendous break on December 21 when a robbery of the Pineland State Bank in Metter, Georgia, included several operatives affiliated with the October Brink's crew. Present were BLA members Donald Weems and Tyrone Rison, the latter of whom was wanted in connection with the murder of an armored car guard. Joining them was a woman named Yvonne Thomas, who, with Samuel Smith, had occupied the very Mount Vernon safe house found after the Brink's robbery.

Smith was the Brink's fugitive who was killed in the gunfight with NYPD detectives just three days after the deadly robbery. Enter David Mitchell and Detective Jimmy Haefner, who went to work on another captured Brink's suspect—Peter Middleton, a.k.a. Kamau Bayette.

Bayette, while not a major component of the coming trial, was in Mitchell's view "critical" to the investigation and coming prosecution. He was allegedly involved in the planning of the Brink's robbery though, in his own words, declined to participate. Subsequent wiretaps of the BAAANA clinic, though, frequently captured him on the phone, and many saw him as the ringleader's "protégé."

We already had a lot to go on tying Mutulu Shakur to Brink's, including the seemingly strange coincidence that after being a daily presence at BAAANA before Brink's, Shakur never returned to the clinic after the robbery. We had seen Shakur often at another address on Barrow Street, however, and from Bayette, Mitchell, and Haefner learned that the Barrow apartment was a safe house rented by Brink's suspect Edward Joseph.

This was that kind of information, in fact, that allowed the JTTF to eventually track Shakur to Los Angeles, where he was apprehended.

Long before the apprehension of the remaining suspects in the case, the work of Mitchell, Haefner, Petersen, and so many others resulted in hundreds of pages of FBI wiretap summaries. As Mitchell observed, the information gathered linked the groups involved in Brink's to other armored-car holdups and crimes in New York and in Georgia. I remember at the time seeing photos of Marilyn Jean Buck, driver and accomplice for the BLA and May 19th group.

Looking over her near-perfect disguises, I was struck by the challenge they represented. Buck showed a dozen different faces and names, and was a highly trained and skilled master of identities on par with an international fugitive or espionage agent. It hit me again that we were on the front line of an entirely new type and level of law enforcement. There were politics and pressure coming from every corner of the job, and rough spots were plentiful, but dedication and willingness to do the right thing was also apparent.

The FBI was used to and wanted the driver's seat, but Ken Walton, Barry Mawn, and I all agreed that the greater good was paramount. Plus preventing our guys from dying was more important than politics or protocol.

Barry Mawn and I often talked over a couple of drinks and after an extremely long day. There was an extremely convenient bar across from 26 Federal Plaza that provided a great location for crying in our beers.

It also provided an opportunity for our adversaries.

We were going twelve, fourteen, sixteen hours a day, and we'd hit that watering hole for a quick drink to decompress, often staying until midnight or 1:00 a.m. Sitting in the bar one night with Elmer Toro, we were hit with the sobering realization that the bartender wasn't the only one watching us. Small groups of people sometimes milled about on the street across from our offices and, one night after a couple of cocktails, Toro was shadowed to the subway. Elmer Toro, the man with the steel-plated El Camino and FALN price on his head.

On multiple occasions, in fact, he was followed to the subway or to his car. If we were a terrorist task force, the FALN and groups like it had built an antiestablishment task force of their own.

Years later, after her arrest, we discovered that Brink's accomplice Marilyn Jean Buck had noted everything. She knew our cars, where our offices were, our faces and habits, right down to the guns we carried.

***

Our initial switch to a more surveillance-based investigation began to bear fruit in January 1982, after we overheard a phone call between Brink's accomplice Anthony LaBorde and his wife, who at the time was at the BAAANA headquarters in Harlem.

LaBorde informed her that he'd been arrested in Philadelphia on a weapons charge. Philadelphia policemen had observed him discarding a gym bag containing a 9mm handgun and ammunition. Despite the fact that he was carrying a loaded weapon and wearing a bullet-proof vest, the cops had no idea whom they'd just collared, though back at the station, his deadly identity was quickly revealed.

Not only was he a known BLA member, he was also wanted in New York for the April 1981 ambush murder of NYPD officer John

Scarangella and the wounding of Scarangella's partner, Richard Rainey. LaBorde figured it wouldn't affect the BAAANA group, but thanks to our wiretap help from FBI Special Ops, his call "home" tied him to the Brink's group, though not to the robbery itself.

Then, a little more than a week later on the evening of January 20, Ken Maxwell, Larry Wack, and Bobby Brandt discovered Donald Weems hiding in an apartment in the Bronx. Maxwell reminded me recently that all the JTTF had to go on at the time was the general location, and we spent days casing the area. They had 149th Street in Harlem and the description of a brownstone, and that was it. Maxwell and Brandt didn't even know exactly who lived there, but info from the street revealed that a fugitive was holed up. So with a stack of Brink's, BLA, and May 19th suspect photos in hand, the two JTTF men hit the area to canvass.

There was a religious-themed store next door to one of the buildings in question, and the owner quickly identified Weems as living just one door over at 295. He even gave them the correct floor and said he was likely home. Maxwell placed a call to the office and got Barry Mawn on the phone.

A short time later Mawn and former A&E Detective Charlie Minch were on the way. When the cavalry finally went in, Weems agreed to come into the hall, though the first out the door was another male subject, dressed in a lime-green negligée.

So much for chivalry.

Weems emerged next, with his hands up, "You got me, man," he said. "You got me." We had to be sure, so Terry Cox pulled up our suspect's shirt and found several bullet scars from where Weems had been shot by police during the Brink's robbery. Then inside the apartment, they found a duffel bag filled with ammunition, a 9mm handgun, and a shotgun.

◤ THE MOST WANTED

By February 1982, Tyrone Rison and Yvonne Thomas had been arrested for the Georgia Pineland bank robbery. Rison quickly flipped and became a key informant.

Once back in New York, he sketched a picture of the central network that was running out of the BAAANA office in Harlem, and the "Action Five," as Rison described them, consisted of himself, Anthony LaBorde, Donald Weems, Samuel Brown, and fugitive clinic director, Mutulu Shakur.

Shakur had recently returned to the city, but instead of moving on him, we set up as much surveillance as Special Ops and our internal resources could muster. The patience yielded a ton of new leads—people and places, including the Mount Vernon safe house that had been occupied by Yvonne Thomas and Samuel Smith. With information Rison provided, we then closed in on Joanne Chesimard.

At his 1987 trial, Rison confirmed that Marilyn Jean Buck had driven one of the getaway cars that took Chesimard to a safe house in East Orange, New Jersey—a house that Buck had also rented. Several months later, Chesimard was transported to another safe house in Pittsburgh, before she fled the country.[90]

The particulars of the 1979 escape and flight to Pittsburgh were stunning. The combined organizations behind Brink's were coordinated and trained. Some of their "above-ground" affiliates and supporters infiltrated various legal and official positions and. though it

---

[90] Lubasch, Arnold H. "Killer Says He Helped in Chesimard's Escape." *New York Times*, December 2, 1987.

was never proven, some on Chesimard's legal team seemed to have stashed guns in the correction facility before the escape.

These accomplices managed to achieve this feat after wearing down the guards. With each visit they brought massive amounts of paperwork and other searchable items, or claimed violations of personal space and—in some cases—sexual harassment. Through a mix of exhaustion and the fear of legal reprisal, some guards simply stopped looking.

**

Coltrane Chimurenga, the Harvard doctoral student turned militant, appeared again on our radar. We didn't know it yet, but Chimurenga was now head of the Republic of New Afrika organization, referenced by a Brink's suspect and overheard in our wiretaps as "a militia that Chimurenga started." Middleton backed up the cryptic statement, "and verified that Chimurenga had taken over a militant unit in the wake of the Brink's arrests."[91]

The picture continued to emerge of just how deep the linkage between Brink's and other domestic terror groups might be headed. As a *New York Times* article of the time stated, "The groups identified by the F.B.I. as communicating through the [BAAANA] acupuncture center included the Black Liberation Army, the Republic of New Afrika, the May 19 Communist Organization, the Black Panther Party, the Weather Underground Organization and the Prairie Fire Organizing Committee." The article continued, "From the first, many of the conversations appeared to the F.B.I to be encoded and secretive, with pseudonyms like 'Spirit', 'Rebel', and 'Applecore' used in place of real names. Transcripts show that the talkers seemed to assume they were being tapped and often reminded each other that they could not speak freely."[92]

---

[91] Larsen, Jonathan Z. "Son of Brink's? A Case of Terrorism or Talk." *New York Magazine*, May 6, 1985, p. 54.

[92] Blumenthal, Ralph. "FBI Wiretaps: An Ear on the Brink's Case." *New York Times*, August 9, 1982.

The true boldness and proximity of our adversaries became fully apparent when a chilling warning was spray-painted across the pink marble wall outside 26 Federal Plaza. It read "Death to the Terrorist Task Force" in blood-red and black paint. It wasn't a particularly rushed job either, but rather a very public and brazen challenge that had clearly taken some time to paint. We could only guess as to whose handiwork the graffiti was, but it didn't matter.

It was a daring announcement to the JTTF that we were being targeted.

The graffiti warning was followed by a mailer that was sent out by FALN supporters. It was titled, "Know Your Enemy: Stop FBI Terrorist Task Force." The ominous correspondence boldly stated the goal. "Victory to National Liberation. Support the Armed Clandestine Movements. Defeat US Imperialism," and included many pictures of JTTF agents and NYPD personnel.[93]

Then, on March 1, four powerful explosions shook the financial district of New York City, bringing both the New York and American Stock Exchanges to a dead halt. The FALN claimed responsibility in a letter left in a phone booth at the scene, which stated that the bombs were "a strike against imperialist forces that are depressing the Puerto Rican people."[94]

So much for silence and our perceived advantage. The FALN, it seemed, was alive and well.

Meanwhile, with information from Tyrone Rison, we moved on Brink's and in the early hours of March 26, the Joint Terrorist Task Force and New York City Police staged simultaneous raids on two safe house apartments and the BAAANA headquarters. The predawn raid resulted in the arrest of several members of the organizations involved in Brink's. After the raids, the combination of wiretaps and

---

[93] Hahn, Richard S. *American Terrorists—The True Story of the FALN*. Seal Beach, California: R. Hahn & Company, Inc., 2011, p 132.

[94] Kroessler, Jeffrey A. "Bombing for Justice: Urban Terrorism in New York City from the 1960s through the 1980s." In *Criminal Justice and Law Enforcement Annual*, volume 6 (new series, volume 1). Edited by Larry E. Sullivan, Staci Strobi, and Dana Greene. Brooklyn, New York: AMS Press, 2014, pp. 63–112.

flipped participants filled in the blanks, including the identity and activities of Silvia Baraldini, a legal aid assistant for the defense at the coming Brink's trial.

Baraldini—as it was later discovered—had been involved as a getaway driver for robberies and provided defendants like Donald Weems with inside information on how to potentially escape from custody.[95] There were insiders at every turn and still more troubling connections where Baraldini was concerned.

After some of the FALN attacks, official communiqués were found at a particular phone booth, one just a few short blocks from her apartment. It was circumstantial evidence, but at Baraldini's home JTTF agents found a carbon copy of a communiqué that offered support for the stated cause of the Brink's crew. The copy was the same as one left at the phone booth, only this version contained handwritten comments later found in final form in a communiqué left for police and press.

As FBI Agent Rick Hahn stated, "It was a damning piece of evidence, clearly linking the two groups of conspirators in a series of bombings."[96]

Baraldini was arrested in November. We ran her information and found a traffic summons issued to her in Nyack, at the very same location of the Brink's robbery and only days before the robbery. This strongly suggested that she was part of the preplanning and assessment. Also in her apartment there were receipts for a money order and a credit card, tying her directly to FALN grand jury participants Ricardo Romero and Julio Rosado and, according to Rick Hahn, "folders labeled 'FALN' and 'Morales escape' along with photographs of Morales before he was injured."[97]

Our heads were spinning over the sheer scope of what we were uncovering. The late spring and early summer were taken up by

---

[95] New York Criminal Justice Institute. *Report of the Policy Study Group on Terrorism*, November 1985, pp. 43–46.

[96] Hahn, Richard S. *American Terrorists—The True Story of the FALN*. Seal Beach, California: R. Hahn & Company, Inc., 2011, p. 131.

[97] Ibid., p. 147.

further evidence gathering and case building, all with an eye toward the fall grand jury, to put even more pressure on the remaining Brink's organization.

***

September fell eerily silent until the early in the morning of September 20, when suspected FALN bombers struck again outside the Banker's Trust offices on Park Avenue. This time the group claimed the bombing was in protest of US support for Israeli aggression against the Palestinian people.

This time the communiqué seemed to take on a tone better suited to the May 19th organization and marked a shift in what the FALN primarily stood for. Suddenly, they appeared as a broader movement aligned with a Marxist revolutionary stage.

Meanwhile, known members of the Brink's—supporting Republic of New Afrika and their leader Coltrane Chimurenga—fell under surveillance by Agent Dave Mitchell, Detective Jimmy Haefner, and others during an expanding investigation. Mitchell and Charlie Minch worked closely with Assistant United States Attorney (AUSA) Kenneth Roth to get authority to bug a telephone in one of their well-protected RNA safe house in the city and as far north as New Haven, Connecticut.

Via current intel, we knew the group was close to an operation, but even with a wealth of warning signs it was a real test trying to convince the legal system that *preventing* a violent crime was better than picking up the pieces afterward.

"When Nyack occurred," Mitchell said, "it wasn't like we were asleep at the switch, but due to the controversy surrounding COINTELPRO and the post-Watergate Church Committee, extremely aggressive restrictions were placed on the FBI, rules that extremely hampered our ability to piece this all together."

Mitchell was spot-on and our adversaries knew it, which was one of the reasons they sometimes splintered into groups like the Republic of New Afrika, or RNA, and the New Afrikan Freedom Fighters, or

NAFF. It was a clever ploy that divided our resources and turned what could have been approved evidence gathering into a deeply controversial and legally shaky investigation of a group that, while affiliated with a known criminal enterprise, hadn't yet done anything.

Fortunately for us, the New Afrikan group had already been involved in violent brushes with the authorities, and once we had the group under wiretap, we discovered that our fears about the RNA's present activities were well founded. They had weapons and were indeed days from conducting an armored truck robbery. More chilling, one of our microphones picked up a rehearsal for the robbery during which Coltrane Chimurenga himself allegedly instructed his operatives on where and when to shoot their victims.

"Always when you, when you say freeze, you're pointing directly, talking about a kill shot, not at his head, because you might miss it." He added, "Got to shoot. *Poom, poom, poom, poom, poom.* You got to shoot. You gonna have to shoot.... Doing like this. This is the biggest area, all this is kill area, all that's kill area. Two shots, dead."[98]

***

A hot, late summer blazed over the city and set records with thermometers bursting well into the nineties. Nowhere was it hotter than behind the scenes of the Brink's investigation as the trial of Donald Weems neared a crescendo.

With our forward progress riding on the verdict, it was make or break. Meanwhile, with the help of the New York FBI and NYPD, we moved on several safe houses, and on September 11, of all days, just two days before the Weems trial ended, FBI agents raided the five known RNA safe houses and made several stunning discoveries.

Various members of the terrorist network were largely without criminal records. Just like the members of the Melville-Jackson United Freedom Front group, they were "successful black middle-class men

---

[98] Lubasch, Arnold H. "A Rehearsal for a 'Stickup': Tape Linked to Brink's Case." *New York Times*, June 27, 1985.

and women." Yet, "a search of the residences uncovered several handguns, an Uzi submachine gun, bulletproof vests, two bombs, sawed-off shotguns, prison guard uniforms, and assorted false identification papers."[99]

One of the captured suspects was Howard L. Bonds who, after talking with Detective Jimmy Cassidy, quickly turned state's evidence and became the key to bringing the rest to trial on weapons charges and conspiracy.

Another staggering find was the hint of a connection between Coltrane Chimurenga and a highly secretive and ghost-like arms dealer named Edward Ransom. According to the FBI's David Mitchell, Ransom had interacted with Chimurenga's group often, helping Bonds and others get bulletproof vests and other items from amenable police supply stores. At one such store, in fact, Law Enforcement Associates in New Jersey, an employee identified Ransom as the man who purchased bulletproof vests for his "nightclub security business."

Later, the FBI traced the address of the fictitious security agency to Ransom's own home address. Through his ties to Ransom, Chimurenga seemed to have amassed a sizable gun collection of his own. Weapons linked to him later turned up in all sorts of places, most notably in the possession of Marilyn Jean Buck.[100]

---

[99] Smith, Brent L. *Terrorism in America: Pipe Bombs and Pipe Dreams.* Albany, New York: State University of New York Press, 1994, p. 108.

[100] Larsen, Jonathan Z. "Son of Brink's? A Case of Terrorism or Talk." *New York Magazine*, May 6, 1985, p. 54.

◤ THE WALLS HAD EARS

David Mitchell and Charlie Minch found the members of Chimurenga's group to be highly skilled at countersurveillance, "going in and out of restaurants, circling blocks while driving, and other methods employed by espionage agents trying to discover a tail."

To make the job still more challenging, "Safe Houses were used and discarded and through meticulous effort, wiped inch by inch of fingerprints and other evidence. Names were changed frequently, phones were constantly juggled," and still "there was more. Agents of the JTTF, observed Chimurenga following a Brink's truck in Manhattan...and learned that Chimurenga and his group had inquired about flight rates and also if [helicopters] could be used in human rescue operations without tipping over."[101] As far as we could tell, the RNA was likely planning a breakout of our Brink's defendants who were about to go on trial.

As fall 1982 chilled into winter, the JTTF and US Attorney's Office fell under siege preparing for the next Brink's grand jury aimed directly at cornering Mutulu Shakur. It was an extremely sensitive and precarious legal endeavor, one that had us attempting to box in Shakur through his inner circle. The result was a court proceeding that would prove extremely problematic for law enforcement and reveal the mosaic of difficulties that clouded the prosecution of politically affiliated groups.

---

[101] Larsen, Jonathan Z. "Son of Brink's? A Case of Terrorism or Talk." *New York Magazine*, May 6, 1985, pp. 56–57.

As an example, in the previous year ten FALN members had been captured in Evanston, Illinois. After the arrest, all ten defendants refused to give their names, and several of the group declared themselves "prisoners of war." Rather than stand trial, they demanded an international tribunal. To back up their position, they asserted that they were being held by a colonial power—one that had seized control of their homeland, Puerto Rico.

One of those FALN defendants, Elizam Escobar, seemed to acquiesce on the issue of guilt regarding many of the group's activities but took special issue with AUSA Jeremy Margolis's use of seditious conspiracy as a prosecutorial approach based on Puerto Rico's status as a colony.[102]

The charge of seditious conspiracy had not been used for years and, in general, referred to activities designed as part of a plan to overthrow the US government. The defendants were also all accused of bombings, kidnappings, and related weapons charges, all of which carried severe and lengthy sentences. So while aspects of Escobar's argument might to him have carried some legal merit, defense attorneys on the FALN side of the table were using these maneuvers for the clouding effect they had on indicting and prosecuting these brazen and deadly political groups.

More important, perhaps, was the effect their position had on the press.

As the case and trials stretched into the following year, and after more deadly bombings occurred, much of the press at the time began to refer to group members and defendants as advocates for Puerto Rican independence. This distinction might be used to justify any anti-American interest, but in terms of my job and the work of the JTTF—to prevent bombs and bullets from flying around our streets—it was our task to protect our citizens and society.

---

[102] Torres, Andres, and Velazquez, José Emiliano. *The Puerto Rican Movement: Voices from the Diaspora*. Philadelphia, Pennsylvania: Temple University Press, 1998, pp. 237–240.

This mission had been especially prominent during the FALN trial the previous February, where the very courthouse itself was threatened with bombing.

In that trial the defendants again took the position that US national law was illegitimate in an international dispute. Yet none of it washed with judge or jury, as Puerto Rico was United States territory, and it was US citizens who had been threatened and killed. During his closing remarks, Assistant US Attorney Jeremy Margolis used a large defense table to great effect, covering the space with seized guns, dynamite, improvised explosives, and ammunition, along with "boxes full of communiques purportedly outlining FALN plans to kidnap prominent Americans and bomb public buildings as part of an effort to gain independence for Puerto Rico."[103]

***

During our early investigation after the Brink's robbery, we focused our attention on an East Orange safe house that had been rented by Marilyn Jean Buck, used by Joanne Chesimard during her hiding.

Before working alongside the Joint Terrorism Task Force, FBI agent Ed Petersen was on the case of murdered State Trooper Werner Forrester, and it was Ed who got the warrant to search the East Orange house. As the FBI closed in, Chesimard was apparently stuffed in the back of a Lincoln Continental and raced to another safe house in Pittsburgh.

Thankfully, her hasty exit left behind a wealth of information including "pages of the FALN bomb building instructional 'In This We Trust,' which had only been found previously in the bomb factory of William Morales...."[104] It was Brink's and the FALN in close proximity.

---

[103] Special to the *NY Times*. "10 Convicted in Chicago F.A.L.N. Trial." *New York Times*. February 12, 1981.
[104] Ibid.

Then we had to constantly maneuver difficult legal territory. Even during the pretrial grand jury proceedings for Brink's, the stakes were upped considerably by the presence of famed defense counsel William M. Kunstler, an imposing legal figure straight out of the radical '60s movements. The man who had once defended Dr. Martin Luther King Jr., Kunstler began laying precedent for a very theatrical defense and, alongside co-counsel Susan Tipograph, tried every angle to derail the trial, even asserting that the FBI's wiretaps were illegal and unconstitutional.

It was a clear salvo aimed to damage the entire proceeding by tying it to the FBI's controversial counterintelligence program (COINTELPRO) despite the fact that COINTELPRO operations had ceased in 1971.[105] Kunstler and team knew it was a reach, but they weren't merely going for legalities, they were also posturing for sensational headlines to cloud the issue and slow us down.

Since many of the members on trial during Brink's were surveilled in the late '60s and early '70s, while COINTELPRO was still in force, Kunstler and Tipograph argued that any FBI intel and personnel were tainted by the program. The eminently capable Patricia Williams, who was assistant United States attorney for the Southern District of New York, had her hands full and, when Kunstler used COINTELPRO as the brush by which to paint the entire Brink's grand jury, the case was in serious peril.

Defense counsel Susan Tipograph had also defended FALN bomber Willie Morales at his 1979 trial, and it was Tipograph who spearheaded the legal maneuvers that got Morales transferred from the Metro Detention Center to the much less secure Bellevue Hospital. Just two days later FALN member Luis Rosado rented an apartment overlooking the ward. Tipograph then suddenly began visiting Morales regularly, and during those visits she began complaining vehemently about searches of her bags and person.

Tipograph was the last one to see Morales, just two days prior to his using a pair of smuggled bolt cutters to tear through his ward

---

[105] COINTELPRO. FBI Records: The Vault. fbi.gov. Web, December 26, 2018.

window and be whisked away by waiting FALN operatives.[106] As a result, during the Brink's trial we had good reason to keep an eye on the defense team behind the scenes, outside of the courtroom.

During the grand jury before the Brink's trial, Kunstler and Tipograph petitioned the court to move all the defendants to the same holding at the Bronx Courthouse. We worried that a breakout might be in the works. It was, after all, eerily similar to how Joanne Chesimard had broken out of jail in New Jersey, so we quickly put the entire Bronx Courthouse under surveillance. For my own part, I took a police-band radio home with me at night and tuned it to the JTTF band.

A few nights before the grand jury proceedings, our surveillance teams began to note a few troubling things falling into place. First, there was construction outside the courthouse, which resulted in holes in the ground and, potentially, hidden access. Then one particular night, our personnel noticed a couple of known FALN assets popping up out of subways or strolling past on foot. Resources were needed, so I placed a call to the nearby 4-4 detective squad and asked the detectives who were on duty to stay on overtime. I also gave them the ominous directive to make a stop at the borough office, grab some shotguns, and stand by.

Then I alerted Ken Walton and Gary Gardner, a battle-tested Vietnam vet and former Army Ranger who had been brought in to replace Barry Mawn after he was promoted to head the Boston FBI office. That was all part of the deadly dance. New suspects at every turn and changes in the Task Force at the same time. We couldn't miss a beat—and thankfully, we didn't.

No breakout occurred, and though we never knew for certain if anything had been planned, with all the telltale signs in place, we couldn't take the chance. It might have simply been a ploy to get us to burn our own agents. Then again, we might have averted a tragedy.

It wasn't over, of course.

---

[106] Weiss, Murray. "Terror-Nest Twist—Lynne's Att'y Suspect in Bomber's Escape." *New York Post*, April 11, 2002.

As the sun rose, I dressed for a better day knowing there had been no breakout. Unfortunately, politics and departmental ego reared their ugly heads, and I got a heated call from a chief down at headquarters.

"Just who in the hell do you think you are?" he thundered. "You got detectives on overtime and you're taking shotguns from the Bronx detective borough." Stinging from the rebuke, I placed a call to Chief of Operations Pat Murphy, and when he heard the tale, he assured me the matter would be addressed.

That was the least of my worries.

ONE STEP FORWARD, TWO STEPS BACK

By all accounts, the coming year looked like it was going to be a good one for us, and as the holidays neared, I was planning to enjoy some time with friends and family—or so I hoped.

On the night of December 16, two bombs exploded simultaneously outside Manhattan, one at the IBM corporate offices in Harrison, New York, and the other at the Elmont, New York, offices of South African Airways. A caller warned of the explosions but did not credit any particular organization. Both devices caused extensive damage. Just as often occurs today, several groups then took credit for the attacks, hoping to get their names and causes into the news.

Initially we suspected the FALN for both devices, as well as the Banker's Trust device from September, and after analysis of bomb debris found at the scene of the Banker's Trust blast, we definitively tied that device to them.

Bomb identification was grueling and detailed work, sifting through debris and damage for tiny fragments of materials, detonators, and wires. Each bomb factory had a kind of brand—the FALN, the JDL, and Omega 7—all had unique assembly and makeup. In each case we found ways to "fingerprint" a bombing, and while that was, again, "after the fact," the evidence proved critical at later trials. Of course, more bombs were on the way.

The next rumble occurred after the bombings at the IBM facility and South African Airways offices. That's when we realized that the United Freedom Front, or UFF, had arrived in our city. The group, which had been formed two years prior, claimed responsibility for ten bombings in all and targeted both military and corporate facilities.

Members of the UFF emerged as belonging to other '60s and '70s radical groups. Some of them were wanted in connection with murders, attempted murders, and bank robberies from Virginia to Connecticut. Others were wanted for the December 1981 murder of a New Jersey state trooper, for example, and the attempted murder of two Massachusetts state policemen in February 1982.

The UFF organization was eerily similar to the Brink's crew that included former BLA, Black Panthers, and May 19th members, only their communiqués were more politically precise, decrying "American Imperialism, exploitation, and/or militarism in Central America, [as well as] protesting South African apartheid policies."[107]

We later discovered that the United Freedom Front also had deep roots in a previous form, the Massachusetts-based Melville-Jackson group, which had taken credit for multiple bombings from April 1976 to February 1979. The Melville-Jackson Unit took its name from two radicals, Mr. Melville, who was killed in the 1971 uprising at Attica state prison, and Mr. Jackson, who was shot to death while trying to kidnap a judge.

The Boston FBI was already on their tail from the February attack on Massachusetts police, but here at the end of the year nobody had put the two events together. Regardless, with a new terrorist group operating in the city, the JTTF settled in for a wild ride.

Then, the big quake hit.

---

[107] "United Freedom Front (UFF)." Military. globalsecurity.org.

PART SEVEN

WALLED IN

NEW YEAR'S EVE

It was around 9:30 p.m. on New Year's Eve, and Joan and I had just arrived at a party. I was just raising a beer to my lips in fact, when the first three bombs went off. Within minutes the coordinated attacks were followed by a phone call.

It was my daughter Joanne. "The office is trying to reach you and said you should call back immediately."

I called from the party and got a quick update. Then I kissed Joan on the cheek and rushed out. The Task Force, city, and country had faced plenty of danger over the previous year, but this was a telling escalation—a brazen reminder that along with a new year, deadlier adversaries were on the way.

Arriving at the scene of the bombings and seeing the aftermath, the carnage and chaos, I stopped cold. Colleagues had been blown up and careers ended. Emergency vehicles were everywhere; their lights strobing over the surrounding city. My whole career, those lights had been a signal that help had arrived or was on the way. That night, they blinded me.

Were we up to this? Were we ready?

Were we already too far behind?

***

The first device, which was made from several sticks of dynamite, detonated outside 26 Federal Plaza at 9:27 p.m. and shattered the windows on three floors. Thankfully no one was injured, but only twenty-eight minutes later, a second device tore through the facade

275

of 1 Police Plaza, nearly severing the right leg of Police Officer Rocco Pascarella. Upon hearing the first blast, he had gone to check on what looked like a discarded box of Kentucky Fried Chicken, and it exploded.

Just five minutes later, Cadman Plaza—the location of the United States District Courthouse—was rocked by a third device. It too blew out windows but, as in the case of the 26 Federal Plaza device, caused no injuries. As this was unfolding, I was in my car and headed to 1 Police Plaza.

Then news reports came over my radio of a fourth explosion, which occurred at 10:45 p.m. outside the Manhattan federal court and the offices of the United States Attorney for the Southern District. There were two bombs at that location, but only one detonated, doing so as bomb squad detectives approached. One of the men, a Brooklyn detective, lost all the fingers of his right hand and was partially blinded. His partner nearly lost an eye and suffered extensive burns. An anonymous call to WCBS Radio included the chilling information that the FALN was responsible.

The attacks not only shook the city, they shook the Joint Terrorism Task Force.

***

While the New Year's Eve attack urgently upped the need for the task force, it also called the into question the existence of the agency. Frantic calls from higher-ups—both city and federal—flooded in.

It's human nature to question and assign blame; just a look at the news and social media proves that. In bureaucracies, though, the acrimony can escalate as budgets are questioned and jobs are on the line. The top-down nature of such an organizational structure places higher-ups in the political and public crosshairs when chinks in the armor seem to appear.

Reactions and assertions ranged from, "I thought we had a terrorist task force!" to the more direct, "Why the fuck didn't you guys know about this?" and, "They're blowing up New York! What in hell are you guys doing about it?"

While understandable, it only slowed down our response.

Meanwhile, no matter where they were or what case they were on, task force personnel rushed to the city to pitch in. While some teams scoured for fragments, others like Jimmy Cassidy and Lenny Cross followed every lead imaginable, even taking to the nearby Metro Detention Center to interview guards and inmates who may have had a window seat for the targets.

In the JTTF offices, Ken Walton pulled me, Gary Gardner, and the entire available staff of agents and detectives into a Saturday morning, all-hands-on-deck meeting. He ran his hands through his usually coiffed hair.

"We're losing," he said flatly. The words fell on our collective shoulders like the weight of the world. In the moment it took me to hang my head, I saw the grim and painful internalizing sinking in around me. *What did I miss?* You could almost see the thoughts. *What hadn't I done?* After a few long moments, Walton shifted his gaze and took a breath and looked around the table from man to man. "What do you need?" He glanced at me and asked, "What could we do better?"

To a man, the response was the same: we needed a dedicated surveillance unit of our own. Our arrangement with Jim Kallstrom's Special Ops unit was great, but too often we got bumped by bigger fish in the Foreign Counter Intelligence caseload pond. Many times we'd be on the trail of targets and information, like guys trying to get into New York from Chicago, only getting bits and pieces of what we needed before losing both our surveillance and then our marks.

Vital pieces had been missed, and one critical bit of human intelligence had slipped through the cracks.

The critical tidbit came to us via a young Chicago policeman named John Eshoo, who just ten days before the attacks observed Edwin Cortes—a known FALN bomb maker—driving a car with New York plates. Eshoo saw Cortes in disguise and wearing a reversible jacket and then again later with the disguise missing and jacket reversed, heading home in his own car.[108]

As Chicago FBI Agent Rick Hahn recalled, "In subsequent meetings with Terjeson, Toro, and other key players in the JTTF, the New York license plate observed by Eshoo in Chicago just before the New Year's Eve bombings was brought up. The information about it had been lost in the shuffle of paperwork streaming through the [task force]. Terjeson made a point of digging it out and over the next few weeks would take the information to a positive conclusion. The vehicle was identified and determined to be registered in an alias used by fugitive Luis Rosado, now wanted for the New Year's Eve bombings."[109]

It was an early game changer and required that the dedicated people in both New York and Chicago be in close communication. In his book *American Terrorists*, Hahn indicated that there was a long-time disconnect between Chicago and New York. It was time to make that connection, and increased surveillance was the key.

For the next twenty days straight, fourteen, sixteen hours a day, we scrambled to move resources. During the early days after the bombings, I spoke with Jim Sullivan, who had given me a few headaches after my joining the task force. Sullivan did his best to help, but there was only so much he could do. As chief of detectives, his control of the NYPD Intelligence Division had been taken by the bureaucracy and moved out of the COD's sphere.

The department closed ranks, and it seemed that the Intelligence Unit might be made into a sacrificial lamb. I next sat down with Barney Mulligan and Deputy Inspector Don Morse of the NYPD's Bureau of Special Services and Investigations, or BOSSI, hoping that they might still be able to provide a good interim solution.

Unfortunately, both Mulligan and Morse worried that some of their guys on the street had been compromised by FALN. We needed

---

[108] Hahn, Richard S. *American Terrorist—The True Story of the FALN.* Seal Beach, California: R. Hahn & Company, Inc., 2011, p. 135.
[109] Ibid, p. 146.

to build a new unit of our own. Of course, FALN wasn't about to wait for us.

A major paradigm shift was in the offing.

According to the 2012 Homeland Security report, the FALN case began as a classic criminal investigation, which meant an after-the-fact reconstruction of events. That in and of itself, and in the time, wasn't a bad thing, but it vividly exposed the evolutionary step law enforcement needed to deal with the new threat of a deeply hidden and obtusely connected network of terror cells.

The entire makeup of the Joint Terrorism Task Force specifically, and anti-terror law enforcement in general, was laid bare. The milestones were there. Fraunces Tavern, bomb factories, explosions at corporate and government offices. In 1974 the FBI had come into the picture, yet things were still so disconnected that it took a seemingly random case involving the Evanston Police to capture those dozen FALN members in Evanston, Illinois.

It was still a case of catching the people responsible for what had happened, rather than preempting what was coming. Our focus had to shift from investigation to intelligence gathering.

The future of our entire effort depended on it.

Of that I was certain, more than ever.

That's not to say that the FALN operations hadn't had a profound effect on fighting terrorism. They did. In fact, the Fraunces Tavern bombing could be considered more of a foundational event than the establishment of Major Case Squad cooperation between the bureau and the department.

According to the Homeland Security report, "After receiving carte blanche from Headquarters, FBI Special Agent Jim Ingram, who was in charge of Foreign Intelligence and Internal Security in New York, created a new and bigger squad with the sole objective of solving the FALN bombings... [and] asked the NYPD to actively join the operation...melding the street savvy, fast-moving, hit-and-run approach of police work with the long-term, examine-everything-and-arrest-later view of the agents."[110]

Coupled with Hahn's outstanding work in Chicago, this led toward the final task force blueprint in many ways. But it was how those resources were used that mattered.

The early 1980s saw several potentially dangerous trends and developments, beginning in the '70s, and all converged just as the JTTF was evolving into existence. These excerpts from Richard Hahn's excellent book dovetails perfectly with my own views on this seminal moment in the history of counterterrorism:

> The 1970's were truly the coming of age of terrorism. Easy international travel, cheap telecommunication and world-wide media distribution all came together to empower any malcontent or opposition to a government to strike out on the world stage with acts of terror. The trade of terrorism was proliferated by governments, leading to many new groups who carried out their own actions for their own agendas. From the Philippines to Ireland, Croatia to Cuba, terrorism began to bloom. With its international community and the presence of offices of governments from around the world, New York was one of the places that conveniently served as a base of operations and a theater for terrorism.

---

[110] Belli, Roberta. *Effects and Effectiveness of Law Enforcement Intelligence Measures to Counter Homegrown Terrorism: A Case Study on the* Fuerzas Armadas de Liberación Nacional *(FALN), Final Report to the Science & Technology Directorate, U.S. Department of Homeland Security*. College Park, Maryland: START, 2012, pp. 11–14.

He then added ominously and pointedly:

> The New York of the 1980's was a far cry from
> the New York of 1974 when the FALN had started
> its campaign of bombing. Terrorists of all bent
> had learned that New York not only had targets
> they could readily attack, but more significantly
> that attacks in New York made world-wide press,
> garnering desperately sought attention for their
> cause. Terrorists of nearly every type acted out in
> the streets of New York.[111]

We saw it all play out. From the antiestablishment groups of the 1960s and domestic terror groups of the 1970s, this brewing storm was fueled by the international networks that led from the PLO's involvement in the terror murders at the 1972 Munich Olympic Games, right to the New York City and Black September/PLO affiliated bombings in 1973.

We had Croatian Separatists, the JDL, and Omega 7. State-sponsored attack in DC in 1976. As Neil Herman had said, it was a new world and a new battleground and, "We began to realize over the years that domestic and international terrorism cases were completely unique. They were over in an instant, with no lingering crime. The evidence blew up and the people responsible always quickly vanished into the woodwork."

Even more unwieldy were the logistics of working with counterparts overseas in Puerto Rico and other countries. The legal hurdles were monumental. At the time Neil was on the Croatian case, but with the FBI office in New Rochelle. Soon he would become heavily involved with the task force, but for the moment we were scrambling to catch up to our ever-larger FALN challenge.

---

[111] Hahn, Richard S. *American Terrorists—The True Story of the FALN.* Seal Beach, California: R. Hahn & Company, Inc., 2011, p. 69.

Then the group struck again, thumbing their noses at us from behind the smoke of January 29 bombing of the FBI office on Staten Island, a building that also included a public post office and recruiting facilities for the United States Navy and Air Force.

The explosive device was left in a second-floor women's bathroom and went off in the early morning hours, causing no injuries. According to my old friend Len Buder, just hours after the blast, an anonymous caller telephoned United Press International in New York and claimed responsibility in the name of the Revolutionary Fighting Group, though authorities at the time said they knew of no organization by that name.

We knew, of course, that the Revolutionary Fighting Group was an arm of the FALN, but with apologies to Len Buder, it made our lives far easier not alerting our adversaries to the fact that we had that information.

The Revolutionary Fighting Group was meant to look like an aligned organization but not connected. We were sniffing ever closer to FALN, so they needed another group to promote the agenda in the public consciousness without risking further exposure to the main organization.

It appeared as if the RFG was tasked with bombing targets late at night, trying hard to avert death and claim as much public relations high ground as possible. Meanwhile, the very same people were ordering the "below ground" activities of the FALN, often including bank robberies, targeted assassinations, prison breaks, and drug deals to fund further activities.

As the 1980s developed, all the eddies and currents of the modern world we know today converged on the ideological battlefront of a new warfare. The Cold War space race with the Soviets had brought us technology. Telecommunication and computer advances then amplified the abilities of foreign governments to better direct activities on American soil.

Evolving tradecraft and the public battleground public opinion caused the game of cat and mouse to become a complex web. We entered a new era, and immediately were playing catch up—though thanks to some fine work out of Chicago and New York, various factors were coming together.

Some of them, bomb fragments.

Recall that one of the FALN New Year's Eve bombs was disarmed by the bomb squad expert Charlie Wells. The explosive was a Hercules brand with a unique date/shift code and "was identified as part of a cache stolen from the Bland Construction Company, located just outside of Austin, Texas... [on] March 3, 1980."[112] The date/shift code referred to the specific timing of the explosive's manufacture, right down to the crew shift responsible. It was like a fingerprint, and through it the stolen dynamite was matched to explosives with the same date and shift found in the home of spring 1982 Nanuet robbery participant Edward Joseph, who had ties to Joanne Chesimard and the group behind Brink's.

It wasn't just a network.

It was a well-trained and formidable organization, one able to lock up their grand jury proceeding over the increasingly political angle of the case, with defendants using their political affiliations as reason to decline testimony. The judge at the time allowed it, which in turn paved the way for the bashing of the FBI and the inference of COINTELPRO. All in all, our ability to bring the Brink's case to trial was undermined.

The FALN followed suit and applied the same game plan. During that grand jury, and after a particularly ugly day of defense protests and motions, lead prosecutor for Eastern District, Jim Harmon pulled everybody aside.

"We gotta do something different," he lamented. "We need somebody on the stand that's not vulnerable to this constant FBI bashing." Then, he looked straight at me.

"You're the guy."

---

[112] Hahn, Richard S. *American Terrorists—The True Story of the FALN.* Seal Beach, California: R. Hahn & Company, Inc., 2011, p. 223.

***

The very next day, I sat in that grand jury and went over the information we had gathered on the FALN investigation. I was the new guy, briefed sure, but in the eyes of that judge and grand jury, was I the guy familiar with every political nuance of the case?

Not remotely.

What I did have, however, was a far lesser connection to the FBI than a career agent. Therefore, I couldn't be so easily painted with the COINTELPRO brush.

Their strategy thwarted, the FALN defendants then refused to testify without valid grounds and were found in contempt.

We were making progress, but...

DAYS OF DOUBT

After the New Year's Eve attack, the city still seemed to be closing in around us, and morale inside the JTTF was at a low point. On any given day, we'd have a May 19th group in a park and alongside known BLA members doing practice maneuvers for what we didn't know. We had JDL bombs going off and Brink's suspects on the loose and the FALN attacking us directly, with no clear picture of their organization. These groups were planning jail breaks and bombings and bank robberies.

The key was resources and surveillance. All remaining walls had to come down and come down fast.

Walton pressed the FBI to help train and fund the unit, and I asked the NYPD to do the same. Light finally began to appear during a breakfast meeting attended by Ken Walton, FBI Director William Webster, Gary Gardner, and me.

At that meeting FBI boss William Webster officially signed off on the FBI's portion of our dedicated surveillance unit. Almost as quickly, Commissioner Bob McGuire and Pat Murphy stepped up and agreed to foot the NYPD's share, as well. People often ask me if these accomplishments and developments made me happy or if I felt pride. Maybe, but what I remember of my own reaction at the time, others have shared as a similar experience. We were gratified to be supported and, in most cases, grimly determined to do more. In short, the moment was only as big as the task ahead.

And we had our marching orders.

Both the department and Bureau ponied up without even really talking to each other. Commissioner McGuire basically afforded me carte blanche on staffing from the NYPD side, meaning I could take guys from anywhere. It was unheard-of, and I took the opportunity and ran with it.

I found guys that were frogmen, undercover guys, you name it. If we could use them, we got them. Only problem was that none of them knew the true scope of intelligence work, relative to the highly honed skills and training of our adversaries. This was going to take time—time that we might not have.

Jim Kallstrom's Special Ops unit came to the rescue again and offered to train our new recruits at Camp Smith in Westchester County, right alongside the FBI's own foreign counterintelligence classes. It was another example of evolutionary and revolutionary cooperation, but it was going to take more men than the task force had available.

One of my next calls was to the citywide Anti-Crime Unit and Inspector Rose. The men and women of the unit were proactive and, in terms of surveillance, ahead of the game. They were the perfect makeup, go-getters, and when I requested fifteen to eighteen of the unit's best, Rose was on board. We both knew of the relative obscurity under which anti-crime people operated, and the opportunity was amazing for them.

It was the perfect start.

I then began calling around to all the precincts where I'd worked and where I knew great leaders and administrators. Thankfully, I got some excellent recommendations but was barely halfway to filling the needed spots.

Detective Sergeant John Loughran from Manhattan Robbery was one of my first personal recruits. Next I called my old conditions car partner Hank Buck, who'd gone back to the Army to bone up on intelligence work and in school studied counterterrorism. When I called, he was ensconced behind a desk at the NYPD's mostly cushy Midtown North precinct, wishing for a challenge, and was going pretty stir-crazy. I remember the call to him like it was yesterday.

"Buck," I said as if we were still in the 2-0, "I need a sergeant and got a spot for you in the task force."

"I'm still in uniform," Hank shot back incredulously, thinking he didn't have the proper departmental stripes. "How can you?"

"Have faith," I joked, knowing the police commissioner himself had given me the authority to tap anybody. "I can give absolution," I offered. "Just be here at Federal Plaza tomorrow morning, and I'll take care of the transfer."

In mere days, Buck and Loughran joined the surveillance unit and were absorbed into groups that we affectionately dubbed "the sneakers" and "the suits"—the detectives and the FBI agents respectively. Hank's education, police and military experience, and time at the academy as an instructor made him an instant fit. I quickly put him to work helping me identify recruits.

Buck had a significant role in training our sneakers.

Smack in the middle of this rush, Commissioner Bob McGuire called and informed me of my promotion to detective commander, which came with a nice raise and a heaping serving of politics. There was no public ceremony, just a private affair with friends and family in McGuire's office. Knowing the maneuvering involved, I called Chief of Detectives Jim Sullivan to see if thanks were in order. Instead, I found that he hadn't been told and wasn't particularly congratulatory.

It was bittersweet, as I had Jim Sullivan to thank as much as anybody for my position in the task force, having helped facilitate my command of the Manhattan Robbery Squad.

Jim Kallstrom was the key to the new squad, helping design and structure our entire training program and then with components of the FBI's Special Ops. He put together a dedicated group to bring us up to their speed, mixing NYPD and FBI people and then training them in techniques and skills many of them didn't yet possess. The new job required a lot more than just field expertise, technology, and surveillance training. The surveillance units needed fluency in legal methodology and evidence gathering, so that legally anything gathered was airtight and squeaky clean for state and federal prosecutions.

***

Kallstrom's grueling surveillance school was a crucible that provided incredible detail in espionage-level intelligence gathering, disguise, and countersurveillance. The men and women of the surveillance unit had to blend into the shadows, note everything: times, faces, plates down to the last detail.

"Some of these guys got so good, they could be a priest one minute and nun the next," Kallstrom observed. The work was methodical, meticulous, monotonous, and often seemed endless. Endurance, focus, perseverance, and dedication were the words of the day. We needed lookouts and networks of tightly choreographed surveillance teams, men and women, who could change looks and locations on a dime. We had to secure stakeout apartments, place lookouts on towers and in the belfries of churches. The job was twenty-four-seven and holidays.

"A lot of times, I had to go away from home for weeks," Elmer Toro noted, "and couldn't tell my family where I was and what I was doing. In reality, we had to do what our adversaries did—stay away from any routine, alter our routes and times, and do everything in a seemingly random manner so we couldn't be predicted."

Morale was particularly important as the job presented what could become crushing anonymity and isolation. These agents got no press coverage and only esprit de corps and camaraderie held it all together. Team and managerial leadership were critical, as appreciation from within could make the difference.

A lot of the time, our offices had the only equipment of its kind in the country. That meant that in the field, we often had to bring our own equipment and rely entirely on our own people, as other jurisdictions just didn't have the same tools and expertise.

The logistics were monumental.

***

By early February, it started to come together, and some truly great agents and detectives were added into the task force; though with the groups we were facing still so well hidden and uncertain, how many would be enough?

One of these new sneakers, as it were, was a guy who even today, prefers history recall him only as "Green One." He knew both brother Tom and Danny Lenahan, and as a young cop had cut his teeth in the dangerous world of undercover narcotics. Green One always looked younger than his years, and his undercover narcotics work usually brought him the role of student or area teen, the guy who infiltrated high schools to make drug buys and take down local dealers selling to kids.

Dealers, mind you, took snitches as badly as they did undercover cops and would show little hesitation in beating up or killing a betrayer of either kind.

Another early standout was Athelson "Kelly" Kelson, a highly decorated Vietnam vet who toured with the battle-tested 11 Bravo Company of the 506th Airborne. Vietnam had been a fire that forged Kelly into a tough, undercover cop, but it would take years before he got to me and the JTTF. Upon his return from war, Kelson worked with the Postal Inspector's Office and then in 1973 joined the NYPD.

In '75, when the city laid off a few thousand cops, Kelly found himself—along with so many others—forced into lesser-paying corrections jobs. Yet he had strengths and experience that most cops took years to acquire. He'd done security and inspection work, and lived through the hair-trigger intensity of war.

"They train you how to stay strong, fight and kill, but they don't train you how to shut it off when you come home," he said. Seeking the familiar pressure of combat, undercover police work and the uncertain life of an undercover narcotics detective called to him. In that pressure-filled role, Kelson stood out and quickly worked his way onto Major Cases.

He had the perfect makeup for the surveillance unit. The only problem was that I had no idea he was out there or available to me. He solved that problem on his own, cold-calling me until I brought him in.

I next looked to the 2-8 Precinct, where old partner and now Sergeant Jerry Gorman was stationed. I got a few great guys from the 2-8 and a real surprise from my past when Gorman suggested this young cop as perfect for the surveillance unit. Described as "a real go-getter, always on the job and doing it all," Jerry was talking about Willie Kennelly, a kid I'd coached in CYO basketball. Thinking back to my coaching time, I remembered how Kennelly used to talk to me about police work, and now, years later, here he was, only two years in the department and already rising to the top.

It took some prying to get him, though, as the humble Kennelly was unsure of what—if anything—he could bring to the task force. Fortunately for us, he had some very personal reasons for finally taking the job. He had worked with the police in Nyack and knew both Edward O'Grady and Waverly Brown, the men killed in the Brink's robbery. This would be his chance to help bring their killers to justice.

Recently Willie recalled how amazing it felt to be welcomed to the JTTF and be part of such a groundbreaking effort. Kennelly was in one of the first groups sent to Camp Smith for training alongside the federal counterintelligence guys. There, he learned how they operated every moment of every day, as if they were under surveillance.

Much like the international spies and terrorists of today.

THE SNEAKERS AND THE SUITS

Not only did our guys have to learn all these so called "dry-cleaning" tactics, but because we didn't yet possess encrypted communications, they had to absorb innumerable codes needed to talk securely. Codes that changed daily.

That may have been our biggest logistical headache, to be sure, and as a precaution we couldn't ever allow our guys in the sneakers division to interact with us at 26 Federal Plaza. They had their own base and their own elaborate ritual of dry-cleaning. Except under the most extreme and secretive circumstances, they were on their own.

Hank Buck noted a major challenge that grew out of the foxhole and secretive unit mentality. As new teams came together and the walls of different training, background, and territory fell away, guys got distracted by their growing friendships. Some got too chummy on surveillance, which was a recipe for mistakes, lost targets, and dead agents.

It was Hank's job to identify this early on, then counsel or break up those guys or find better pairings. Hank also helped with diversity, which was important to the department and to me personally. It was also critical to our surveillance capability. We were trying to prevent attacks from Black Panthers, BLA, Weather Underground, and more, meaning a patchwork of ethnicities and backgrounds.

Our new units needed to reflect the same diversity.

As you might imagine, the police force in 1983 New York was decidedly white, and the FBI almost entirely so. Until we reached full staffing, whatever that would be, we needed not just dozens of new detectives, but new police officers and FBI agents. Wherever they came from, they had to be quickly and completely familiar with every inch of the city and be able to change directions, clothes, and locations—sometimes hourly.

None of this would have been possible without the help and support of FBI Agent Paul Philip, who among his many roles and accomplishments, served as assistant director in charge of FBI training worldwide and as special agent in charge of the Miami and San Juan, Puerto Rico, field divisions. As an African American, Philip helped lead the charge to recruit more minorities. We also recruited gay and lesbian cops, breaking down every barrier and evolving the job. We operated without bias and without the politics of the day, and I'm extremely proud to say that we pulled it off.

For example, when I needed Asian representation for surveillance, I got exactly what I needed in Chinatown. After I pulled up to two well-regarded officers, handed them my card and asked them to come to 26 Federal Plaza for interviews. They were thrilled by the opportunity and took the jobs that were offered.

It was a wonderful and transformative time to be in law enforcement—though for our adversaries, not so much. When one of the Chinatown officers, now a detective in the task force, appeared in court to prosecute a weapons-buy case, a stunned suspect commented, "My God, they are an equal opportunity employer!"

That wasn't even half of it. We also needed a lot of new people just to cover our surveillance needs. If one of our targets looked around and even remotely suspected or "made" one of our sneakers, another sneaker needed to be ten steps away to pick up the trail.

The only effective way our team members could learn to be excellent intelligence operatives was by real-world practice—the very same activity that could get somebody killed. To address that potentiality, Walton, Gardner, and I had to be very careful about whom we approved and why. Eventually, we ended up with such a diverse group that I joked to Walton, we had everything but an Eskimo.

"I've got one on order," I assured him.

The street unit was key for tracking the network of bomb makers, and terrorist couriers eschewed cars. They preferred walking and public transportation, both of which were conducive to dry-cleaning. They even avoided air travel when possible, to stay off flight manifests and the need to deal with false identification and airport security.

Therefore, partnering with the New York City Transit Police became paramount to us. We needed their expertise in the subways, so I made a call to transit head Chief Jim Meehan and asked to meet.

"Jim," I said over lunch, "I need five of your best people." I wanted a top transit cop on each unit, so we would have an insider who knew the hidden ways to move through the city. Meehan was receptive, and his people proved so valuable that a month later I asked Jim for three more.

Teaming with Transit also gave us access to what was called the "gold phone," which allowed us to stop and hold any train in order to disrupt or delay marks we were following. We used this new tool to preempt terrorist operations, divert and slow couriers, anything to disrupt without actually revealing our presence.

It was a deadly serious game, since we might inadvertently cause an accident, put a sneaker in danger, or facilitate an escape. At one point, a nearby bank was robbed right while we were trying to stop a target group from pulling off the same kind of heist at another institution. When we moved our team in, we found it wasn't our bank—or our targets. Life in the big city was pretty complicated like that.

As you might guess by the designation for Green One, we coded our teams by color. Every morning, we had a two-part meeting, us at 26 Federal Plaza and the sneakers at one of their off-site locations. The only point of contact was John Loughran, acting as liaison.

Some of the issues we faced in the early days involved career paths. There were levels to reach in the NYPD—shields, promotions, and opportunities. We needed rewards for the guys in the unit. For the transit guys, we made sure they got grades and shields, and we tried to build in rewards for FBI agents that would mirror their NYPD counterparts.

***

With the FALN and Omega 7, it was a grueling race against time on an immense and ever-expanding obstacle course. As Neil Herman described, "Surveillance on the FALN and groups like them, was a monumental task. The organization and those like it, were generational and you (even as an individual case agent) had to understand their thought process and longer-term goals. You had to immerse yourself, not just track and watch."

Another challenge we faced was the view from outside. The public *and* the department had a very short memory. Causes shifted with the headlines, and politicians came and went with their own agendas. How could we consistently fight twenty-plus years of ideology, when our leaders and the prevailing political motivations changed every two to four years?

We had plenty of hits and misses.

Early in 1983, for example, some Chicago sneakers "made" a known courier at O'Hare Airport and observed him heading to a flight to New York's LaGuardia. This was perfect, since a flight was the easiest way to track a target. The sneakers on the case contacted headquarters and gave us a full description, but Chicago was stretched thin and couldn't get an asset on the plane. So as soon the plane's hatch was closed, they effectively passed the job to us. Red flags and questions were everywhere.

Why's this guy coming?

Who's he going to meet with?

What are they planning?

What if we lose him?

We took solace in the fact that that he was trapped on a plane, but sometimes a target was so good at disguise, they seemingly vanished. Such was the case here. While on the plane, our courier changed clothes and emerged from the flight dressed as a woman, so we followed the wrong guy out into the terminal.

Remember, even with Freddie Mendez providing us information on tactics and structure, we only had bits and pieces.

As potentially disastrous as these near misses could be, they were still opportunities that taught us to be more adept. We soon started to see more pieces of it and fully grasp the massive scope of what we faced.

We'd be on this one "ball" (target), doing all this dry-cleaning, and suddenly we'd see a new guy or gal whom we hadn't seen before. As a result, we made a new connection, discovered a new piece of the puzzle. Sometimes they were sleeper agents, used on rare occasions. Other times they were new players. It didn't matter. We had to log, track, and note it all.

Our surveillance teams would sell hotdogs, be homeless people, and act as Con Ed utility workers. Our targets *always* knew they were being watched, and we spent as much time hiding in plain sight as they did.

Just having our unit out there slowly began to alter or interrupt some of our opponents' plans. It also helped that the NYPD gave us surveillance taxis and cars reserved for NYC special ops, and the FBI kicked in with planes and helicopters and all the fancy toys. Most of these assets, however, could only be used once or twice and then had to be rotated or replaced, or our surveillance would be easily discovered.

In the early days there was little money for that, so before we were fully operational we sent out EMTs or fire departments units to areas where intel said a suspicious group might be casing a target for a bombing or an attack. We grabbed for anything we could—motorcycles, cabs, buses, you name it.

It was a deadly chess game on so many levels, involving different regions and states, some places we'd never yet set foot.

There was a "plus" through the constant shifting of teams. The moving of surveillance assets as the need required provided two immediate benefits. First, our surveillance teams picked up a *ton* of experience, which they were able to share. The second, and perhaps more significant, advantage was that by being rotated so frequently, our guys were harder to identify and track.

Field investigators, as well, were able to slide over to hot situations and leads. The increased experience and expertise there also brought in fresh perspectives, resulting in many investigative breakthroughs. The Joint Terrorism Task force was coming together and, more critically, coming to a life of its own.

THE PRICE OF INFORMATION

In mid-February 1983, an informant approached the JTTF's Sammy Perola with news of a robbery of guns and ammo in Marathon, Florida. Sammy was a well-connected cop in the system and had been Deputy Commissioner Pat Murphy's old radio car partner.

Between them, they knew everybody.

Sammy's contacts were legit, and his intel was top shelf. He was told that two males and one female suspect were en route to the Baltimore, Maryland, area and headed to the Bronx in a 1974 Chevrolet van with Florida tags. We knew the cache of stolen weapons might be headed into the arms of one of our domestic terror groups, so Perola notified Dan Lenahan.

Perola and Lenahan brought the situation to my attention. At face value, this wasn't entirely the purview of the task force, but with those weapons headed for a February 21 date with the Capri Whitestone Motel in the Bronx, and a potential Washington's Birthday arms deal, I placed a call to Chief of Detectives Jim Sullivan and asked his opinion. I figured Jim would steer me to the Burglary Squad or one of his guys, and they'd run with it, but he surprised me.

"That's your problem, not mine."

Taking that as a tacit go-ahead, I headed into Ken Walton's office and announced, "We got something going here." It seemed like it would be a great drill for us. Walton agreed and directed me to get Gary Gardner to plan logistics. While this unfolded, we asked Sammy Perola's informant to make contact with the group and position us as members of a terrorist organization interested in buying the goods.

When the suspects agreed to sell, we knew we were dealing with some very bad guys. Still, the possibility existed of a shootout with weapons traffickers. Gallows humor ensued with guys kidding me that the whole holiday operation was a play for overtime and extra pay. I'll admit, I wanted this operation. Looking back on it now, I suppose I may have jumped the gun a bit.

I set up a meeting with the precinct commander at the 4-5, gave him the full picture of what was about to go down, and got his logistical support for the area around the motel. I didn't want any surprises with who was going to be there and where they would be positioned.

Then after conferring with Supervising Special Agent Gary Gardner, I got the teams and equipment assembled, including a New York City Police helicopter to track suspects from above, and asked Gardner to ride shotgun in the copter, a job he'd done in Vietnam. He quickly agreed.

February 21 was a Monday, and at 7:50 a.m. we assembled at the 4-6 Precinct with bulletproof vests, visible shields, IDs, and guns at the ready. Gardner and I handed out assignments as we all looked over a floor pan of the motel and detail on the surrounding area. Team members were briefed on positions and manpower by Special Agent Jimmy Lyons and Detective Charlie Minch. We had little to go on except for the description of the van, and time and place of the deal.

We had one more bit of information, though, and it was the aspect of the situation that bothered me most. There was a partial ID on one of the participants. He was known as "Bongo" and, according to our informant, had a particular taste for guns and violence. Our plan was to not take chances and to box the van in as soon as it pulled into the lot, in order to get the situation under control as quickly as possible.

The element of surprise was our best weapon, though I ordered the team to take no action except by my direct order. With Gardner and the police helicopter dispatched to watch the van's approach to the city, we took off in five or six unmarked police vans, one containing Ken Maxwell and Detective Ken Cohen and the other, Sergeant Dan Lenahan and Special Agent Vincent Piazza.

The plan was to position the vans in spaces spread apart on the lot so they could move in from either side to box our target. Two more male and female teams of agents were assigned to unmarked vehicles, stationed at either end of the motel parking lot, with still more personnel stationed inside the motel to bar entry and serve as lookouts. Two marked NYPD patrol cars were on nearby perimeter assignment.

Sammy Perola drove me to the motel in an unmarked car and with Gardner and copter crew circling the Cross Bronx Expressway, we did one last check that everybody was in position and in radio contact. We then pulled our unmarked car onto a service road adjacent to the motel, where we had an unobstructed view of the entire scene.

February 21 presented us with a raw and frigid morning, barely twenty degrees under a gray sky and with gusty, biting winds. Sammy readied a shotgun, and I was armed with my service revolver. I hadn't used my gun all that much in my police career, outside of shooting up a car, but still I was calm, assured that we'd thought of everything and had the right team in place.

That calm was quickly tested, as around 11:00 a.m. Gary Gardner radioed that our target van was observed proceeding east on the Cross Bronx Expressway and exiting south onto the Hutchison River Parkway.

They were just blocks away.

Then as the blue Chevrolet van entered the motel lot, a focus came over me that I hadn't felt since my hallway dance with Teenager. I took a breath. It was my call, and as the blue van appeared and darted through my field of view, even at a distance it looked large and imposing. The vehicle moved slowly toward an empty parking space near the green unmarked police van occupied by Cohen and Maxwell, where it stopped briefly.

Suddenly it backed up.

I reached for my radio but held back as the van was then maneuvered into another open spot near the grass divider between the motel and the service road where Perola and I were positioned. The change gave me a very good look at our suspects, a white female driver, a white male front passenger, and another white male located between them.

As the van stopped in the space, I scanned the area for bystanders and those who might unknowingly walk into a potential line of fire. We were ready, we were clear, so I glanced at Sammy and keyed the radio.

"Take 'em."

The choreography went perfectly as both vans moved in to block the suspects, Maxwell and Cohen's van in front and Lenahan and Piazza's to the side. Sammy Perola and I raced into the lot and jumped out with guns drawn. As my feet hit the pavement, I heard the helicopter above as it moved low over the motel. From inside, Gardner started calling out over the loudspeaker, alerting the area of the police presence and commanding the trio in the van to surrender peacefully.

For me, time slowed.

There was the copter above and van in front, the task force guys moving in from all around. It all became one complete picture, and in the middle of it all, training took over and any possible consequences vanished.

Then, time just started again, like hitting play on a paused movie. The van abruptly lurched forward and rammed the one holding Maxwell and Cohen. Doors flew open, and I began bellowing.

"Police! Get out of the van with your hands up!"

The team around starting shouting with me as I crouched into firing position by the driver's side door. That's when I saw the male passenger by the window bring his arm up from out of sight. He had a gun, but instead of pointing it at me, he took aim through the front window, directly at Ken Maxwell and Ken Cohen. I saw at an angle and through the windshield that both of my guys were in the line of fire. Ken Maxwell raised his shotgun and started yelling.

"GUN! GUN!"

And "DROP THE GODDAMN GUN!"

Next thing I knew, bullets began flying as the suspect and Maxwell exchanged volleys through the van's front window.

As we discovered later, Bongo was that passenger, and he was as dangerous we had been forewarned. In the hail of bullets and buckshot, Ken Maxwell's shotgun nearly took off half of Bongo's face.

Bongo lurched back, grabbing at his own head and face. The guy in the middle dove toward the back of the van, where I could see a large suitcase of sorts, and I realized he was likely going for some heavy artillery.

He stopped after Sammy Perola emptied a couple of shotgun shells into the side of the van, between the guy and that case.

Shotgun blasts shattered the side windows of the van and sprayed my face with glass, which stunned me for a beat and, in that moment, the van was swallowed up by a sea of remaining task force personnel.

It was over just like that.

As the woman driver was pulled from the van, along with the other two, we found a Derringer handgun, a silver .25 caliber and a 9 millimeter, all within Bongo's reach.

Then looking into the back of the van, I saw it. The motherlode. That silver case was indeed full of deadly weapons, seventeen pistols in all, along with seventeen rifles and shotguns, twenty knives, and a canister of Chemical Mace. Later, after the press showed up, with his flair for the dramatic and former-reporter instincts, Ken Walton put a neat bow on it and deadpanned.

"They were supposed to meet us, only they did not know it."[113]

That afternoon after a debriefing, the group of us headed out for a celebratory drink. We celebrated three things. First, that the mission had succeeded and the guns were seized. Second, that nobody died. Ken Maxwell later said that it was the first time in his career that he had shot somebody. He got through it knowing that the choice ultimately came down to Bongo or himself and some of our guys.

Lucky for Bongo, too, we had Gary Gardner in the helicopter above and those two precinct cars moving in. Without the police

---

[113] Buder, Leonard. "3 Seized in Bronx Shootout in Police Ruse to Buy Arms." *New York Times*, February 22, 1983.

helicopter available for a medevac, Bongo would certainly have died from his wounds.

Last, we celebrated that the Joint Terrorism Task force's reputation was enhanced, and with it our ability to thwart future acts of terror. While we hoisted our drinks, the successful operation hit the airwaves, and the bar became hushed as a reporter came on screen to mention the great work of the JTTF.

Guys cheered and toasted.

It felt great.

***

The feeling didn't last though, as that evening the Bronx District Attorney's Office got involved and demanded that all law enforcement involved in the shootout appear in a grand jury the next day. That didn't sit well with me as our guys needed to decompress. They were shot at and had lots of other pressing duties in regard to the operation.

Proper justice and legal considerations aside, this was going to go according to a more human-based schedule, and not according to DA Mario Merola's media calendar, so I made a call to Ken Conboy, the former Manhattan ADA at the Rackets Bureau, now the NYPD deputy of Legal Matters. Conboy, as you may recall, was part of the Squitieri case and was very supportive of my desire to hold my guys back until more appropriate time.

It seemed to me that there might be political motivations coming out of Merola's office. The Bronx DA rather publicly made it clear that he felt the FBI wasn't being helpful enough with a high-profile case that involved a ranking government official in Washington. With politics trumping justice, and without voicing the true nature of my suspicions, I asked Conboy to intercede, and he helped delay the grand jury until a time that was more customary and appropriate.

Without a doubt guys would be grilled at that grand jury, questioned concerning every detail, especially Ken Maxwell for wounding Bongo. It was a near perfect operation and, as we call it in law enforcement, a "good shooting," if that's really a possible thing. But as the grand jury neared, we sensed the trouble brewing, exactly as you'd expect.

Each of the others in the blue van that day—the women driver and middle passenger—pleaded out. Entered a guilty plea in the hope of getting a reduced sentence. Only Bongo waited, and, sure enough, on the stand Kenny Maxwell got the brunt of it with defense attorneys asking him about the size and caliber of his weapon.

"A Remington shotgun," Ken replied.

The attorney for Bongo turned to the judge.

"And my client had a little .22."

Such was the way of law enforcement. We did our best to question every aspect of our own motives and actions, only to have them all thrown back at us later and in the most explosive and suggestive manner possible. We got through it, of course, but it left a bitter political taste in my mouth.

***

While this was going on, we had sneakers and suits in transit between New York and Fort Smith, Arkansas, where they were trained in counterintelligence by FBI Special Ops. Guys were also shuttled to Brooklyn's Floyd Bennett Field for training by local FBI.

The back and forth was frenetic and included the higher-ups. During the early part of 1983, Ken Walton, Gary Gardner, and I were hopping on and off planes to FBI Headquarters in Washington, DC, for meetings with Buck Revell, the assistant director in charge of criminal investigations (including terrorism). We met with Director Webster himself on several occasions, in both DC and New York. The ability to speak directly to leadership was unprecedented access and critical to our mission's success.

We also made a lot of trips to Los Angeles and Chicago to interface with our investigative counterparts.

TARGETS IN A BOX

Brink's informant Kamau Bayette, along with previously captured Republic of New Afrika insider Howard L. Bonds, began filling in an even larger picture for us by helping unravel the mystery of the New Afrikan Freedom Fighters, a more recent construct affiliated with the many groups behind Brink's.

Bayette's and Bonds' information pointed us to RNA leader Coltrane Chimurenga, a close friend and associate of BLA's Mutulu Shakur and by most accounts, the founder of the RNA According to Bayette and Bonds, the RNA was well organized and used the same tactics as their forbears, placing safe houses and headquarters in extremely insulated locales and planning brazen breakouts, most notably the rescue of Donald Weems (Kuwasi Balagoon) before his trial.

From initial telephone traffic gleaned via pin registers, case agents David Mitchell and Charlie Minch realized that the RNA was well along in operations, with supplies, weapons, and vehicles to accomplish an as-yet unidentified task. It all seemed to be approaching fast, and by late spring our dedicated surveillance unit was nearly up to speed.

We still struggled with the occasional washouts and motivation issues. Team leadership—the kind we found in Green One—proved critical to keeping guys focused on what mattered and why they were living months of their lives basically invisible.

To help focus the guys, I brought in two of the policemen who had been badly wounded in the New Year's Eve bombing, Police Officer Salvatore Pascarella and Detective Anthony Senft. Seeing cops in uniform, missing hands and fingers and blinded, allowed reality to sink in. This wasn't meant to be personal, mind you, but we wanted our guys to see that for our adversaries, it was *decidedly* so.

The surveillance tool was already a game changer, but in the task force some started wondering where their careers would go if the need for our organization began to wane. Therefore, it was extremely important to impart to the men and women of the unit that they were the start of a new aspect of investigation and that their experience would not only become a key to their own futures, but also essential to the future of law enforcement.

To me, they were all top-level investigators-in-waiting, and many of them would continue to have that chance even if reassigned. For the moment, though, we had no concrete idea that what we were going to uncover on the FALN alone was only the tip of a massive mountain. Our surveillance investigators would be busy for quite some time.

Then, we got word that a known "aboveground" FALN member was headed to New York by train. He was a public figure without much of a record for us to go on, but his brother was Luis Rosado, an FALN fugitive wanted in connection with the 1980 armed robbery of a car dealership in Highland Park, Illinois. After being caught and arrested, Rosado skipped out on bail and vanished. That's when his FALN connection came to light.[114]

Here we were, faced with the appearance of his brother, an aboveground FALN supporter, choosing at eighteen-hour train ride over an easy flight. The choice of transportation raised alarms—he would only take the train to avoid the security of air travel or, more ominously, to carry something that would be hard to get on a plane.

We deployed our surveillance forces.

Even before the train left Chicago, Ken Walton, Gary Gardner, and I were sitting in the JTTF control room, agreeing that we needed to "get somebody on that train." We didn't just want agents in the cars, we wanted a guy right next to our target, so we hatched a plan to disguise a task force detective as a blind traveler, dog and all, and sent

---

[114] Rosado, Luis. Wanted Section. www.fbi.gov.

him down to the NY Institute for the Blind to get some pointers on how the blind interacted with the world around them.

With the potential that Rosado might be a bomber, the key to the plan, of course, was the dog, a bomb-sniffing canine that had previously been trained as a service animal.

We chose Albany as the perfect spot to get our teams in place. After the Chicago train arrived, our team got on, and in one of the cars, our "blind" detective found Rosado in a seat by the aisle. Above him in the overhead luggage rack, there was a large and imposing suitcase. Our asset took the aisle seat across from him and settled in for the ride.

When they got to Penn Station, Rosado took the bag down, and our man cued the dog. For a few awkward moments, the seemingly friendly pooch sniffed and pawed at Rosado, with the detective apologizing for his overly friendly animal.

There were no traces of explosives. Did that mean he had been sent to throw us off, while the real bomb courier came via another route?

That whole year we tracked known members on and off trains in New York while our Chicago counterparts did the same in Illinois. Some of our opponents were so good, on and off trains, jumping up and down stairs and changing looks and wardrobes on the fly, that a lot of our guys got "made" in the confusion.

One particular surveillance involved forty-eight members of our force, spread out through the city and following just one subject, but our target was so adept at dry-cleaning that he lost them all. In another case, one of our targets was on the subway platform at 14th Street and seemed to have made one of our agents who was dressed as a homeless man. As the guy stared and slowly approached, our agent embraced his vagrant role, turned and took a leak off the platform and onto the tracks.

It may have saved his life.

Task force detective Kelly Kelson recalled a surveillance on Coney Island where two subjects split up, one getting into his car while the other took to a nearby building and emerged on the roof. The whole thing was a setup to blow our cover. This was how our adversaries lived and breathed, always testing and observing. They learned from their mistakes and made constant adjustments, just as we did.

Rick Hahn and the guys in Chicago were pretty busy uncovering safe houses and more couriers. Joint operations between New York and Chicago uncovered plans to break leader Oscar Lopez out of the federal prison at Leavenworth, Kansas, during a transfer to a medical facility. We turned the tables when the FBI chose not to apprehend Lopez and his coconspirators. Instead they merely interrupted the breakout by changing the transport schedule. The breakout was thwarted, and several members of the "below-ground" were observed changing plans. When they did, we followed, and more safe houses were uncovered, allowing AUSA Jeremy Margolis to help us get bugs and cameras into even more locations.[115]

Of course, our adversaries expected as much and had planned even more contingencies. When we managed to get listening devices into their safe houses, they'd always meet with TV sets and radios blaring, and sat close together so we couldn't pick out words. Kallstrom and FBI Special Ops responded by creating custom electronic filters to cut through the noise. It was a cold war of electronic arms and methods.

***

Mid-April brought the trial of Brink's participants Cecil "Chewy" Ferguson and Edward Joseph. From the start, the hearing proved a complex tangle of logistics and legalities.

Ferguson and Joseph were tried along with four other affiliated members of the Weather Underground, which helped us bring interstate and RICO charges to the table, to go along with robbery and murder. Held at the small courthouse in Goshen, New York, the trial

---

[115] Belli, Roberta. *Effects and Effectiveness of Law Enforcement Intelligence Measures to Counter Homegrown Terrorism: A Case Study on the* Fuerzas Armadas de Liberación Nacional *(FALN), Final Report to the Science & Technology Directorate, U.S. Department of Homeland Security.* College Park, Maryland: START, 2012, pp. 25–26.

created both an instant media frenzy and security nightmare. No matter how tightly we secured the outside, chaos reigned within the building as ideology and politics took center stage.

The FBI's David Mitchell observed the trial with case agents Bob Cordier and Ken Maxwell. Mitchell talked about the circus atmosphere that had dropped into the lap of Federal Judge Kevin Thomas Duffy, a man noted as a fair but tough magistrate.

Duffy presided over three of the country's most infamous international terror cases, two involving the Osama bin Laden–led 1993 World Trade Center bombing and bin Laden's thwarted plot to blow up a dozen passenger airliners over the Pacific Ocean. By the time of Brink's, Duffy had already cemented his considerable reputation by presiding over the Paul Castellano Mafia murder trial. Never one to shy away from the difficult cases, Duffy quickly had his hands full as Brink's defendants refused to talk, called themselves prisoners of war, and through their attorneys—Jesse Berman, Chokwe Lumumba, and William Mogulescu—displayed a mix of open disrespect and downright antagonism for the entire proceeding.

As noted crime writer Colin Evans wrote about the case, defense attorneys Bill Mogulescu and Jesse Berman tore into the credibility of both Joseph and informant Bayette (Peter Middleton), effectively getting their testimony blocked. This left only cooperating witness Tyrone Rison, a development the defense publicly celebrated as "a defeat for the government."[116] The defense then built its case on the belief that as the Brink's robbery was merely the expropriating of money taken from African Americans through the institution of slavery, one could not charge a crime against criminal activity.

From there, the trial devolved.

At one point, a defendant charged the bench and Judge Duffy. It was a scary moment that required a federal marshal to draw his sidearm and intervene. Still, according to David Mitchell, sympathy in the jury ran high since Rison, a confessed murderer, would walk free while Joseph and Ferguson took the rap. Thus, in September, they

---

[116] Evans, Colin. "Weatherman Brink's Trials: 1983." law.jrank.org.

acquitted both men of murder, only convicting them of being accessories after the fact. It was especially frustrating for Mitchell, Maxwell, Cordier, and the rest of the Joint Terrorism Task Force—doubly so when damning new evidence was found against Joseph.

As David Mitchell recalled, "Even during the trial, we never stopped working and with the defense trying hard to undermine Rison, we located Cecil Ferguson's gun, buried near where Rison recalled it might be. Halfway through the trial, in fact, and after a long search, we recovered the weapon which had lain undisturbed for two years. We flew it to the FBI lab in Washington where forensics and ballistics tied it to the shooting and to Ferguson."

Trying to be overly fair, Duffy disallowed it, stating, "You have more evidence than you need." That gun would have changed everything, though the tough-minded Duffy, citing confusion over the verdicts, still hit Joseph and Ferguson with twelve-and-a-half-year terms.

***

A lesser-known aspect of the trial that bears mentioning is why key planner Tyrone Rison refused to participate in the robbery. On the one hand, Rison thought the plan was flawed and didn't include proper escape routes. On the other hand, the actual motive for the crime was suspect.

For all the courtroom bluster of fund expropriation and striking a blow for civil rights, much of the real need for cash, according to Rison, was drugs.

According to FBI officials at the time, "The purpose of the robbery was to replace money that had been used for narcotics, and to get additional money for more narcotics," an assertion backed up by one of the defense attorneys who stated, "This thing is so complicated...and different people were in it for different things. Some of it was corrupt."[117]

---

[117] Farber, M A. "Changing Views of Brink's Case: Narcotics Allegations Emerge." *New York Times*, March 7, 1983.

The trial also presented eerie similarities with the 1981 trial of the members caught in Illinois, those suspected in connection with the New Year's Eve attacks, as well as other bombings such as the one at Mobil Oil.

None of the people brought in, both in Chicago and New York, testified in court. Even the ones we eventually tied to the New Year's Eve plot asserted their rights as prisoners of war and attacked both the proceedings and the court as having no jurisdiction in their case.

Under the skilled guidance of AUSA Jeremy Margolis, the government compiled overwhelming evidence of their guilt, but the defendants remained defiant if not outright hostile. At federal sentencing some even made direct threats to the judge and others in the courtroom.

One, Carmen Valentin, shouted to the judge, "If I weren't chained, I'd try to take care of you right now!" He continued, "All those who have partaken in this illegal and vicious trial will not be exempted for the righteous and just revolutionary procedure. There will soon be judges, marshals, member of the jury, prosecutors, agents, all of you—some of you will be walking on canes and in wheelchairs. Revolutionary justice can be fierce. Mark my words."

As a second state trial got underway in July, the case against Judith Clark, David Gilbert, and Donald Weems was far more focused on Brink's and Brink's alone.

"Here the charges related entirely to the Brink's robbery," Colin Evans explained, "allowing the jury to concentrate more fully on the facts of one case, rather than be confused by several."[118]

That being said, the circus atmosphere of Judge David Ritter's courtroom was exacerbated when the three co-defendants chose to represent themselves. During the trial, Gilbert, Clark, and Weems repeatedly interrupted the proceedings by shouting anti-state and

---

[118] Evans, Colin. "Weatherman Brink's Trials: 1983." law.jrank.org.

-government condemnations and political slogans. At the height of the theatrics, the trio stormed out of the courtroom with Gilbert yelling, "All the oppressors will fail."

Judith Clark then chimed in, "Death to U.S. imperialism."[119]

[119] Ibid.

As the first trial began and a month before the second unfolded, the pressure rose along with the May mercury.

The United Freedom Front emerged to strike again, this time bombing an Army Reserve building in Uniondale, Long Island. The blast blew out glass and damaged the structure, but thankfully the UFF members were careful to avoid deaths, having called surrounding businesses ahead of time to advise people to avoid the area.

At the time we knew little about this extremely clandestine Massachusetts-born group but had to catch up fast and do so using thinly stretched resources. As our investigation began to converge with work done by the Boston FBI, the UFF turned out to be a very difficult adversary with a long history and pedigree. Formerly known as the Jackson-Melville Unit, what would become the UFF had been born in the early 1970s after a Massachusetts prison meeting between militant Vietnam veterans, Thomas Manning and Raymond Levasseur.

A mixture of middle class Black and white members who were well-entrenched in neighborhoods and communities under assumed names, the UFF had kids in local schools and cover jobs, and would pick up and leave at the slightest hint of attention.

Once alerted, they assumed new identities and addresses, forcing their own children to live on the run, many of them not even realizing what their parents were up to. Until the UFF, many of the revolutionary groups we tracked had young members without kids, but these guys used their own families as part of their cover.

Fortunately, Boston FBI and Massachusetts law enforcement had by then formed a kind of task force of their own and reached out to coordinate with us in New York. The growing investigation began in 1982 and took on the name "BOS-LUC," which combined the host city and middle name of original UFF ringleader Ray Luc Levasseur.

The massive investigation included the task force and elements of the FBI, NYPD, BATF, plus departments from Maine to Ohio and as far south as Pennsylvania and New Jersey.[120]

Then, our already-full dance card had a new name added.

***

In early June 1983, a surveillance team monitoring a Chicago safe house watched through their hidden cameras as known bomb maker Edwin Cortes trained Bronx-born activist Alberto Rodriguez on how to build a bomb.

Then later at night, a surveillance team watched as the same pair cased a series of military facilities in the Chicago area. In July, the same pair were surveilled inside their safe house "talking about the final details of the bombing plot, including a discussion of what to include in the communiqué and where to send it."

The bombing was set for the July 4th holiday weekend and the "decision was made to stop the investigation and intervene before the suspects were able to carry out their plan."[121]

As the heat rolled in, it was on. The robberies and other activities were interrupted seemingly by sheer chance and circumstance, including a "happenstance" interruption the Chicago FBI used to disrupt the bombings of those military facilities outside Chicago.

---

[120] BOSLUC. History. fbicollector.com.

[121] Belli, Roberta. *Effects and Effectiveness of Law Enforcement Intelligence Measures to Counter Homegrown Terrorism: A Case Study on the* Fuerzas Armadas de Liberación Nacional *(FALN), Final Report to the Science & Technology Directorate, U.S. Department of Homeland Security*. College Park, Maryland: START, 2012, p. 27.

Each time we diverted assets, it was done by greater design as we watched the group's response and identified more operatives. While it seemed a brilliant strategy, it was also because we had no other choice. We knew the FALN had more safe houses and bomb factories, both in Chicago and New York, but didn't know where or how many. So we had to rely on the double-edged sword of inviting attacks in the name of uncovering the rest of the group's apparatus.

Eventually the FALN put the pieces together on the seemingly random disruptions, which forced us to burn some guys and move in, grabbing some safe houses. This meant letting other perpetrators vanish into the shadows.

***

The Omega 7 investigation came to a head when group leader Eduardo Arocena was arrested in Miami.

Arocena had been wanted in connection with a 1980 plot to assassinate the Cuban ambassador to the United Nations in New York. Informants led the FBI to him, he was apprehended, and at some point he'd be back in New York to face the music.

We'd be waiting.

Agent Joseph Valiquette, also a spokesman for the FBI, tried to reassure a worried public that the Omega 7 group was no more than fifteen or so people, though the group—after failing in their attempt on the diplomat—boldly murdered an embassy attaché six months later. Arocena headed an extremely violent and active organization that over the course of seven years was responsible for multiple murders and bombings from Miami to New York City.

Then in August 1983, the National Guard Armory in the Bronx was rocked by a powerful explosion, blowing a hole in the side of the building and destroying a nearby truck. The UFF had struck, and New York was again under attack by what University of Alabama Criminal Justice Professor Brent L. Smith called "undoubtedly the most successful of the leftist terrorists of the 1970s and 1980s."

In his book *Terrorism in America: Pipe Bombs and Pipe Dreams*, Smith mentions how then FBI spokesperson James Greenleaf described the search for the UFF as "the most extensive and the longest investigation in New England." The group used public phones and mail drops, all while hiding in plain sight.[122] Initially, what we had on their identities was a blank slate, though we did possess forensic evidence from bombings that included pocket watch fragments, part of a timing and detonation mechanism.

As fall arrived, Omega 7's Eduardo Arocena was brought to us for questioning, and his arrival at FBI Headquarters provided a unique and up-close view on the challenges and decisions we encountered on a daily basis dealing with theses "political" groups. Facing down Ken Walton, Gary Gardner, Larry Wack, Bobby Brandt, and me, Arocena knew he was looking at heavy time as the group's mastermind. Rather than face his own music, Arocena promised that if we let him go, he'd flip on his whole organization.

How could we make that choice? Do we let a vicious bomber out, a guy responsible for deaths and destruction, or do we lock him away and see what reverberations then echo through his group? Some argue that while taking out bin Laden helped cripple al-Qaeda, for example, others argue it created more splinter and satellite groups in their wake.

When Arocena openly admitted to us that parts of his group were too violent and needed to be removed, how were we to trust that he didn't just want us to get some of his internal competition out of the way? Ken Walton summed it up best after the interview.

"This guy pisses ice-water."

***

On October 11, we moved on the NAFF and arrested nine members of the group. Searches of their safe houses provided a bonanza

---

[122] Smith, Brent L. *Terrorism in America: Pipe Bombs and Pipe Dreams*. Albany, New York: State University of New York Press, 1994, pp. 110–111.

of weapons and ammunition, as well as explosives and plans for prison breaks.

Meanwhile, within days of President Ronald Reagan sending troops into the island nation of Grenada in response to a violent Marxist revolution there, the FALN—under increasing pressure on US soil—seemed to ratchet up the battle offshore. A light antitank weapon system (LAWS) rocket was fired at the FBI building in Hato Rey, Puerto Rico.

Detective Elmer Toro, who spent a lot of time back and forth from Puerto Rico, later stated that the FBI's computer room was the intended target and the Boricua Popular Army, also known as Los Macheteros, knew exactly where it was. Before the rocket could be fired, though, a small child had walked behind the shooter, causing him to flinch. The subtle movement sent the LAWS rocket into the nearby US Department of Agriculture building, instead.

That night, the separatist Los Macheteros still issued a communiqué that stated the attack was in retaliation for the Grenada invasion. What we didn't yet know was that the rocket attack was also in retaliation for a joint JTTF and FBI operation against Los Macheteros and FALN bank robbers in the States.

***

Four weeks prior to the rocket attack, a Wells Fargo bank in West Hartford, Connecticut, was robbed of around seven million dollars, at the behest of Los Macheteros planner Juan Segarra Palmer and leader Filiberto Ojeda Rios, who while also a Macheteros was a founding member of the FALN.

Both men, operating out of Boston, celebrated both the bank job and rocket attack. Unbeknownst to them, however, the Rios event gave the FBI the information needed to connect both the robbery and rocket. Since they used a clandestine network of vehicles, secretive contacts, and locations to smuggle the money out of the country, we began to close in.[123]

After the rocket attack, we sent task force members to assist local authorities in Puerto Rico. Detective Sergeant Dan Lenahan led the group. Green One went, too, and the operation was even more secretive than our domestic ones. Our teams landed at highly protected military bases, from which they were divided into small units and sent off to different hotels.

With the bank investigation proceeding and this operation unfolding, connections between the two events slowly emerged. The FBI opened an investigation called FEDROC, which found evidence from the scene that tied the LAWS weapon to a US device left in Vietnam. Finding the car used in the attack, the FBI identified and tracked a Los Macheteros member to a safe house where conversations took place about having the exact sum of seven million dollars at the group's disposal.

When the FBI checked to see if anybody was missing seven million dollars, the Hartford Police were quick to say "yes."

A raid on the safe house revealed a huge cache of documents confirming the involvement of Filiberto Ojeda Rios and, through him, the FALN. Our domestic adversary wasn't just a proponent of Puerto Rican independence, it was part of a well-connected and multifaceted terror group.[124] The dots connected, we closed in on Rios, and the organization appeared to have been compromised.

At this point the Omega 7 group, with their leader in custody, was lying low. This freed us up to work closer with the US Attorney's Office to roll out grand jury proceedings in preparation for the major court cases that would follow.

Guys in the surveillance units noticed the slowdown and, as Green One put it, began to worry that it might mark the beginning

---

[123] Mahoney, Edmund. "Chapter Six: A Rocket Attack, an FBI Revelation." *Hartford Courant*, October 28, 1983. Web, February 22, 2019.

[124] Mahoney, Edmund. "Chapter Six: A Rocket Attack, an FBI Revelation." *Hartford Courant*, October 28, 1983. Web, February 22, 2019.

of the end for their time at the Joint Terrorism Task Force. There was some foundation to their fears, since when the brunt of a given problem seemed to have been addressed, the bureaucracy often saw it as an opportunity to pull the plug and divert resources to other endeavors—sometimes even pet projects.

In this case, the slowdown didn't last long.

***

On the night of December 13, 1983, a phone rang in the Navy District Recruiting Office at East Meadow, New York, out on Long Island. Through the line came a warning for the center to evacuate, saying that three bombs were set to go off in just twenty minutes.

At 11:39 p.m., the Nassau County Police Department responded to the scene and in the now empty building discovered two black briefcases. They placed bomb blankets over both. At 11:48, both devices exploded harmlessly.

While this unfolded, two more calls came in, one to the offices of the local paper *New York Newsday*, and the other to the offices of the news service United Press International (UPI). Both callers stated they were members of the United Freedom Front and focused on a communiqué stating opposition to US involvement in Central America.

The very next night, UPI New York was called again, this time with a warning of two more bombs in front of the Queens offices of the Honeywell Corporation. The caller said that these bombs, too, came courtesy of the UFF, and in protest of US involvement in Central America. NYPD responded and successfully removed the devices to the department's bomb range at Rodman's Neck in the Bronx, where one of the devices was rendered inoperative and disassembled.

This gave us a pocket watch mechanism that could be traced to the bombers, but the question remained: Who exactly was the United Freedom Front?[125]

We had our hands full again.

---

[125] "United Freedom Front (UFF)." Military, globalsecurity.org.

◢ SPECIAL EVENTS

Another bomb went off on January 29, 1984, and again courtesy of the United Freedom Front.

After they phoned in the warning, the powerful device shook the Queens Equipment Repair Facility of the Motorola Company. We got lucky, too. Despite the warning, two uniformed cops had already arrived at the scene and found a canvas bag hanging from a door. It was brightly marked with the word "Bomb," and the cops joked about poking it, certain it was a gag. They were barely far enough away, though, when it went off.

A communiqué found at the scene identified Motorola as a defense contractor and therefore considered part of the United States military intervention in Central America and Puerto Rico.[126]

***

In February the Jewish Defense League returned after a quiet 1983. Seemingly under cover of the Jewish Direct Action organization, they unleashed a firebomb at the Soviet compound in Manhattan.

Then on March 19 another UFF bomb tore through the IBM building in Harrison, New York. This blast came in protest of IBM's sale of computer parts to the apartheid government of South Africa. The UFF was on the rise, and this seemed a portent of more ominous

---

[126] McGill, Douglas C. "Bomb Damages Queens Building; Radicals Claiming Responsibility." *New York Times*, January 30, 1984. Web, January 9, 2019.

things to come. Hindsight, too, indicated that the FALN may have helped the UFF as a cover and diversion.

Then it was the JDL's turn again as a dummy hand grenade was delivered to the Greenburgh, New York, town hall, where a Soviet film was being shown. After the scare, the JDL did its usual dance, denying involvement before later suggesting that JDL members may have been involved.

What the JDL didn't know was that they were being watched, and that the sneakers—including Green One and Ken Maxwell—were closing in. Forensics of the time clearly tied the bomb fragments and design from several devices to the same JDL bomb makers.

The hard work of Green One and Ken Maxwell combined bore fruit. They identified a guy named Murray Young, who was present at many of the JDL demonstrations and protests. It turned out that Murray was the record keeper for the JDL and active in their financial affairs.

Careful surveillance and a bit of luck revealed that Murray was also an active participant in the JDL bombings. It all came together years later, in 1986, after a bombing at Lincoln Center's Avery Fisher Hall. The JDL device only partly exploded and, it its wake, offered plenty of usable evidence. What a Lincoln Center security guard saw, though, gave the team of Green One and Ken Maxwell their best lead yet.

Just before the firebomb was placed, an alert security guard spotted a big sedan as it left the scene. It was later determined that the car was a close match to one owned by none other than Murray Young. After obtaining a search warrant, agents from the task force entered Young's apartment and found the matching bomb-making materials. Murray was quickly brought in and promptly flipped, allowing Maxwell and Green One to surveil and then apprehend more of the JDL's infrastructure.

***

The year 1984 also saw the long overdue appointment of an African American police commissioner, and long-time cop Benjamin Ward was the obvious choice.

Ben wore many hats in the NYPD, earning stripes as a chief, deputy commissioner, and commissioner in the Housing Authority. Ward had earned law degrees, worked in the Civilian Complaint Review Board, and ran the Department of Corrections, making him as well-rounded a candidate as could be found. Ward came in under Mayor Ed Koch and, regardless of his many accomplishments, immediately felt the heat of budget and resources.

Ben was forced by sheer practicality to look at the Joint Terrorism Task Force as a unit on the wane. Some in the department hierarchy started squawking that they needed our detectives back on the street and "not sitting on their butts in the JTTF." Thus, even with the UFF emerging from the shadows, this new administration would prove to be our next big test. It showed vividly that we had to be as proactive with our own brass as we had to be with our adversaries.

I invited the new commissioner to come to the task force for a full briefing. When Ben Ward saw the intel and active investigations we had going, his head spun. Before he left, he assured me that there would be no cutting of resources and pledged all we needed to continue our work. We never heard about breaking up the band again, though it always seemed as if we were teetering someplace between the street, the budget, and the politics.

Thankfully, a job well done sometimes delivered its own rewards. One such reward came to me in the form of an invitation to be the keynote speaker at the February 1984 Conference of the American Society for Industrial Security, now ASIS International.

Since 1955, ASIS has been the go-to organization for training and maintaining the edge in all aspects of corporate and private security. Held at the St. Regis Hotel in New York, the ASIS opportunity was a way to share my own experiences, and I hoped that the value of teamwork and cooperation might prove a valuable example to military, corporate, and commercial security agents.

There were one hundred twenty-eight guests in attendance that night, and I was peppered with questions for a solid twenty minutes after my talk.

The ASIS conference was also a great opportunity to network, and network I did, especially when two gentlemen approached me after my wrap-up. They introduced themselves as Jim Tierney, a former NYPD policeman and the director of security for Time Inc., and Jim McDonald, the security chief for HBO. They wanted to talk to me about the 1984 Summer Olympic Games, scheduled for Los Angeles.

It hadn't fully occurred to them that individual venues and their own people might be vulnerable to terrorist attack. Aside from the 1972 Munich games, not many in the United States seemed to consider a contingency for such an attack on native soil. The admission from Tierney and McDonald intrigued me and got me thinking about an entirely new level of terrorist threat—going after the big-name and big-money target of a major sporting event. For the first time, I began thinking of what might come next for me beyond the JTTF.

***

Due to the city's financial plight, there hadn't been a captain's test in years, which severely hampered any further upward mobility for me within the NYPD.

As if on cue, 1984 started bringing opportunities my way that would involve sweeping decisions on my part. It began when Jim Tierney called to invite me to meet with his executive board to help assess their security plans for the Los Angeles Olympic Games. My plate was still full, however, but I agreed to consider the opportunity and left it at that, though the words "sports" and "security" began to rattle around in my head.

It was strange—1984 may have been the first time in my professional career that I thought about what *I* wanted outside the department and police career. I talked with Ken Walton, and he supported my checking it out. So a few days later, I was at Time Inc. headquarters on 6th Avenue meeting with the executive board and giving a presentation regarding the task force's work against domestic terrorism and how it might apply to the Olympics.

I advised the board that, as far as we knew, there were no known threats to the event and further explained that the JTTF received regular information from throughout the world, so we would be on alert to any hint, no matter how outwardly trivial. I assured them that they could call on me at any time to give them the latest. Aside from recommending the needed precautions on the ground, I didn't think I had all that much to add.

Tug Wilson, a former British frogman and underwater explosive expert, made a very theatrical pitch and zeroed in on the five-star luxury liner that was set to house numerous executives from major corporations during the games—among them the many VIP guests of Time Inc. Tug championed his crack team of underwater explosives experts and how they could do major inspections each day, along with unscheduled security monitoring on board.

Rather ominously, as I recall, Wilson explained that tourist ships had been a favored target of terrorists before, and I thought I heard a board member's knees knocking during his talk.

Then as the meeting broke up, I was approached by Robert L. Miller, the publisher of *Sports Illustrated*, who, flanked by Jim Tierney, formally asked if I would become part of the *Sports Illustrated* security team for the Olympics in Los Angeles. I was flabbergasted but hesitated at responding. Miller remained undeterred, turned to his senior security official, and directed that he make sure I accept.

"Whatever it takes," he added with a wave as he walked away.

It was nice to be wanted, sure, but there was plenty of work still to be done elsewhere. Also, I couldn't figure out *why* they wanted me specifically, until I found out that Jim Tierney was ex-NYPD, and thought me best qualified. Still, I told both men that I needed to talk with ranking officials in the FBI and NYPD before considering any offer and then left for home, all the while, trying to wrap my head around what had just taken place.

How could my stock over the past two years have risen to the point of having the best job in law enforcement and now an opportunity to work the Olympics?

***

Back on the job, the brass on both sides of the JTTF saw the Olympic offer as a great piece of PR and a real feather for the organization, even commenting that if I turned it down, one of them would go in my place.

It would take all of my remaining vacation and more to work the event, and that was going to affect my family, though the nice bump in money would make up for some of that pain.

Joan laughed it off and said that if I played my cards right, maybe there would be more vacation in our future. This from the woman who spent our first anniversary in night court. Regardless, I knew she was right. She usually was where I was concerned.

So I decided to accept.

All that remained was for me to figure out my salary—I hadn't done this level of moonlighting before. *Where's Tug Wilson when I need him?* I'd also need a team, so I reached out to John Loughran, who had been so instrumental in helping build the task force. Bringing him on board would be a great way to reward him and tap his expertise at the same time.

With my brain kicking into long-term thinking, I called *Sports Illustrated* and accepted the offer. Immediately weekends were filled with assessing a local team, the availability of LAPD officers, and city resources. If anybody knew the lay of the land in LA, it was my old FBI buddy Tom Elfmont, so I made arrangements to fly west and interview a group of candidates from surrounding police departments.

Elfmont got word out to cities and municipalities as far away as San Diego, Oakland, and San Francisco. After we trimmed our list to the finalists, we asked the top choices to come to the semi-secluded Barnabey's Hotel in Manhattan Beach. There, Tom and I spent considerable time with the candidates. Thankfully, only the best of the best seemed to have answered our call. Not only were they quick on their feet and adept in policing and security, they were equally impressive as they grilled us back about the job and the Olympics. Once again, I was happily relying on an incredible network of people to handle the forces swirling around.

And once again, yet other unforeseen forces were circling.

***

I knew very little about the mastermind of the 1984 Summer Games, Peter Ueberroth, though by 1984, it had become apparent to the world that he possessed a brilliant mind for both sport and business. Ueberroth came into the Olympics via Hollywood icon David Wolper, the producer of huge hits like *Willie Wonka and the Chocolate Factory*, *Roots*, and *L.A. Confidential*.

Years before the LA Games, David had brought the travel mogul in as a potential investor in a professional volleyball league involving many Hollywood power types. While the power players in the room saw big money and NFL-sized franchises in the sport, Ueberroth quickly dressed them down, asserting that unless their league started small and built from there, it would quickly die. Wolper and his colleagues basically ran Ueberroth out of the room and their new league went broke soon after.

Five years later, in 1978, Wolper—given the monumental task of organizing the Summer Games in Los Angeles on a fixed budget, with a local referendum against using taxpayer money, and with profit for the city in mind—went straight back to Ueberroth, who as Organizing Committee President, skillfully mixed corporate sponsorships and city money to set a new standard for funding Olympic games.

Previously, the Olympics had been sponsored by a vast list of companies, all of which ponied up money to be one of the crowd. Ueberroth brilliantly changed the rules and capped the number of sponsors, thereby making funding for the event far more exclusive. As a result, the LA Games took in more than ten times the endorsement money that the previous 1980 Winter Games in Lake Placid had.[127]

---

[127] La Rocco, Claudia. "Rings of Power: Peter Ueberroth and the 1984 Olympic Games." *Financial History Magazine* (spring 2004). Web, January 22, 2019.

Ueberroth also favored using existing venues like the iconic LA Coliseum over building spectacular new structures that might never achieve profitability after the games were over. As fellow committee member and president of Southern California Edison Howard Allen put it, "We wanted someone to run the Games; we didn't want the Games to run us."[128]

Again, while I knew little of Peter, it certainly seemed that some on his staff and those around him came to notice me that summer. One was Charlie Bear, known as Ueberroth's right-hand man and personnel officer for the Organizing Committee. He befriended me just before the July 28 opening ceremonies.

I also spent a lot of time with Jim Tierney, and we hit it off not just because of our shared NYPD background, but also because we were both creating a new type of security for the Olympics. During the Games, for example, I wanted the guys Tom Elfmont and I had picked to be readily identifiable by the dignitaries they were protecting yet also be able to blend seamlessly into the crowd. We put them all in Oakland A's baseball caps and each carried a shoulder bag that I later found out, to my amusement, the VIPs assumed contained an automatic weapon.

They were first aid kits.

I also met Edgar "Ed" Best, who was the vice president/director of security for the Olympic Organizing Committee. Ed had formerly held a major leadership position in the FBI and was well known and well thought of by many of my colleagues in the JTTF.

Ed gave me some good ribbing over my job at the Olympics, commenting on my ability to do my JTTF job and moonlight at the same time, but it was Ed who had the big job, coordinating the efforts of fifty-plus law enforcement agencies. I was just one of the guys.

Or so I believed.

During a dinner with Tierney and Bear, the latter asked what I was planning to do after leaving law enforcement.

---

[128] Kennedy, Ray. "Miser with a Midas Touch." *Sports Illustrated*, November 22, 1982. Web, January 17, 2019.

"Get a real job," I jokingly replied.

The comment got a laugh, but a couple weeks after the Olympics ended, Tierney called me in New York and mentioned that Major League Baseball was beginning its search for a new head of security and that I should toss my hat into the ring.

Honestly, I don't recall my feelings at the time, as it was so far from my radar. Sure, I'd been eyeing the private sector but just the thought of returning to my childhood and teen passion of America's pastime, not to mention to be able to do so via my law enforcement career, seemed a complete pipe dream.

Little did I know, but not long after my speaking appearance at the ASIS Conference in New York, Peter Ueberroth had accepted the job as the incoming commissioner of baseball, replacing Bowie Kuhn. He was taking Charlie Bear with him.

Behind the scenes, the wheels were turning...

LEVELING THE PLAYING FIELD

After the Olympics, still more of the items on the JTTF agenda were being ticked off. The Croatian and Omega 7 groups had been severely compromised, and while the FALN work was ongoing and some key Brink's fugitives—namely leader Mutulu Shakur and key accomplice Marilyn Jean Buck—were still at large, we seemed to be getting on top of things.

Baseball returned to my awareness when on October 14 when, along with about twenty-eight and a half million other fans, I settled in to watch game five of the 1984 World Series. The first pitch was tossed out by Detroit Tigers' legend and 1983 Hall of Fame inductee George Kell, who settled in to watch the game alongside Vice President George H. W. Bush and the new baseball commissioner Peter Ueberroth. The Tigers carried a 4-1 lead into the eighth inning, and more than fifty thousand paying customers geared up to celebrate their team's first World Championship since the 1960s.

Outside the stadium, tens of thousands more gathered, but their celebration quickly devolved into rioting as drunk and delirious fans began overturning cars and setting fires. Bolstered by a criminal element, more inebriated fans joined in the mayhem and turned the area around Tiger Stadium into a virtual war zone.

Even before the last out, alarmed Secret Service agents were aware of the mayhem and whisked the vice president out to the parking lot.[129] Then after the game ended, the crowd outside jumped

---

[129] Thomas, Steve. "The Night the Detroit Tigers Won the 1984 World Series." Detroit Athletic, September 21, 2014. Web, October 13, 2017.

the stadium turnstiles and joined the growing riot inside, tearing up the playing field and surrounding ballpark, forcing famed TV announcer Vin Scully to report the destruction from under his desk in the press box.

Within minutes, the riot was reported all over the world and became a black eye for both the city and the sport. I admit that after the Olympics, the "hows" and "whys" of Detroit did rattle around in my head, though aside from my experiences with the NYPD and some moonlighting jobs, I didn't know enough about the logistics of the Tigers' facility to reach any real conclusions.

A couple of weeks later, my phone rang again, and this time, it was Major League Baseball's head of security, Harry Gibbs, who asked me to visit him at the MLB offices in New York. It was a complete cold call, and I had no inkling of what Gibbs would be asking me, aside from maybe some help with security planning after the '84 World Series. It sort of made sense when coupled with the calls I'd gotten from Jim Tierney about general sports security ideas, but when it sank in, the offhanded comment previously made by Tierney about tossing my hat into the ring for the MLB security job, suddenly hit home.

Was I about to be interviewed?

Let me say here that Harry Gibbs, who passed away in June 2018, was as solid a guy as can be and the genuine article. The soft-spoken Gibbs, who had cut his teeth in security as part of JFK's Secret Service detail, said he was considering me for a position heading up Eastern Region Security as part of his office and, to his credit, told me the full extent of the concerns as expressed by Commissioner Ueberroth, many relative to the World Series riot.

Nobody had anticipated what unfolded in Detroit. It was an incendiary mix of a depressed city, insufficient security, and an overabundance of alcohol, and while I only knew about the Detroit riots as a fan, I tried my best to sketch out for Gibbs some of the things I might have paid attention to as an active law enforcement administrator. After the meeting ended, Gibbs thanked me, and that seemed to be it. I figured I was mistaken about the job.

I couldn't dwell on it, anyway. For me, the JTTF was still the only game in town.

***

That November, we caught a huge break on the United Freedom Front case, when the hard work of the Joint Terrorism Task Force and Massachusetts-driven BOS-LUC investigation led to the Cleveland, Ohio, arrests of five of the organization's key members, including FBI Top Ten fugitive Raymond Luc Levasseur; his wife, Patricia Gros; Richard Charles Williams; Jaan Karl Laaman; and his girlfriend, Barbara Curzi.

Upon searching their homes, FBI agents from New York, New Jersey, Massachusetts, and Rhode Island hit the motherlode. There were UFF communiqués and bomb-making materials that matched the pocket watch devices found at UFF bombings, along with detailed notes for bomb placement at various locations that matched previous UFF bombings at facilities like IBM.[130] Evidence gathered in Ohio helped lead investigators to two more members of the group hiding out in Norfolk, Virginia. They were found with caches of automatic weapons and still more bomb components.

In the original Ohio raid, we found the very handgun used to kill New Jersey State Trooper Philip Lamonaco in 1981, and this discovery opened our eyes to the scope and deeply embedded nature of the UFF, and the group's disturbingly secretive and insular cell structure. Carefully hidden in suburban life, the group's members rarely had contact with any greater organization outside their immediate area and acted like sleeper cells.

To this day, though the UFF has faded thanks to the incarceration of its key members, it's unclear who pulled their strings or where they got their training and funding. No concrete ties were ever found between the group and other organizations or foreign governments.

---

[130] Hanley, Robert. "Ohio Suspects Tied to 10 Bomb Blasts." *New York Times*, November 9, 1984.

Still, the UFF would present a major haul for the task force and another protracted legal challenge for the US Attorney's Office.

We'd seen it before in trials for Brink's, the Croatians, and Omega 7, and at the time both Gary Gardner and I cautioned the federal judge overseeing the arraignment in New York, telling him to expect some kind of outburst in the courtroom. Sure enough, the day of the arraignment Levasseur and his compatriots went crazy during the proceedings, rushed the bench, and screamed taunts and threats. As Gary and I watched, US Marshals had to use stun guns on Levasseur, and he hit the floor at our feet.

The judge jumped up and fled the courtroom.

Before the year ended, one of the last three known Brink's fugitives, Susan Lisa Rosenberg, was arrested at a storage facility in Cherry Hill, New Jersey. The Weather Underground member had been sought for two years and was implicated in the 1979 escape of Joanne Chesimard. Rosenberg and Timothy A. Blunk were apprehended by a combination of chance and training after Officer Mark DeFrancisco spotted the pair wearing very obvious wigs to hide their identities.

All in all, it was a strange but telling end to the UFF, but a grim foreshadowing of an ever more complex counterterrorism landscape.

◢ LATE INNINGS

Sure enough, 1985 brought big changes in the Joint Terrorism Task Force and big changes in my life.

The first big turn came late in January when excellent detective work brought us closer to Brink's frontman Mutulu Shakur. Special Agent Dave Mitchell and Detective Jimmy Haefner were on the case alongside Charlie Minch and Jimmy Cassidy.

Previously, in a Baltimore safe house used by Brink's fugitive Marilyn Jean Buck, Haefner and Mitchell had found a letter that led to a schoolteacher in Los Angeles who identified Shakur and a female companion as a couple who sometimes lived next door and watched her kids. This woman knew them as "Skip" and "Betty," but we knew more. Shakur's female companion was Laverne Dalton, who also went by the name Nehanda Abiodun and was a known member of "the Family" that carried out the Brink's robbery, and "included members of the BLA, Republic of New Afrika, and Weather Underground."[131]

Under the direction of Special Agent Mitchell, a JTTF team was quickly sent to LA to participate in an undercover takedown. Task force agents were more than NYPD and FBI personnel—we were deputized US Marshals, which meant we could seamlessly work across state lines and carry our firearms in doing so. Charlie Minch, Neil Herman, and David Mitchell were among the assets sent to Los Angeles, but we also needed guys who could blend into the

---

[131] Smith, Harrison. "Nehanda Abiodun, Black Nationalist and 'Godmother' of Cuban Hip-hop, Dies at 68." *Washington Post*, February 12, 2019. Web, February 25, 2019.

streets of Compton. We needed another minority surveillance unit, so I also dispatched Kelly Kelson and his partner, Wally Williams, to join the operation.

In LA we quickly picked up Shakur's trail, and it led straight to one of the BAAANA founder's associates—more like his protector. This member of one of the groups behind Brink's was providing Shakur with money, safe houses, and IDs.

As mentioned previously, these guys used extremely sophisticated tactics of countersurveillance and counterintelligence. One tactic entailed obtaining the ID of a deceased person so that when run through the records, it would check out as a real person.

Shakur and Dalton were constantly on the move and eventually took the names David and Claudia Bryant, a clear reference to FBI agent David Mitchell, who stated, "It was aimed at me and their knowledge of who was on their trail."

David's full name is David Bryant Mitchell.

Our first order of business was to follow Mutulu Shakur's suspected support apparatus and get intel and photos of how the group sustained themselves. Once we identified Shakur's "handler," we put him under constant surveillance, even using an FBI plane with infrared heat cameras aboard. We discovered that our target played basketball at a local schoolyard, so over the course of two or three weeks we clandestinely got seven of our people into the nightly game.

It was mission critical that Kelly Kelson and his team were from the same areas and backgrounds as the Brink's crew, and could use that familiarity to better blend in. I also needed some detectives who knew Shakur on sight, from his work at the Lincoln Detox Center in Harlem. To get them I had to ruffle some feathers, and First Deputy Commissioner Pat Murphy helped me smooth that all over.

It came together one February night at a schoolyard in Compton, after Shakur's protector mentioned to one of our guys that he needed to leave the game for what he called "an important 9:00 p.m. meeting." He then backtracked around a mostly deserted and shuttered-for-the-night, commercial area of Compton, eventually landing at a partly dismantled phone booth. "Partly dismantled" because the phone's ringer had been deactivated as to make no noise.

There he stood, constantly checking his watch, and at precisely 9:00 p.m. he picked up the silent phone and started talking. He then hung up and stood there for about five or so minutes, when suddenly from out of the darkness came Mutulu Shakur.

Our LA team closed in.

The pursuit had lasted three and a half years, and it ended up in the bushes where Shakur hid and finally surrendered.

When he was brought in, the wanted fugitive had eleven cents in his pocket, a California license in the fictitious name "Eugene Allen," and a list of phone numbers that led to some chilling connections.

"Three or four of the numbers were for payphones in Atlanta, Georgia," Agent David Mitchell recalled, "and in locales frequented by an individual named H. Rap Brown."

H. Rap Brown eventually took the moniker Jamil Al-Amin and became a leading figure in the United States Muslim community. As David saw it, the possibilities of linkage between domestic terror groups and Muslim extremists wasn't something new, but to some, it hearkened back to the same kinds of international influence and funding that helped spawn and cultivate so many of the domestic associations we pursued in the JTTF.

When Shakur went on trial in 1988, in fact, a mysterious character witness showed up in his defense, and it was none other than H. Rap Brown, who later went on trial for murdering policemen. As a 2001 article in *American Spectator* told it, "H. Rap Brown was a founder and later chairman of the Student Non-Violent Coordinating Committee, whose definition of non-violence included his famous boast: 'We're gonna burn America down.'"

In 1967 Brown incited a mob to torch two city blocks in Cambridge, Maryland. "It's time for Cambridge to explode, baby," was his punch line. Then in 1970, while serving as the fugitive "Minister of Justice" of the Black Panther Party, Brown made the FBI's Most Wanted list for the first time. A shootout during the attempted robbery of a bar on New York City's Upper West Side left him and two police officers injured. Brown did five years in New York prisons, during which time he experienced a jailhouse conversion to Islam and took the name Jamil Abdullah Al-Amin.[132]

After we captured Shakur, our surveillance started to find some of our connected targets going into the same Brooklyn mosque where Omar Abdel-Rahman, a.k.a. the "Blind Sheikh," held court. The Blind Sheikh was convicted in 1995 as the mastermind behind the 1993 terror bombing of the World Trade Center—the first such attack made under the direction of what later became known as al-Qaeda.

---

[132] Pipes, Daniel. "The Curious Case of Jamil Al-Amin." *American Spectator*, November–December 2001.

◣ THE CALL-UP

As spring training started up in Major League Baseball 1985, I was called to report again to the commissioner's offices in New York, this time to meet up with Ed Durso, the executive vice president and chief operating officer of the league.

Suddenly, things got very serious. I admit I got caught up in it and quickly went out and purchased Peter Ueberroth's book *Made in America* so I could study every page.

Peter had just been named *Time* magazine's "Man of the Year," and his written words provided incredible clues as to what he personally wrestled with during the 1984 Olympics. They were items, I might add, that presented opportunities for solutions that I hoped to bring to baseball as security director.

The many worries circling the games included the palpable fear that Soviet agents might attempt to disrupt the proceedings in revenge for the US boycott of the 1980 Summer Olympics in Moscow. Ueberroth also spoke of concerns beyond foreign intrigues and possible terrorism, but I couldn't spend too much time dreaming of my own solutions. The more immediate needs of the JTTF were always close by.

***

In May, the Baltimore FBI alerted the JTTF that their surveillance unit had picked up the trail of Brink's fugitive Marilyn Jean Buck en route to New York City. According to the FBI, Buck was accompanied by Linda Sue Evans, who had harbored her since the deadly Brink's holdup. They were reported to be in a light blue sedan.

Aside from Mutulu Shakur, Buck was the last of Brink's fugitives left, and we quickly rallied all available task force assets including "sneaker" Willie Kennelly, who by then had become a trusted right-hand to John Loughran. Wille came into the JTTF partly to help find justice for his friends Edward O'Grady and Waverly Brown.

Incredibly, he was about to get his chance.

With the FBI ready to pass the ball to us, Ken Walton, Gary Gardner, and I quickly set up in our command post as the pair was picked up by our surveillance. It all seemed to be going smoothly until they began to show signs that they knew what we were up to. Still we tracked the duo into the city, where they began meandering, driving in circles, before finally slipping into a safe house on Giles Place in the Bronx. For most of the day we sat tight, assessed the situation, and tried to figure out the best and safest place to apprehend them. We didn't want a shootout and weren't hot on the idea of entering the mysterious unknown of the safe house.

Once it got past midnight, Ken Walton—surmising that Buck and Evans had likely gone to sleep and the situation was stable—went home for a quick nap. That left Gary Gardner and me holding the fort. After a time, Gardner too went to the nurse's office for a catnap.

Not long after he left, Marilyn Jean Buck and Linda Sue Evans emerged wearing new clothes and wigs. They hastily jumped into their car and sped off. Within moments, a tail of vans and cars followed them to the nearby Van Cortland Park area, where Evans and Buck again seemed to get spooked, abandoned their car, and vanished.

On scene, John Loughran jumped into action and, in a dangerous move, hit the streets on foot. He discovered a motel a short distance away. Sure enough—and fortunately I might add—Buck and Evans had stopped for the night. It was a perfect opportunity to close in. While Buck and Evans were resting, we got the US attorney on the phone and obtained permission to wire their car for sound.

Given the unpredictability of the situation, it was a harried and nervous operation. Special Ops had to break into the car and remain undiscovered.

At 6:00 or 7:00 a.m., Buck and Evans emerged from the motel, got back into their car, and proceeded up Route 9, carefully avoiding major highways and attempting to hamper any clear view from surveillance aircraft above. They were right to try, since there was an FBI plane with agents on board, listening in. That feed was relayed to JTTF headquarters, and we got a rare inside peek at the tense and paranoid lives of these wanted fugitives.

They were extremely nervous about being followed and several times talked about stopping. Knowing things could develop quickly, I radioed ahead to my team and directed them to take the pair at the first-best opportunity.

Our fugitives and their ten tails got near the mid-Westchester town of Dobbs Ferry, and the skittish duo threw us another curve. Buck didn't like the look of a local Dobbs Ferry cop who happened to pull out behind them. Certain they were being tailed, Buck and Evans spoke about ditching the car, going to a local diner, and then catching a train out of the area.

Yet they didn't rush. Even if they thought they'd been spotted, these were the careful actions of trained individuals, and had we not been listening, they might have worked.

Then we had our opening.

Buck and Evans pulled the light-blue sedan into the lot between a gas station and the back of the brick and blue metal Mayflower Diner. Ten FBI cars and vans moved in to surround them. Willie Kennelly and partner ended up the closest, moved in to cut them off, and as the two agents jumped out of their van, Buck froze. Evans took off for the nearby Mayflower Diner, an entourage of agents in pursuit.

Buck reached to her thigh and under a long rust-colored top. Willie Kennelly, who had a shotgun in his lap, quickly realized that he didn't have time to maneuver out of the car and take aim. She was about to get the drop on him. In a flash he lunged for Buck and got hold of her hair, but the wig came off in his hands! Her hand emerged with a .38-caliber revolver and in seconds, Kennelly and Buck were struggling for their lives.

More frantic FBI agents and NYPD detectives rushed over.

"Get down!"

"Gun! *Gun!*"

Willie still had the shotgun in one hand and Buck's hand in the other, when a fellow agent grabbed the shotgun, allowing Kennelly, in the heat of the moment, to hook Buck with his free arm and slam her head-first into the hood of the car.

The long-standing fugitive was finally in custody.

Willie Kennelly was the guy who put the cuffs on Marilyn Jean Buck, though he always stressed that about twenty other agents and detectives made the arrest with him. He said that time had slowed down as the car door opened and recalled the takedown as a form of combat scenario. In just a few moments, the world spread out around him. He saw a kid pumping gas a few feet away and people walking on the street nearby. All in the span of seconds, Kennelly saw the cars driving past, some slowed or stopped.

"It was strange," he said. "I had to consider that people could get hurt. People on the Brink's crew had already escaped jail and killed cops and security guards. If we hesitated, people could get shot in the crossfire, and Buck and Evans could get away. It was the culmination of my police training and my JTTF experiences and this was exactly how and why it was supposed to fit together."

"The other guys joked that I was gonna have to pay for the dent in the hood, though," he added. Buck had been a fugitive for eight years in all, dating back to before the Brink's robbery.

Linda Sue Evans, meanwhile, had made the unfortunate choice of running into the Mayflower Diner and ducking into the bathroom, in the hope of climbing out a back window. The window was too small, and she was apprehended holding a loaded 9 millimeter at the ready. She had worked part-time in Connecticut and was also tied to the May 19th communist organization and "was said to have been a part of a 'support apparatus' that helped members of the Brink's robbery gang with hideouts, false identification papers, communications and other assistance."[133]

***

At the US Attorney's Office, we were met by the familiar face of lawyer Susan Tipograph, who made sure both Evans and Buck didn't utter a word to us. Meanwhile, both women began furiously noting every single detail of the proceedings, and Marilyn Jean Buck, for her part, got busy putting together three or four yellow legal pads of everything that went down prior to and after her arrest, including names, ranks, and full descriptions.

If it was an attempt to shake us, we'd been through far too much to care. More likely the two were looking for any and all angles through which to fight and steer the arraignment and court case ahead.

Later in the day we searched the Giles Place safe house and learned from the building manager that the apartment had been rented by a schoolteacher—a woman who, according to the manager, wore a different wig each month and walked with a limp. Marilyn Jean Buck, who had shot herself in the thigh escaping the Brink's robbery back in 1981, had sustained a pronounced limp from that wound.

Buck went on trial at the end of 1985 and in January 1986 received the first of her lengthy sentences, stemming from a federal weapons charge in connection with her arrest. The fact that she had carried the weapon across state lines, coupled with two prior convictions, later landed her in court again to face an eight-count indictment of racketeering, armed bank robbery, and three bank robbery–related killings.[134]

---

[133] McFadden, Robert D. "Fugitive in 1.6 Million Brink's Holdup Captured." *New York Times*, May 12, 1985.

[134] Reilly, William M. "Fugitive Charged in Connection with 1.6 Million Brinks Robbery, Convicted," UPI, January 17, 1986.

As Willie Kennelly described, it was a high-pressure operation to bring her down and provided a rare inside look at the tense, pressure cooker that was the surveillance unit of the JTTF.

***

As the whirlwind year kept churning, I was called for another interview at Major League Baseball, with Chief Operating Officer Ed Durso. Toward the end of discussion, Durso leaned back informally.

"Kevin, you've been all over, on lots of high-profile assignments, the FBI, terrorism, big cases." He leaned forward. "You'll be able to take in some ball games. It'll be a nice change for you."

The statement gnawed at me. I wasn't coming to baseball to coast, and I recall suddenly sitting straight up in my chair and taking umbrage.

"Ed, I'm not looking to semi-retire. I'm looking to be part of an active group and with them, make a difference in the sport." My words hung over the table a moment, before Durso blinked, and smiled again.

"I understand."

Sometime later, Durso admitted to me that in his mind, anyway, my answer to him was the moment I got the job.

But I didn't know what was coming, and when several weeks went by, it began to feel like a merry-go-round. Then another call came, and I was hustled into to a meeting to discuss the financial aspects.

I'll admit, that was when I started to daydream. There I was, bat in hand and back at Cowboy Land ready to finally hit that ball over that wall. It was maybe the first time in my life I thought I could really bring something to such a large organization. My family was ecstatic over the idea, of course; the job was high-profile but, maybe more important, safer and less demanding.

Then, it happened again, and the line from MLB went deafeningly silent. I suddenly felt that all I'd accomplished was the ignominious feat that ballplayers call the "golden sombrero," oh-for-four with nothing but strikeouts.

***

Soon after, the politics of law enforcement circled again, only this time taking down my mentor and boss, Ken Walton.

We knew from the rumor mill that higher-ups were looking to move him. Ken Walton was a quintessential boat-rocker when it came to getting the job done, but his flamboyant style grated on some of the more conservative elements in the FBI. Just as I was considering the private sector, Walton too seemed to be looking for his next move.

A few weeks later, Gary Gardner and I were called to Walton's office and, upon entering, met Tom Sheer. He was the assistant special agent in charge and a close friend of Ken's. The door was closed, and a teary-eyed Walton informed the three of us that he had just been notified of his transfer to the Detroit FBI. It was big post, for sure, but a very visible demotion from the Joint Terrorism Task Force.

We were shocked but more upset at how hard it was hitting our leader and boss. The three of us tried hard to pick up his spirits, and I was so ticked off that I offered to retire on the spot, suggesting that Walton and I open a security business. If Ken Walton had said yes, my career would have ended there, but instead he looked at me with that wry smile.

"You get your pension right away," he said, "but I would have to wait a couple more years." He didn't say no, mind you, but the conversation moved on to other matters.

We still had work to do.

Before he left, Ken Walton signed a picture for me.

"*We did it our way,*" he wrote. "*All the way—Ken Walton.*"

I think the Bureau broke Ken Walton's heart, and all of us knew that day that he would likely never fully recover from it. Ever the professional, though, Walton did amazing work as head of the Detroit FBI until his retirement in 1988.

I'm saddened to say that while we kept in touch for a time, Walton and I eventually drifted apart, and it's sadder still to report that he passed away in 2016 at age seventy-six, after a battle with cancer.

Ken Walton was one of the best leaders I knew.

THE LAST TASK

At the end of 1985, the Joint Terrorist Task Force was awarded an NYPD unit citation for outstanding work in the arrest of more than one hundred domestic terrorist suspects and an incredible decrease in attempted bombings.

Sure, there would be plenty of work ahead, but for this iteration of the JTTF, citations were appropriate—not just by nature of deserving them, but as awards generally come at the end of things. You could feel it in the halls after that, new guys were coming in, leadership was changing, and it was a truly good cop or FBI agent who knew that too long on one job was a recipe for stagnation and therefore trouble.

The winds of change began to die down, and by 1986 the last of our major cases came to a conclusion. In March, the seven captured members of the United Freedom Front were convicted of conspiracy, receiving sentences ranging from fifteen to fifty-three years.

Not long after, I was introduced to Admiral James L. Holloway, who was the executive director of the Vice President's Task Force on Combating Terrorism. The distinguished Holloway was also a member of the President's Blue Ribbon Commission on Defense Management and had come to the New York FBI and JTTF offices to discuss our work and successes.

Barely a year before, Congress had met to discuss the issue of terrorism but strangely only invited the CIA and not the FBI. It wasn't necessarily an oversight, but a combination of long-term effects.

In a 2008 interview, Agent Richard Hahn explained, "In April 1978, Mark Felt, L. Patrick Gray, III (the acting FBI director from 1972 to 1973), and Edward S. Miller, (who had served as the head of the bureau's intelligence division), were indicted for ordering warrantless searches that were part of the FBI's investigation of the WUO (Weather Underground Organization)."[135]

This was COINTELPRO.

According to Hahn, Gray's charges were dropped in 1980, and presidential pardons cleared Felt and Miller in 1981. Hahn noted, "[B]ut the prosecutions highlighted to special agents the personal legal dangers surrounding domestic terrorism cases. Not surprisingly, counterterrorism assignments were widely seen as 'career killers,' or as one former special agent recalled, 'Nobody wanted this and management, not just in the field but at FBI Headquarters, wanted nothing more to do with this....'"[136]

Certainly, the success of the JTTF—as well as task forces in Chicago, LA, and around the country—had changed that, along with the clockwork combination of federal, state, and local law and legal resources involved. As a result, government bigwigs were paying more attention to the FBI and its effectiveness in counterterrorism.

Previous to meeting Admiral Holloway, I was invited to lecture at the Command and General Staff College in Leavenworth, Kansas. There, I met Colonel James H. Fraser, the chief of the Terrorism Counteraction Office. Both Holloway and Fraser subsequently recommended me to a Clemson University Conference on Terrorism in June near Myrtle Beach, South Carolina. It was an honor just to receive such a prestigious invitation and to serve on a panel no less.

Quite strangely, baseball reappeared as Peter Ueberroth's office called with an invite to Shea Stadium to meet Peter and watch a game between the New York Mets and Los Angeles Dodgers. I sat in the owners' box with Mets General Manager Frank Cashen and Ueberroth.

Summer arrived, and I had my hands full again with another security job, this time for the prestigious Operation Sail and the July

[135] Richard S. Hahn interview by Brian R. Hollstein. April 15, 2008. Transcript, Society of Former Special Agents of the FBI, p. 20.
[136] Ibid.

4th Liberty Weekend Celebration. The sweeping event was to be a perennial version of the famous 1964 World's Fair Parade of Ships; it also celebrated the Statue of Liberty's centenary. The monument to freedom, hope, and immigration officially would reopen after a two-year restoration, making the statue a prime target for terrorism. More than thirty thousand spectator craft were expected for the parade, and the July 4th fireworks spectacular was billed as the largest pyrotechnic display in American history.[137]

Since many areas around Liberty Island included federal reservations, the Joint Terrorism Task Force would be brought into the security mix. President Reagan was attending, as were justices from the Supreme Court, French President François Mitterrand, and other prominent world leaders. The result would be a bevy of security people from various regions and governments alongside the Coast Guard, NYPD, the US Navy, Secret Service, and the smaller and more specialized Presidential Protection Detail.

It was going to be a huge, complex, and extremely daunting job.

***

As the June Conference on Terrorism drew closer, I began to grow impatient about the baseball job and began to convince myself that they were jerking me around.

So much was still going on in the task force, and with other outside opportunities calling, I worried that if I put all my eggs in one basket I'd lose them all. I'm not sure what exactly pushed me over that edge, but I recall picking up the phone, calling Ed Durso, and advising him that if I didn't receive word in the next ten days of MLB's interest, I was moving on.

I hung up, feeling uneasy that in days, I would be interacting with Ed Best at the Clemson Conference. In my mind, I knew that Best was likely Ueberroth's first choice for the job, but he had already moved

---

[137] Operation Sail. Events. 1986. opsail.org. Web, January 22, 2019.

on to Hughes Aircraft. Maybe Ed would be watching me on Peter's behalf.

Then again, maybe I'd just buried myself with that phone call.

All I could do was continue with my job, so I did my best to leave it all behind as Joan and I flew off to Myrtle Beach. My career up until that point had been all-encompassing, the hours grueling, and it was wonderful to give Joan a few days in the sun.

Joan was thrilled with what she believed might be another chapter in our life together. From bullets to bombs, long nights away to dangerous undercover operations, a life lived far less under pressure would certainly be a welcome change. Meanwhile, though confident of my career opportunities, I was still unsure as to what exactly lay ahead.

***

I'm not sure I slept much that night, but I know I needed the rest.

The event the next day was a heavy-hitting affair and packed such notables as Admiral Holloway and noted terrorism professor Colonel James H. Fraser. Both men filled out an already all-star panel that featured Alabama Senator Jeremiah Denton Jr., who was the chairman of the Subcommittee on Security and Terrorism, and Dr. William R. Farrell of the Naval War College and author of the 1982 book *The U.S. Government Response to Terrorism.*

Dr. Farrell and I were already friends, and I was happy to see him on the panel. As a young man, the Bronx-born Farrell joined the Air Force Office of Special Investigations before being pulled toward the Vietnam War. At the last moment he was sent instead to Japanese language school, then shipped to Japan for intelligence work.

Farrell studied the Japanese Red Army, an international terror group whose stated purpose was "to overthrow the Japanese Government and monarchy and to help foment world revolution." The group carried out a bloody 1972 massacre at Lod Airport in

Israel, as well as two Japanese airline hijackings and an attempted takeover of the US Embassy in Kuala Lumpur.[138]

At the conference, Dr. Farrell found many of the analytical documents and conclusions to be disconnected. As he put it, "Everybody was writing from their silos." I had seen it myself in both the NYPD and Joint Terrorism Task Force and had met and worked with amazing men and women who looked beyond those very silos and helped make a world of difference.

The conference was rounded out by the highly decorated Major General T. Eston Marchant, CBS News Congressional Correspondent Ike Pappas, Clemson economics professor Clinton H. Whitehurst Jr., and my friend Edgar Best.

"How'd the FBI let you out?" he said with a friendly jibe.

I wasn't sure if he was complimenting me or needling me for taking the side job.

***

As the two-day panel got rolling, each person spoke at length on issues of domestic terrorism, beginning with the seemingly esoteric but legally important defining aspects of terror and terrorism.

Critical to unifying the international community and locking down legal guidelines, the issue was a difficult one. In the past, acts of sabotage and political assassination had touched off world wars. Then terror had gone underground, splintering into ethnic and group ideologies over national and international disputes. These interconnected and nimble groups of radicals served a range of masters from individuals to foreign states.

What they shared, though, was the level of violence, now aimed at corporate interests or command and control infrastructure. This redefined the theater of operations as a mobile war zone, with some groups declaring that innocent victims were guilty by association.

---

[138] Japanese Red Army (JRA). Federation of American Scientists. fas.org. Web, October 10, 2018.

Newsman Ike Pappas struck a real chord when he talked about the tangled relationship between terror and the media. "The terrorists who blow up our buildings and hijack our airplanes and murder our citizens have learned very rapidly how to use the power of television to further their causes. Terrorists are operating on a simple principle these days: Make the act so horrible that it will attract worldwide attention and then, when you've got that attention, try and deliver your message through television. Sadly, it's almost like marketing."

Ike talked about how he'd been in LaGuardia Airport just five minutes before the 1975 bombing. His response had been to get people out rather than let more in, and his reaction had been formed during the crucible of war. Ike had been a correspondent in Vietnam and knew the Vietcong playbook which called for the detonation of a first bomb as a ruse to lure rescuers and Good Samaritans into the path of a second.

His chilling conclusion was that if the media simply ignored or downplayed these acts, the terrorists would escalate them until the results were so horrific, they would be felt and seen by all. The solution he proposed was more cooperation between media and law enforcement to get the story covered but not aid the terror agenda.[139]

***

For my part, I talked at length about the evolution in the way terror groups looked at society. Ominous signs were everywhere, as intertwined groups seemed to view an entire world of potential targets.

Tied to these targets was a patchwork of ideological goals as narrow as community and as far reaching as the geopolitical Marxist agenda. I cautioned the conference that there was an escalation of terrorism on the horizon, that these now generational groups could

---

[139] Pappas, Ike. "State and Local Responses to Domestic Terrorism." Conference Proceedings, the Strom Thurmond Institute of Government and Public Affairs, June 9–10, 1986. Clemson University, pp. 32–33.

only be partly controlled by recognizing their appetite for violence and making their intended targets harder to get to.

American soil much more easily could be targeted by groups in the US inside of which foreign nationals and home-grown agents could easily hide and operate. It was a slippery slope indeed of rights and legalities that required a delicate mix of operations, legal and ethical standards. The makeup of the Joint Terrorism Task Force was a powerful tool and example, as it combined assets and people from all over the country, pooled information, and had the unique ability to operate as a mirror to embedded terrorism.

Ed Best made one of the more telling points at the conference. "Our best defense in this country is to not deal with terrorism as a political matter, but as a criminal matter." This salient point had been repeatedly backed up during the prosecution of the various members of the Weather Underground, Black Panthers, and May 19th Organization during the Brink's case. After the 1981 indictment of the initial defendants, Rockland County District Attorney Kenneth Gribetz called the defendants' political feelings "irrelevant" to what he felt was a murder trial.

Ed Best also described attacks done by agents who often were trained by foreign states, funded through bank robberies or drug sales that also, at times, involved foreign entities and governments. Often these attacks were carried out using weapons provided by regimes outside the country.[140]

The unifying element at that time was criminal enterprise, and criminal acts by US citizens on US soil. Ed gave a shoutout to the JTTF, stating that the nation couldn't "deal with a complicated terrorist incident in the United States unless you have the cooperation of law enforcement, because it involves, in most cases, several jurisdictions."[141]

---

[140] Best, Edgar. "State and Local Responses to Domestic Terrorism." Conference Proceedings, the Strom Thurmond Institute of Government and Public Affairs," June 9–10, 1986, Clemson University, p. 11.
[141] Ibid., p. 13.

The immersive conference took my mind away from baseball and back to the JTTF, and after a few days of sun and relaxation, Joan and I started thinking about what else the future might hold for me.

We returned to New York and found a note waiting for me on our kitchen table, scrawled on the back of a paper plate by our son Kevin.

"Dad, call the commissioner."

I looked at Joan.

Commissioner of Police? I wondered.

Sanitation?

Parks and Recreation?

What?

I actually called the police commissioner, then was about to dial the fire commissioner when it suddenly dawned on me.

Was this it? The job offer or the end of the game?

It was neither; it was an invitation for Joan and me to attend the Yankees-Red Sox game that night at the Yankee Stadium. We had just come off the plane from Myrtle Beach and had to scramble just to make the first pitch.

RETURN TO COWBOY LAND

JOAN THE CLOSER

There I was, in the "House That Ruth Built." Joan and I were seated between the commissioner of baseball and Dr. Bobby Brown, the American League president.

The first home team long ball came courtesy of Yankees' lead-off hitter, Ricky Henderson, who drove a Rob Woodward pitch into the stands to make the score 5-1. As the Bronx crowd erupted, fans jumped onto the roof of the Yankees' dugout to celebrate. Peter Ueberroth turned to me.

"Did you see that?"

As I watched Henderson round the bases, I commented on the pitch, then realized that my potential future boss was asking me about the breach of security.

Strike one.

Soon after, though, Joan gracefully excused herself, and Ueberroth, thinking she was going for a refreshment, stopped her.

"Joan, they bring food to us here." She simply smiled.

"We just got back today and left in a hurry to get here. I just wanted to check on the kids."

With what I felt was the first strike against me, Joan instantly evened the count. Just after she got up, I noted Ueberroth surreptitiously nodding to Bobby Brown. He liked that we cared about our family.

The game continued into the seventh, when the commissioner turned to me again.

"We have to decide on this security job. Why don't you come down to Park Avenue tomorrow and we'll talk about getting it done?"

Just like that.

The rest of the game was a blur, and while a furious Yankee comeback stalled at 7-6, the Joan-led comeback won the day. The entire drive home, we were a mix of stunned and buoyant. At one point, my beautiful wife shot me one of her humbling smiles.

"You know I got you this job," she purred.

Looking back, I believed Ed Best was the main reason for the opportunity, something that Peter Ueberroth recently verified. Though in baseball parlance, Joan was the closer.

The next day in his office on Park Avenue, Peter Ueberroth officially offered me the job as director of security for Major League Baseball. I was over the moon, and when I saw the actual offer, I was floored. The security for my family would be huge.

Thirty walls would await me now, each one marking the outfield boundary of a highly valuable professional sports team's domain, my new domain.

Getting over them would prove another story entirely.

***

Just after the meeting with Ueberroth and outside on the street, a uniformed NYPD officer caught my eye as he headed up the street. I looked into that young face at the start of the journey and reflected on just how far I had come and the amazing opportunities that the NYPD had given me.

▲ EPILOGUE

As July arrived, so too did the Liberty Weekend in New York and with it my last day on the job as co-commander of the Joint Terrorism Task Force.

Tall ships paraded New York Harbor, fireworks lit up the night sky, and large crowds enjoyed the festive atmosphere in a safe and secure environment. I recall watching the tall ships sail by and feeling a kinship with those sailors, all celebrating America with the wind at their backs and going, to some extent, where the currents took them.

Each ship seemed a moment in my long career, both in memory and in celebration. The entire event was a multinational success.

Judge William Webster, director of the FBI, attended, as did Marine Corps Commandant Paul X. Kelly. Both men stopped in at the task force command center to meet with our team, and Webster thanked us for our outstanding three-year success record, as well as the intensive planning and organizing that went into the Liberty Weekend event.

Director Webster approached me with General Kelly at his side and mentioned that he'd heard all about the baseball job. Turned out Judge William Webster was a frequent tennis partner to Peter Ueberroth.

Not many secrets in the intelligence community.

According to Webster, Ueberroth had asked for the judge's opinion of me.

"You got the job," Webster said with a grin, "so I guess he didn't accept my recommendation."

KEVIN M. HALLINAN

The last night of the weekend celebration, General Kelly and Judge Webster invited me to join them and other FBI leaders aboard the USS *John F. Kennedy*, where we dined with the ship's officers and were given a tour. It was an experience I will not forget, and as I stepped off of the US Navy launch that evening, my whole career seemed to sail off into New York Harbor, though I will admit to eying two futures.

Wanting to bring all my experience and expertise into baseball was of course, paramount, but I also wanted to leave the Joint Terrorism Task Force with everything I had. My replacement would be John Loughran, and I provided him with as much advice as I could.

"You're going to have a tougher job than I ever had," I said. With the swirl of political, procedural, and legal issues ahead, the dwindling resources courtesy of short-sighted government administrators with eyes on the next projects, I feared the challenges ahead. Threats to the nation's security were only growing broader and more complex.

I watched it all in my mind as the ships went past.

***

Looking back, I realized that I had mainly been part of two very big families during my working life. The first being my own and the second the New York City Police Department.

Being a cop presented me with an intricate and intriguing lattice of people, places, and procedures, a humbling larger-than-life journey into an entire universe of serving others. It certainly wasn't an easy career, but, thankfully, any disappointment that had to be dealt with over many years of such a trying career tempered me.

When walking the beat and interfacing with people in pain, helping a young mom give birth, investigating crimes of desperation or depravity, I felt each and every moment as it became a personal and inseparable part of me. Like a grand life lesson, the career constantly offered two choices: harden from it all or empathize and understand. As I slowly grew into the job and career, I was even able to find passing moments of connection and appreciation for my adversaries, as the sum of my experiences began to blend into an amazing human tapestry of people and places, of clues and patterns.

The times when the system broke down, cases were lost, and leads went nowhere and were sometimes crushingly heartbreaking and demoralizing. Some guys on the job gave up; some hardened; some broke the rules and even the law. You had to learn from it all to stay effective and keep going.

From the beat and through the windows of a patrol car, I saw so much history and lived each moment as fully as possible. Twenty-five years flew by, and somewhere in the blur, I grew to enjoy the unexpected challenges of each day.

***

I hope that my tale serves as a reminder of the human network required for effective public safety as well as the importance of empowering each and every part of it. There are some telling developments in the history of law enforcement that occurred during my time out there. The circumstances we faced, during the times we did, allowed us the opportunity to develop a generation of investigators who together built a new model against a new and ever-evolving face of crime.

In terms of today's world I will say this: too much compartmentalization, while a major and deadly strength of terrorist organizations, also points to a potential and deadly weakness in law enforcement. Communication and the breaking down of inter- and intra-departmental walls is one of the most effective and important strategies I learned in my twenty-five-year police career.

Certainly, specialization is a critical and important tool, but only in the right hands and only when properly shared. We all too often forget the generational challenges of counterterrorism, the human networks and relationships that transcend and easily elude a system that is more often governed and budgeted in two-, four- and six-year increments. The militant groups of the '60s directly led to those of the '70s and '80s and the seeds sewn in the 1980s have led to today.

What seeds and patterns are we not looking at together, collectively? What parts of this never-ending puzzle are being overlooked via lack of resources, politics, and just sheer ignoring the lessons of the past?

If you are involved in law enforcement, or planning to be, I hope this book in some way does for you what the people and voices here have done to guide and inspire me. If you get the chance and are so inclined, find the Robert McAllister book, *The Kind of Guy I Am*, and see how you measure up.

I spent a lifetime trying to figure out the kind of guy I was and, in some ways, I'm still looking. My wife, Joan, knew, as did each and every one of the other amazingly significant individuals who coached, mentored, and partnered with me.

As for my personal adventure and what I ultimately take from it, I believe legendary baseball announcer Jack Buck said it best at a baseball owners meeting. When asked about his amazing run, Jack recalled his wife asking him one night, "Jack, if Jesus Christ came down to earth and came up to you, what would you say to him?"

Jack replied, "I'd say, 'Lord, why have you been so good to me?'"

**My police academy graduation – July 1961. (I'm
in the top row, third from the left.)**

With Hank Buck – Circa 1987.

With my first patrol car – Circa 1965-66.

Ad for WCBS-TV *Police File* with Chris Borgen – Circa 1973.

**In New Orleans during the Middle Management
Exchange Program – 1972.**

**At my desk in Research and Planning at the Chief
of Detectives Office – Circa 1973-74.**

Former Senator John Glenn's ticker tape parade after flying on
the space shuttle Discovery. My son Tom is driving. – 1998.

With FBI Agent Ken Maxwell – Circa 1986.

Liberty Weekend with FBI Director William Webster and
Marine Corps Commandant Paul X. Kelly – 1986.

**My promotion to lieutenant with
Bob McGuire and Pat Murphy – 1979.**

**Graduation from the FBI National Academy,
with William Webster – 1979.**

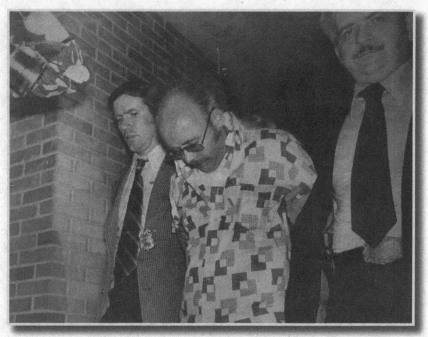

**Apprehension of murder suspect Joe Delany,
with Detective Tom Kelly – 1977.**

FALN mailer, identifying members of the Joint Terrorist Task Force that they had been surveilling and following – 1982.

My sergeant's desk at 8th Homicide, with detectives John
Rogan, John Taldone, and Tom Moroney – Circa 1978.

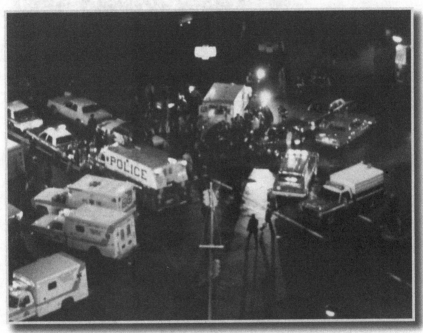

The bomb scene at 1 Police Plaza, New Year's Eve – 1982.

FBI supervising agent Kenneth Walton. JTTF – Circa 1983.

The shootout scene at the Whitestone Motel – 1983.

My FBI graduation with my family – 1978.

Ken Walton and Bob Johnson at the JTTF Command Center during the capture of Marilyn Jean Buck – 1985.

With Ken Walton – Circa 1984.

Sergeant Al Howard and detectives Richie Paul and Ron Marsenison, Bruckner Expressway shootout scene, 138th Street War – 1976.

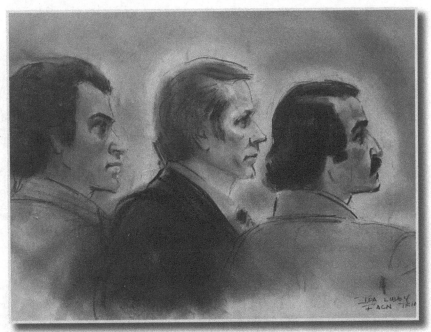

With anonymous FBI Agents, FALN Grand Jury – 1982.

Talking to detective Jack McCann in the hallway where I faced
off with "Teenager" Jamie Villa, 138th Street War – 1976.

With my future wife Joan
when we were teens – 1958.

My NYPD rookie photo – 1962.

8th Homicide, Team C: Mike McTigue, Jack
McCann, Ron Marsenison, Charlie Summers, Tom
Davis, John Meda, and me – Circa 1977.

My sons Kevin Jr. and Tom. Both are now in the FBI – 2006.

Some of the JTTF staff, from a commendation
ceremony. For obvious reasons, the surveillance
teams could not be photographed – 1985.

A PERSONAL NOTE FROM KEVIN M. HALLINAN

Once retired from Major League Baseball, life brought me together with John Petrullo and POPPA, a fantastic volunteer organization that describes itself as an organization of "Helpers Helping the Helpers."

POPPA, or the Police Organization Providing Peer Assistance, came into being in 1996, after twenty-six NYPD officers committed suicide in just two years. Today, POPPA's vast network of volunteers offers twenty-four-seven support, quick response teams, and an extensive catalog of resources from mental health support to alcohol and drug abuse counseling. Today, approximately two hundred active and retired uniformed members of the NYPD act as peer support officers or (PSOs). The organization's work is strictly confidential. The idea is to get retired cops' help and to better equip active ones for the many rigors of the job.

Upon hearing of the program, my first thought was that I had seen men and women from the beat to the detective squads suffering under stress so many times. Now, I was going to be able to be one of the guys waiting on the other end of that line. Like this very book, working with POPPA is my form of payback for all of the incredible people and experiences that law enforcement has given and continues to give to me. While the part we play may be small, it's everything to the people that call.

Police officers are very particular kinds of people, kind of like islands. They consider themselves the helper and never the ones that seek help. Most of us share a personality trait—duty to others, well above duty to self. Law enforcement agents are famous for burying feelings and always looking strong. Still, our most powerful tool is our kinship and a helping and supportive voice to those who too often mistake pressure for weakness, and any tiny mistake as a failure. POPPA delivers the message that it is a sign of strength and responsibility to ask for help. It makes you stronger and better for your family and those around you. It also makes you a better law enforcement officer. Most people don't realize the incredible grind of the police officer's job, the moment-by-moment judgment required, the gravity of even the slightest mistake. POPPA is a godsend, and I'm honored to do my part. And while this vital program only exists in New York, I'm hoping to do some small part to change that.

A portion of this book's proceeds is going to POPPA. It is the very least I can do.

If you are an active or former NYPD officer reading this book and wish to help out or need assistance, don't hesitate to contact POPPA at 212.298.9111 or 1.888.267.7267.

▰ ACKNOWLEDGMENTS

In closing, I'd be remiss not to mention the following individuals who took a significant part in this literary journey with me. To the last, they supported, pushed, cajoled, or otherwise helped me get this project over the finish line...

On the law enforcement side, FBI Agent Rick Hahn's groundbreaking antiterrorism work with the Chicago FBI was not only a critical proof of concept for the JTTF in New York, his riveting book on the subject and his wonderful encouragement were extremely helpful and appreciated. To better coalesce the investigative powers of the NYPD and FBI into a more unified force, the late Jim Kallstrom almost singlehandedly created a new textbook for surveillance. Jim's unique insider look at how the FBI helped empower the JTTF inspired entire sections of this book. The same goes for former FBI Agent David Mitchell, whose dogged investigative work spanned several states and helped build our national counterterrorism network. His dramatic stories and supportive friendship were critical to me then and now. I also want to acknowledge former NYPD Commissioner Robert J. McGuire, an encouraging and inspiring force from day one. A big proponent of the community aspect of better policing, Bob's influence is easy to spot all along my journey. Former assistant director of the NY FBI Office, Tom Sheer, was one of my most trusted counterparts in the JTTF. A "get your hands dirty" type, Tom's attitude and friendship were powerful inspirations personally and professionally.

On the business side, award-winning journalist and author Howard Blum always knew a good story when he saw one, and thankfully, one of them was mine! Howard offered constant encouragement and a fantastic roadmap for maneuvering the publishing minefield. I can't mention Howard without the late Leonard Buder. Both were working at the NY Times when the 138th Street War story broke, and both taught me the importance and lasting lessons of great journalism. If you've read this far and taken something of value from this book, please join me in thanking Howard and Len for helping point me in the right direction. My good friend, New York University professor Lee Igel is a force in the sports medicine and security sphere. After I retired from baseball, Lee stoked the fires that led to this book by generously inviting me to speak to his classes on matters of sports security and leadership. During my time in Major League Baseball and beyond, David Gavant was a crucial partner in creating programs to better protect the sport, its teams, and players. The security of our national pastime would not be what it is today without his exceptional talent and determination. Peter V. Ueberroth is a true visionary and the man that gave me my big at-bat in baseball. He was also a demanding boss who always encouraged pushing the envelope and looking for the next mountain to climb. When first interviewed for this book, Peter picked up right where he left off and encouraged me to finish the job ahead again.

In terms of finalizing the manuscript, a few more key folks need to be acknowledged. My niece Laura Cannon was a constant cheerleader and organizing force who provided much-needed support and steady counsel throughout the process. While co-writer Rob Travalino and I were in the thick of things, my highly talented second-cousin, the accomplished author Mary Beth Keane, generously shared essential lessons from the publishing trenches. She also provided the initial contact that kickstarted this book's journey to market. Procured by Mary Beth, literary agent Chris Calhoun stepped up next to offer important early advice. In his first shot across the bow, he suggested Post Hill Publisher Anthony Ziccardi. Mr. Ziccardi was not an easy sell at first, but we won him over. Without his gracious guidance, time, and support, and the critical, creative work of Maddie Sturgeon, Devon Brown, Melissa Smith, and the team at Post Hill, this project would not have come together. Upon completion of the